WOMEN, GENDER AND CRIME

WOMEN, GENDER AND CRIME

Sue Strickland-Lord

SOCIETY Publishing

www.societypublishing.com

Women, Gender and Crime

Sue Strickland-Lord

Society Publishing
4164 Lakeshore Road
Burlington, ON L7L 1A4
Canada
www.societypublishing.com
Email: orders@arclereducation.com

ISBN: 978-1-77956-395-8 (Hardcover)

ABOUT THE AUTHOR

Sue Strickland-Lord is a college lecturer in Social Sciences, lecturing for over twenty years in several UK colleges. She specialises in Criminology and has a 1st Class degree in Criminology from the University of Winchester and a MSc in Criminal Justice, with merit from the University of Portsmouth. Sue achieved particularly high grades in her dissertations with pass percentages at 85% and she has been able to pass on those skills to many of her students who have excelled in their educational achievement.

Sue works hard to introduce students to the world of Criminology and inspires students to research the subject thoroughly and understand it fully to support their own academic writing. Many of her students have gone on to gain their educational aspirations and go on to work in areas such as criminal justice, policing, law and prison services.

Her own career as also included working with vulnerable victims and writing educational programmes within prison reform.

TABLE OF CONTENTS

LIST OF FIGURES

ABSTRACT

Women, Gender, and Crime is a book that explores the connection between gender and criminal conduct. It illuminates a subject that is frequently disregarded in mainstream conversations about crime and the justice system. By specifically centering on women and gender, the book offers a more all-encompassing comprehension of the intricacies associated with crime and its effects on individuals and society. An important focus of the book is the impact of gender norms and stereotypes on the criminal justice system. This study analyzes the influence of societal expectations on the experiences of women throughout the entire criminal justice process. This analysis is essential for illuminating the prejudices and disparities that exist within the system. The distinguishing feature of this book is its interdisciplinary approach. This study incorporates insights from sociology, criminology, psychology, and related fields to offer a detailed comprehension of the connection between women, gender, and criminal behavior. This interdisciplinary approach enhances the analysis by providing greater depth and complexity, making it a valuable tool for scholars, students, policymakers, and professionals across different disciplines. The book is also inclusive of a broader readership, encompassing individuals with a general curiosity in comprehending the societal and cultural factors that impact criminal behavior and the legal framework, especially as it pertains to women and gender. The text is written in a lucid and accessible style, making it appropriate for readers from both academic and non-academic backgrounds. Through the act of reading this book, individuals will acquire a thorough and inclusive understanding of the primary subjects and debates within the realm of Women, Gender, and Crime. They will acquire a more profound comprehension of how gender influences the way crime is experienced and the functioning of the criminal justice system. The book will also foster critical thinking regarding the influence of gender norms and stereotypes on our comprehension of crime and criminal behavior, urging readers to contemplate alternative viewpoints and strategies for tackling these matters.

PREFACE

Women, Gender, and Crime provides a thorough analysis of how gender and criminal behavior intersect. This book is significant because it illuminates a subject that is frequently disregarded in mainstream discussions on crime and criminal justice. By specifically directing attention towards women and gender, it offers a more intricate and all-encompassing comprehension of the intricacies surrounding crime and its effects on individuals and society as a whole. The book also examines how gender norms and stereotypes impact the criminal justice system, influencing the experiences of women at all stages of the process.

This book is necessary because it fills a notable void in the current body of literature on crime and criminal justice. Although there is a considerable amount of research on crime in general, there is a limited amount of studies that specifically concentrate on women and gender. This book seeks to address the lack of information by offering a thorough examination of the main topics and discussions in this field, utilizing various theoretical viewpoints and factual data.

The book's uniqueness and value lie in its interdisciplinary methodology, which incorporates perspectives from sociology, criminology, psychology, and other relevant disciplines. The book provides a comprehensive and nuanced understanding of the intricate relationship between women, gender, and crime by incorporating perspectives from various disciplines.

This book will appeal to a diverse audience, encompassing students, scholars, policymakers, and professionals in the disciplines of criminology, sociology, psychology, and gender studies. Additionally, it will attract individuals who have a curiosity in comprehending the societal and cultural influences that mold criminal activity and the legal system, specifically in relation to women and gender. The book is composed in a lucid and approachable manner, rendering it appropriate for both scholarly and lay readers seeking to enhance their comprehension and insight into this significant subject matter. There are multiple advantages for readers who choose to read this book. Primarily, it will furnish them with a thorough and current synopsis of the principal matters and discussions in the domain of Women, Gender, and Crime. By actively interacting with the content presented in the book, readers will acquire a more profound comprehension of how gender influences the experiences of crime and the criminal justice system. Additionally, readers will gain insight into the wider social and cultural environments in which these processes occur. The book will prompt readers to engage in critical thinking regarding the impact of gender norms and stereotypes on our understanding of crime and criminal behavior. It will encourage readers to explore alternative viewpoints and strategies for addressing these matters.

– Author

CHAPTER 1

HISTORICAL PERSPECTIVES ON WOMEN AND CRIME

Contents

The field of gender and crime research is currently experiencing a high level of innovation and activity, as highlighted by Carrington & Death (2014). It is essential for criminologists and historians to consider gender as a crucial factor when examining criminal activity. One significant development in the field of crime analysis is the inclusion of gender. This addition has greatly enhanced our understanding of various facets of criminal behavior in both men and women. It has shed light on the underlying motivations behind criminal activity, the organizational structures of crimes, the prosecution of offenders, and the portrayal of crimes. Furthermore, it is crucial to acknowledge that criminal behavior can be greatly influenced by gender norms and the socioeconomic conditions that individuals, both men and women, find themselves in. As a result of these gender stereotypes, there existed a widespread bias against women and crime. It was believed that women were only capable of committing crimes that were traditionally associated with their gender, such as moral transgressions, witchcraft, and abortion. Prejudices have historically influenced the way prosecution practices were carried out based on gender, and they continue to affect the assumptions made by researchers studying crime today (Carrington & Death, 2014) (Figure 1.1).

Figure 1.1. *Women criminology.*

Source: Criminology (2024).

Similar to how contemporary views on criminality were influenced by gender, early criminological and historical studies also adopted a comparable methodology. When discussing the issue of criminality in relation to women, scholars often emphasize prevailing views on women's victimization, passivity, and innocence. When it comes to female crime rates, some criminology academic publications argue that we are currently experiencing significant historical shifts. To truly comprehend the criminality of women throughout history and in the field of criminology, it is imperative to recognize that women can indeed be offenders. Additionally, it is crucial to delve into the influence of gender as a contributing factor to criminal behavior.

Early research on women's criminality often relied heavily on quantitative data as its foundation. Historically, there has been a prevailing belief among criminologists and historians that women were less inclined to engage in criminal behavior compared to men. It was also commonly assumed that gender disparities in reported crime remained consistent over time (Williams, 2000). Early studies on the history of crime often dismissed the involvement of women in criminal activities. Beattie's work from the 1970s is still highly regarded for being the first to delve into the discussion of women in criminal contexts. However, it is worth noting that the subject of criminal women was not commonly the focus of research in criminology or crime history. This was due to the prevailing belief that women were less likely than men to engage in criminal activities. Various studies have found that women's involvement in criminal activities is either minimal (due to lower rates of criminality) or tends to be specific to gender, such as prostitution or infanticide. As a result, these crimes require a distinct analytical framework compared to male crimes (Williams, 2000). It is widely acknowledged in the field of criminology that men have a higher rate of criminal activity compared to women. This gender disparity in crime rates has been recognized as a well-established and widely accepted phenomenon.

1.1. THE EVOLUTION OF WOMEN'S ROLES IN SOCIETY

Throughout various societies and across a significant span of history, women have often been regarded as inferior to men. Historically, there was a significant disparity in the education levels between girls and boys. Historically, women often found themselves marginalized from professions and positions that provided them with opportunities for economic or political influence. Following marriage, the women often relinquished any money they had to their husbands. They were denied the right to vote and had limited legal rights. Women were also expected to conduct themselves in a manner that aligned with societal norms. Their main responsibilities revolved around being mothers and spouses. According to Momsen (2019), they were often praised for their physical appearance rather than their skills, and were described as submissive, kind, and compassionate.

Despite these circumstances, numerous women achieved remarkable accomplishments, led captivating lives, and played significant roles in intriguing historical periods. The recorded history often focuses on the dynamics of power, encompassing conflicts, rulers, politics, and the economy (Momsen, 2019). Throughout history, there has been a significant presence of individuals who held positions of power and influence, often belonging to a particular demographic. History, for the majority of individuals, has often been perceived as "his story." Due to significant limitations on women's influence, there is a scarcity of records documenting their actions. Historical narratives predominantly focused on male figures until the 1970s.

Historians and archaeologists have traditionally held the belief that women's activities were primarily confined to the domestic sphere, lacking excitement or significance, and therefore not deemed worthy of documentation or scholarly examination. Women's history was often dismissed or overlooked in the past because of prevailing perceptions about what constituted "real" history. Historical records have predominantly highlighted the lives of women from noble and royal backgrounds. In contrast to their White or affluent counterparts, individuals from working class backgrounds, Black individuals, or women from marginalized groups faced even lower chances of having their history recorded. Within historical texts, the interplay of class, race, and gender created a complex web of marginalization and limited agency, as noted by Momsen (2019).

It is worth noting that the perspective on women's history and other underrepresented histories has undergone a significant shift in the past 50 years. It is evident that an increasing number of women have been able to pursue studies and establish careers in the fields of history and archaeology. One cannot deny that expectations have undergone a significant shift, and the concept of equality has experienced a notable increase due to the influence of feminism and the broader social changes that have taken place. The study of social history, which sheds light on the experiences of working-class and female populations, has become increasingly popular. It has become increasingly evident to institutions such as universities and museums that embracing diversity and decolonizing their narratives is of utmost importance. However, it is important to acknowledge that significant progress still needs to be made, considering the centuries-long existence of certain societal norms and practices (Momsen, 2019).

There is a significant number of stories pertaining to women that have unfortunately been overlooked or have not been properly documented. In addition to the exceptionally affluent and powerful, the women whose stories have been documented are those who defied societal norms. A small percentage of individuals who achieved success in a world predominantly controlled by men or challenged the male-dominated structure are the individuals who took on roles as activists, artists, explorers, and inventors. This sentiment is captured in the popular saying, which suggests that women who conform to societal expectations are less likely to leave a lasting impact on history. Although it is indeed inspiring, it does not provide a comprehensive understanding of the experiences that the majority of women face in their lives (Momsen, 2019).

1.2. GENDERED PERCEPTIONS OF CRIMINALITY

Gendered perceptions of criminality refer to the biases and preconceived notions in society that influence how different genders are viewed in relation to crime (Evans & Jamieson, 2008). Perceptions can have a significant impact on how crimes are reported, examined, and prosecuted.

1.2.1. Stereotypes in Society

Throughout history, there has been a prevailing perception that men have a higher tendency to engage in criminal behavior, particularly violent crimes. On the other hand, women are often regarded as less prone to violence and more susceptible to becoming victims of crime. Prejudices can have a significant impact on the criminal justice system, leading to potential biases in sentencing. This can result in women receiving more lenient sentences while men may face harsher ones (Evans & Jamieson, 2008).

1.2.2. The Impact on the Criminal Justice System

Gendered stereotypes can have an impact on victim support programs, potentially leading to a lack of adequate services for male victims due to resource allocation that sometimes favors female victims. In addition, it is worth noting that certain crimes, which deviate from the traditional gender narrative, may not receive the recognition they deserve. This includes instances of violent crimes perpetrated by women or cases of domestic abuse where the victims are men.

According to Evans & Jamieson (2008), the percentage of women involved in arrests for various offenses is relatively low, at around 25%. Furthermore, it is believed that these individuals pose a lower risk of reoffending and have limited chances to engage in criminal activities. They are considered suitable for incarceration and may not face identical charges upon apprehension. Additionally, they may receive more favorable treatment during the process of criminal sentencing (Evans & Jamieson, 2008).

According to criminologists and feminist theorists, these empirical results can be explained by the influence of gender roles. It is worth noting that crime rates, regardless of the method used to measure them, consistently show that men commit crimes at a significantly higher rate compared to women. This finding has been supported by various studies. Research has consistently shown that there is a higher representation of women in prostitution offenses and property offenses such as fraud, forgery, embezzlement, and theft of property. On the other hand, men tend to be more commonly involved in offenses against individuals, such as assault.

It is widely recognized among criminologists that gender disparities in crime are a universal phenomenon. It has been observed that men tend to engage in various types of offenses at much higher rates compared to women. However, it is worth noting that when it comes to prostitution offenses, the gender disparity is not as pronounced. When it comes to serious offenses, there is a noticeable difference in criminal activity between genders. However, when it comes to minor crimes, this difference becomes less pronounced.

According to Evans & Jamieson (2008), there is a significant disparity in arrest rates between men and women. The data shows that men are arrested at a rate of 7,480 per 1,00,000 people, which is more than four times higher than the arrest rate for women, which stands at 1,475 per 1,00,000 women. It is common to observe differences in criminal behavior between genders in western nations. In Canada, the frequency of women being detained by the police is significantly lower compared to men. According to official data from nine provinces obtained through the Incident-based Uniform Crime Reporting Survey, it was found that only one-fifth of all individuals charged with a crime in 2005 were females aged 12 and older. During that particular year, the number of women who were arrested amounted to 1,080, which was significantly lower compared to the arrest rate of men, which stood at 4,193 per 1,00,000 population. This means that the arrest rate for women was one-quarter lower than that of men.

1.3. THE INVOLVEMENT OF WOMEN IN CRIMINAL ACTIVITIES

The involvement of women in criminal activity, although historically less prominent than men's, is a significant subject in the field of criminology. In this section, we will delve into the various types of crimes committed by women, the frequency of their involvement, and the factors that shape their criminal behavior.

1.3.1. Nature of Participation

It is important to acknowledge that women are involved in a wide range of illegal activities, encompassing violent crimes, drug trafficking, and white-collar crimes. However, due to the influence of gender norms and societal expectations, women often find themselves with different responsibilities compared to men. There are instances where women may become involved in criminal activity as accomplices or counterparts due to coercion or influence from their male counterparts.

1.3.2. Types of Crimes

Based on statistical data, it has been observed that there is a higher tendency among women to engage in property crimes such as fraud or theft, as compared to men. Furthermore, individuals are increasingly becoming active participants in drug-related offenses, both as dealers and consumers. While less common, instances of violent crimes committed by women are not unheard of. There have been documented cases of assault and even murder (Halder & Jaishankar, 2011).

1.3.3. Influencing Factors

Various factors can contribute to women's participation in criminal behavior, including their financial status, previous experiences of abuse, substance addiction, and mental health issues. According to Halder & Jaishankar (2011), it is possible for women to resort to criminal activities as a means of resistance or survival in response to patriarchal pressures and gender inequity.

Despite the ongoing gender disparity in the criminal justice system, there has been a noticeable increase in the number of women participating in this field. This can be attributed, at least in part, to the progress made in addressing other socioeconomic gender inequalities. With the increasing independence of women in modern times, there has been a corresponding rise in the potential for criminal activity. Despite the progress made in achieving social equality, there still exists a disparity in the way police and judicial institutions handle female offenders compared to their male counterparts. One potential way to address the salary gap between skilled and unskilled female workers is by implementing policies that incentivize female education. By doing so, we may see a decrease in crime rates among underprivileged women. According to Halder & Jaishankar (2011), there is evidence to suggest that implementing policies that encourage marriage and parenthood could potentially contribute to a decrease in female crime rates.

Men make up the majority of criminals, while there has been an increase in the percentage of female offenders. There is still much that remains unknown regarding the factors contributing to gender disparities in criminal behavior, as well as the changes occurring in the gender gap. According to Halder & Jaishankar (2011), policies that aim to address prevention, punishment, and rehabilitation have failed to consider gender differences. Female involvement in the criminal market has been largely overlooked in the economic literature, despite extensive research on gender convergence in the labor force. In order to effectively combat crime, it is crucial to thoroughly analyze the gender difference in the crime market, closely track its evolution over time, and accurately pinpoint the primary factors contributing to it. It is crucial to investigate whether there are behavioral variations between men and women in the criminal market and, if so, determine the primary causes of these disparities (Halder & Jaishankar, 2011).

Various factors can influence an individual's decision to engage in criminal activities. These factors include the chances of getting caught, the potential consequences of being convicted, the practicality of serving time in jail, the expected financial gains from illegal activities, the availability of lawful employment options, and the individual's level of risk aversion. On the other hand, most economic research on crime tends to focus exclusively on males. Comprehending the complexities of women's involvement in crime is greatly hindered by the undeniable variations in motivations between genders. These distinctions also imply that it is necessary to implement different measures in order to reduce the probability of engaging in criminal activities (Halder & Jaishankar, 2011).

1.4. LEGAL RESPONSES TO WOMEN'S CRIMINAL BEHAVIOR

According to Brown (2004), there have been significant changes in the way the law has responded to women who commit crimes. These changes reflect broader shifts in society's perception of women's responsibilities in relation to crime. In this section, we will delve into the various aspects of rehabilitation, sentencing procedures, and gender-specific concerns within the judicial system.

1.4.1. Procedures for Penalties

Historically, there has been a discrepancy in the severity of punishments for similar offenses between men and women. This can be attributed to the perception that women are less of a threat or due to factors such as their responsibilities in childcare (Brown, 2004). With the increasing awareness of gender bias in the criminal justice system, there has been a noticeable trend towards adopting more gender-neutral sentencing practices.

1.4.2. Programs for Rehabilitation

Rehabilitation programs for female offenders often address a range of specialized requirements, such as treatment for substance abuse, mental health services, and assistance for victims of domestic abuse. There is a growing recognition of the importance of gender-responsive programming that considers the unique trajectories that women take towards engaging in criminal behavior.

1.4.3. Considerations Specific to Gender

The judicial system is undergoing changes to better serve the interests of women. As an illustration, courts now provide childcare facilities and consider the impact of incarceration on families. Restorative justice approaches that focus on making amends and reintegrating offenders into society have gained significant popularity in recent years (Brown, 2004).

1.5. FEMINIST CRITIQUES OF TRADITIONAL CRIME THEORIES

Throughout history, the act of committing crimes has often been attributed to men, as it has been linked to traits such as aggression and masculinity. Historically, the number of women involved in criminal activities has been relatively low. However, when women did engage in such behavior, the prevailing explanations often focused on their deviation from traditional gender roles.

This perspective suggested that the characteristics associated with female criminality were inherent to women. Various explanations have been proposed to understand causation, such as the mono-causal theory. This theory delves into gender-role explanations and examines how societal expectations can be challenged. Some theories suggest that physical anomalies, various psychological and social disorders, moral decay, and illness may contribute to this phenomenon (Ferguson, 2017).

In a broader perspective, it is often argued that women tend to exhibit higher levels of law-abiding behavior compared to men. Additionally, they are less likely to engage in criminal subcultures or delinquent activities. However, it is worth noting that criminological theory has not extensively considered these aspects when it comes to women.

Starting in the 1970s, feminist criminologists launched a rigorous critique of the prevailing theoretical foundations in criminology.

They highlighted that these explanations were not comprehensive theories of female crime, but rather perpetuated stereotypes that reinforced sexist notions about women (Ferguson, 2017). The feminist approach to criminology is a constantly evolving field that highlights the impact of sexist ideological practices and patriarchal oppression on the understanding of female criminality (Ferguson, 2017).

1.5.1. Traditional Theories and Female Crime

1. **The First Psychoanalytic Theory:** One can also analyze Sigmund Freud's perspective on women and their actions, noting his tendency to interpret them through a lens shaped by masculine experiences and understanding. According to Freud, the presence of female criminality can be attributed to "penis envy," a concept within his psychoanalytic theory (Ferguson, 2017). According to Ferguson (2017), this method proposes that young girls experienced feelings of inferiority and jealousy upon realizing their lack of a penis. The trauma experienced by these women has never truly dissipated; rather, it has become deeply ingrained in their psyche. Women who considered themselves to be typical attempted to compensate for their perceived disadvantages by seeking male attention or engaging in activities that were unique to their gender, such as becoming pregnant.

   According to Ferguson (2017), women who were unable to find a male spouse often resorted to committing crimes in an attempt to pass as men. Freud successfully established a connection between female "sexual delinquency" and prostitution within his theories. He discussed the connection between this phenomenon and the Oedipal syndrome, which involves experiencing sexual attraction towards the parent of the opposite sex. Female offenders may engage in promiscuous behavior as a sexual alternative due to societal restrictions on incest. However, their inability to find true satisfaction leads them to constantly seek new partners. This concept can be seen as a parallel to the Freudian theory of "penis envy," which stems from women's desire for male attributes. Freud's approach to treatment primarily focused on the use of intense psychoanalysis. Freud approached the description of female criminal behavior differently from male criminal behavior, offering his own perspective on the matter (Ferguson, 2017).

   The notion that women are expected to adhere to societal expectations of gender and the potential consequences of deviating from these norms were reinforced by the belief in women's inherent inferiority and the unexpressed desire for a different anatomy. According to Ferguson (2017), the underrepresentation of women in our criminal justice system and the lack of attention given to them in criminological theory can be attributed to the argument that criminal women are in need of assistance due to their illness.

2. **The Late Otto Pollack:** In his book The Criminality of Women, Otto Pollack (1950) offers a unique male perspective on female criminality.

Based on the research conducted by Pollack, it has been observed that women tend to engage in criminal activities with a primary focus on sexual motives, while men are more inclined towards committing crimes driven by financial motivations (Ferguson, 2017). It is worth noting that there are certain behavioral differences between women and men. Some studies suggest that women may exhibit higher levels of strategic thinking and adaptability, while men may display more assertiveness and passion in certain situations. Female crime often involves activities such as prostitution and stealing, which can be driven by a desire to acquire items that are seen as attractive to men.

Women possess a range of qualities, encompassing both favorable and unfavorable traits. Women possess certain virtues and compassion that make them well-suited for roles such as wife and mother. However, it is important to acknowledge that, like anyone else, they are capable of engaging in criminal behavior driven by traits such as cunning, retaliation, greed, and untrustworthiness. Adhering to their established duties was the sole method of maintaining control over their "dark side." According to female theorists, the perpetuation of this sexist stereotype of women is highly effective in upholding social control. It achieves this by reinforcing existing social bonds and discouraging any questioning of the established status quo (Ferguson, 2017).

Pollack recognized this phenomenon, suggesting that the lack of male action against female criminality may be attributed to its reinforcement of traditional gender roles, where women are seen as dishonest and submissive, ultimately boosting men's self-perception. While it is true that women may engage in different types of criminal behavior compared to men, it is important to consider the societal factors that may influence their choices. For instance, women may be compelled into certain circumstances that contribute to their involvement in crime, rather than solely being driven by different motivations (Ferguson, 2017). According to Pollack, the presence of distinct female traits is believed to contribute to the development of female patterns of crime. It is suggested that women may exhibit certain behaviors that are unique to their gender. It is important to consider the various factors that may impact individuals, such as their social standing, roles, possibilities, and social expectations.

3. **The Theory of Roles:** An alternative perspective in understanding female criminality is through masculinity theory, also referred to as

sex role theory. This approach focuses on the influence of societal gender roles rather than biological or psychological factors. There are two main concepts that are encompassed in this.

- In many cases, crime is seen as symbolically masculine due to the association of traits like boldness, toughness, and aggression with masculinity. This perception often leads to the assumption that criminal behavior is motivated by masculinity. A man who commits crimes can be seen as an example of male virility.
- Women's higher tendency to conform can be attributed to the notion that they are not suited for engaging in criminal activities. According to Ferguson (2017), women are less likely to engage in unlawful activities that are traditionally associated with men.

There is a belief that women who possess more masculine traits are more prone to participating in criminal behavior. Their engagement in criminal activity can be seen as an unauthorized expression of these societal expectations. As per Ferguson (2017), the rise in crime rates among women and the changing trends in female criminal behavior, particularly in relation to drug use, have been linked to certain masculine characteristics. In addition, there is a belief that female criminality can be seen as a reflection of traditional female gender roles. For example, when women engage in criminal behavior, they may transition from being consumers to shoplifters, or from cashing legitimate checks to cashing fraudulent ones. Once again, the portrayal of female criminals perpetuates the stereotype of them as sexual misfits. Their "rebellious" behavior is often attributed to a lack of positive and healthy attitudes towards women. Sex role theory has faced criticism for its focus on attributing reasons for women's involvement in crime, such as "role frustration" and "under socialization," without acknowledging the lack of evidence supporting the notion that women commit crimes for different reasons than men. This concept offers limited understanding of actual female offenders in the real world. It solely focuses on the description of how behavior is influenced. The issue at hand fails to acknowledge the historical and cultural marginalization of women, as well as the underlying structural factors that contribute to gender inequality (Ferguson, 2017).

1.6. INTERSECTIONALITY AND WOMEN'S EXPERIENCES WITH CRIME

Understanding the intricate dynamics between various social strata, such as gender, class, and race, is facilitated by the concept of intersectionality. Intersectionality offers valuable insight into the diverse experiences of women involved in criminal activity and those who are victimized by it.

1.6.1. The Impact on Sustaining

It is important to recognize that women's experiences with crime are diverse and shaped by various intersecting identities. Take into consideration that a woman's socioeconomic standing has the potential to impact the types of illegal activities she may be more inclined to engage in. In addition, it is worth noting that the manner in which the criminal justice system handles cases involving women can be impacted by factors such as race or ethnicity. This, in turn, can lead to disparities in terms of the frequency of arrests, the types of charges brought forth, and the severity of sentences imposed (Dancig-Rosenberg & Yosef, 2019).

1.6.2. The Impact of Victimization

Intersectionality plays a significant role in the influence of victimization. There is a possibility that women belonging to marginalized groups have a higher likelihood of becoming victims of crimes such as human trafficking or domestic abuse. In some cases, individuals may face challenges in accessing support services or encountering obstacles in seeking justice due to prejudice or cultural norms.

1.6.3. Implications for Practice and Policy

In order to effectively address the diverse needs of different groups of women, it is crucial to have a comprehensive understanding of intersectionality. The approach advocated here emphasizes a comprehensive strategy for victim assistance and crime prevention, considering all the factors that influence women's experiences of crime.

1.6.4. Challenges in Implementing Intersectional Theories

Implementing intersectional approaches in the criminal justice system can be challenging due to several obstacles:

1. **Institutional Opposition:** Opposition to change may be present within reputable institutions. Given the nature of legal systems, it is important to recognize that incorporating intersectionality requires a significant shift in the approach to handling cases. This is because legal systems often require time to adapt and adjust to new perspectives and considerations.
2. **Identity Complexity:** Addressing discrimination and disadvantage in intersectionality is a complex task, as it involves navigating multiple overlapping identities. Developing policies that encompass every possible scenario can be quite challenging.

3. **Gathering and Examining Data:** It is crucial to have accurate information that encompasses the diverse experiences of individuals. It can be challenging to gather and evaluate data when there is a lack of resources or regular procedures in place.
4. **Instruction and Training:** In order to gain a comprehensive understanding and effectively apply intersectional principles, it is imperative that law enforcement officials, legal professionals, and support staff receive proper training. In order to keep pace with the ever-evolving dynamics of society, it is imperative that this training be conducted on an ongoing basis.
5. **The Allocation of Resources:** In order to adequately address the diverse needs of different populations, it may be necessary to allocate additional funding towards intersectional approaches that provide specialized services and support networks.
6. **Balancing Systemic Change and Individual Needs:** Intersectionality highlights the importance of personal experiences, while also calling for necessary structural adjustments. Indeed, finding a balance between these two qualities can prove to be quite challenging.

1.7. THE LEGAL CLASSIFICATION OF POVERTY AND WOMEN AS CRIMINALS

Globally, the number of incarcerated women and girls exceeds 7,40,000. Women constitute a minority, accounting for only 7% of the total global inmate population. However, when comparing the rates of incarceration, women have experienced a more rapid increase of 60% since 2000, whereas men have seen a growth of 22%. According to Balfour & Comack (2021), around 19,000 children and their mothers are currently in prison. The study conducted by the Justice for Women High-level Group reveals that discriminatory societal norms pose substantial obstacles to achieving equal rights. These barriers are further intensified by additional disadvantages such as poverty. However, despite the detrimental impact of imprisonment on women and their families, specifically their children, studies suggest that poverty plays a significant role in the increasing prevalence of women being incarcerated. Across the globe, the predominant demographic of incarcerated women consists of individuals who have been accused of or convicted for non-violent offenses (Balfour & Comack, 2021). A significant number of individuals are given short prison sentences solely due to their inability to pay bail or fines (Figure 1.2).

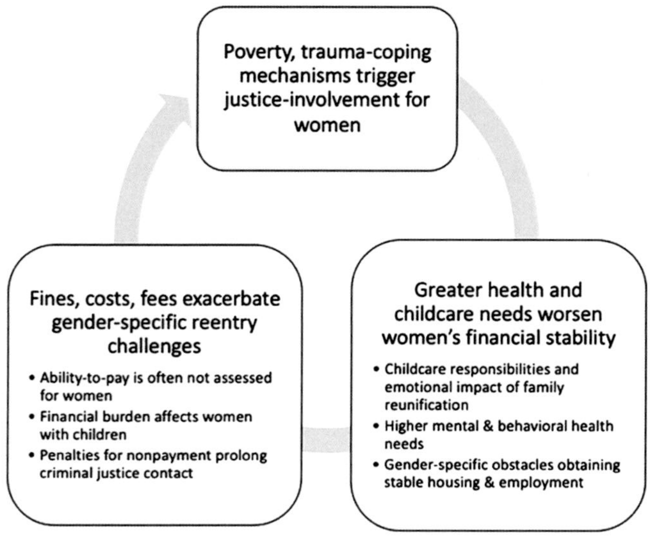

Figure 1.2. *The cycle of financial instability and justice involvement for women.*

Source: Servon et al. (2021).

The concept of "criminalization of poverty" refers to the perception of poverty as a criminal act or as a catalyst for increased criminal behavior, with a particular focus on women and other marginalized groups.

1.7.1. Improved Engagement with the Criminal Justice System

Residing in neighborhoods with a strong police presence, facing financial inability to settle fines or fees, and engaging in survival-related offenses such as theft or sex work are some factors that contribute to poverty leading to increased encounters with the criminal justice system.

1.7.2. Gender Imbalance's Impact on Women

Women may have a higher vulnerability to being criminalized for being poor, especially if they are the main caregivers or single parents. They often face additional challenges such as a lack of affordable childcare, unstable housing, and limited employment opportunities.

1.7.3. The Process of Criminalization

Impoverished women who become ensnared in the criminal justice system may find themselves trapped in a recurring pattern of being apprehended, found guilty, and incarcerated. Their financial predicament may exacerbate due to this cycle, rendering it more challenging for them to escape poverty.

1.7.4. Policy Implications

In order to address the criminalization of poverty, it is essential to implement policy reforms that give priority to decriminalizing survival behaviors, providing social support services, and creating economic opportunities for women. Individuals with limited financial resources may experience a substantial negative effect from the fines and expenses imposed by the criminal justice system, often exacerbating their financial hardships. The consequences of fines and fees on individuals with low income encompass:

1. **Perpetuating Poverty:** Imposing fines and fees can compel individuals with limited incomes to sacrifice essential needs such as sustenance, housing, or healthcare. This can lead to an inescapable cycle of indebtedness and destitution, which poses significant challenges to overcome.
2. **Challenges to Reintegration:** Financial consequences can also impede reintegration after being incarcerated. These barriers could hinder individuals' ability to secure housing, employment, or education, thereby obstructing their efforts to begin anew.
3. **Implications for Legal System:** Failure to pay penalties and fees may result in legal consequences, such as additional fines, mandatory community service, or potential imprisonment. This has the potential to deepen individuals' involvement in the criminal justice system.
4. **Imbalanced Impact:** Communities that are marginalized due to their race and economic status face a greater burden of fines and fees. This is because they are more likely to be financially unstable as a result of systemic injustices.

1.7.5. Revisions to Policies to Tackle Penalties and Charges

Here are some practical policy modifications that could be implemented to address the impact of fines and fees on individuals with low income:

1. **Utilizing a Variable Payment System based on Income Level:** By implementing a sliding scale for fines based on an individual's income, it ensures that the penalties are proportionate to their financial ability.
2. **Community Service Options:** Providing community service as an alternative to monetary fines can offer a fairer solution for individuals who cannot afford to pay.
3. **Upper Limits on Fines and Fees:** To prevent excessive financial burdens, it is advisable to set a limit on the maximum amount of penalties and fees that can be imposed.

4. **Elimination of Specific Charges:** Eliminating fees for non-essential services such as public defenders and probation supervision can alleviate the financial strain on individuals with low incomes, without compromising public safety.
5. **Reducing Incarceration based on Debt:** Legislation that prohibits incarceration as a consequence of failure to pay fines and other expenses could potentially disrupt the detrimental cycle of criminal behavior perpetuated by poverty.
6. **Automated Pardon or Reduction of Fines:** Implementing automated systems that allow individuals with low incomes to have their fines reduced or forgiven can gradually mitigate financial penalties.

The issue of poverty criminalization is a complex problem that has a disproportionate impact on women. To effectively tackle this issue, it is crucial to consider the underlying causes of poverty and provide affected individuals with comprehensive assistance. Individuals with limited financial resources can experience severe consequences from fines and fees, exacerbating the cycle of poverty and criminal behavior. Reforming these practices is crucial in order to establish a criminal justice system that is more egalitarian.

1.8. THE PARTICIPATION OF WOMEN IN ORGANIZED CRIME

This section will focus on the main roles that women have in drug trafficking, human trafficking, and migrant smuggling. It will specifically highlight the various illegal activities that women are involved in within these economies, ranging from subordinate positions to leadership roles. Narratives that depict women as "victims" or "passive participants" often overlook the reality that women have taken on diverse roles within criminal economies, including positions of authority. The reason for this is that gender establishes a hierarchical distinction in conventional male and female roles (Balfour & Comack, 2021).

1.8.1. Drug Trafficking

The global cocaine trade, which encompasses drug trafficking, has relied on a multitude of workers involved in different stages of production, distribution, and sales for the past three decades. The allocation of tasks between males and females often mirrors power imbalances that arise from societal expectations regarding gender roles. However, there are notable exceptions that warrant investigation. For the sake of clarity, it would be advantageous to analyze the cocaine trade by dividing it into its three primary components: production, international transportation, and retail (Figure 1.3).

1. **Coca Collectors and Temporary Workers:** Traditionally, women have been employed as agricultural laborers in rural areas, especially during the time of crop harvesting. Although women generally engage in domestic service tasks, some of them also participate in coca picking. Conversely, men are typically responsible for the coca harvesting process (Balfour & Comack, 2021). According to Balfour & Comack (2021), the Ideas for Peace Foundation in Colombia asserts that women who work as day laborers or coca pickers are also obligated to carry out domestic tasks at home, effectively constituting a second employment.
2. **Cooks:** Due to the remote locations of these facilities, women are recruited to prepare meals for the workers while coca is being chemically processed. Despite receiving higher compensation, female cooks employed in large laboratories operated by armed organizations are still bound by a code of conduct and face the potential danger of being harmed during their work or while commuting to and from the facilities.

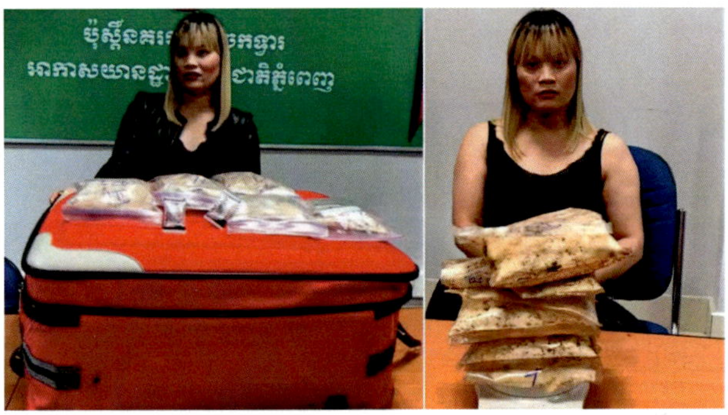

Figure 1.3. *An Australian woman charged with drug trafficking in Cambodia.*

Source: SBS News (2018).

3. **Agricultural Workers:** The majority of female coca growers tend to the cultivation of a family plot. In addition to harvesting coca leaves, they also engage in the manufacturing of cocaine paste. In certain circumstances, they might also be the individuals responsible for distributing the primary form of cocaine. In addition, they may also have the responsibility of coordinating the labor of the pickers during the harvest, making arrangements for meals, and managing the collection of their wages. Traditionally, it is the responsibility of female farmers to manage the recruitment of pickers and negotiate fair trade agreements.

4. **Drug Traffickers:** These women, being the most susceptible point in the drug trafficking process, transport drugs. Griselda Blanco, known as "The Godmother of Cocaine," played a crucial role in pioneering the use of "mules" to transport cocaine and marijuana into the United States market. She consistently utilized this method for drug trafficking.

Women who participate in micro trafficking or serve as "drug mules" often choose these dangerous and poorly compensated occupations due to financial constraints. Individuals may find themselves ensnared in the criminal underworld as a result of their drug dependency or connections to a partner or relative engaged in illicit drug trade (Balfour & Comack, 2021).

1.8.2. Migrant Smuggling

Migrant smuggling refers to the practice of transporting individuals across borders, whether by land, sea, or air, in order to profit financially.

The criminal economy in Latin America is highly lucrative due to the significant influx of migrants in the region. Due to their geographical position, a significant proportion of migrants journey northward from Colombia and Panama to the United States. Colombia is extensively crossed by trafficking routes, commonly originating in Ipiales near the Ecuadorian border, and terminating in Turbo near the Uraba region close to the Panamanian border. Subsequently, individuals involved in illegal trafficking, commonly referred to as "coyotes," may facilitate a migrant's transportation via boat to Panama or direct them to undertake the perilous trek through the treacherous Darién Gap jungle. The cost of this crossing is contingent upon the migrant's country of origin, ranging from $7,000 to $20,000 (Balfour & Comack, 2021). Women play diverse roles in the illicit transportation of undocumented migrants across borders and between nations in Latin America (Figure 1.4).

Figure 1.4. *Colombian police take down criminal group behind human trafficking.*

Source: Interpol (2021).

1.9. THE INFLUENCE OF GENDER ON SENTENCING AND PUNISHMENT

The sentencing phase of the criminal justice system was chosen because evidence suggests that this is the stage of the process where the most significant discrepancies exist in the way different genders are treated in terms of the sentences they are given. The claim is substantiated in academic literature through the analysis of authors who have investigated the impact of gender as a variable on an individual's sentencing, and whether the severity of the sentence aligns with the crimes they have committed. The issue of whether individuals of different genders are treated equally when being sentenced for similar crimes could be used as a foundation for justifiability. The topic will primarily examine two theories: the Double Deviance theory and the Chivalry theory.

1.9.1. Chivalry, Selective Chivalry, and Paternalism Theory

Otto Pollak posited the theory that women in the criminal justice system are granted more lenient treatment than men due to the concept of chivalry towards women (Bontrager et al., 2013). Subsequently, paternalism is typically perceived as a subsequent element to the noble aspect. According to this hypothesis, women's leniency or favoritism is attributed to the perception of law enforcement and courts that women are vulnerable and childlike, thus requiring their protection.

Given that Pollak's research may be deemed antiquated, we aim to assess whether any elements of the theory remain relevant to the current practices of sentencing in the criminal justice system. Selective chivalry refers to the modification of the theory of chivalry by paternalism. The implication is that only Caucasian women and individuals from privileged socioeconomic backgrounds are eligible for the leniency associated with the concept of chivalry. Multiple studies have been conducted on various types of crimes, and the findings have analyzed the possible influence of chivalry on sentencing decisions (Bontrager et al., 2013).

1.9.2. Double Deviance/Evil Woman

The principle of double deviation posits that certain women are subjected to penalties for supposedly committing two transgressions. They are seen as having violated the law and cultural norms regarding what is considered acceptable behavior for women (Bontrager et al., 2013). They are subsequently evaluated on the basis of having committed two offenses. According to this hypothesis, a woman's adherence or violation of social norms may result in either demonization or leniency.

The Double Deviance theory, also referred to as the Evil Woman theory in some cases is a concept in criminology. While some women may receive more lenient treatment under this concept, it may seem like a form of selective chivalry. The notion that women who deviate from these gender norms are subjected to harsher penalties compared to males who commit the same transgressions is markedly distinct. Despite committing identical crimes, women who conform to this notion and are perceived as doubly deviant are considered more culpable in this scenario, leading to more severe punishments (Bontrager et al., 2013).

CHAPTER 2

GENDER DISPARITIES IN CRIMINAL OFFENSES

Contents

There are intriguing patterns that emerge when analyzing the variations in criminal behavior based on gender. It is important to note that criminal behavior is not limited to one gender. However, it is evident that the level of participation in criminal activities varies significantly between men and women (Figure 2.1).

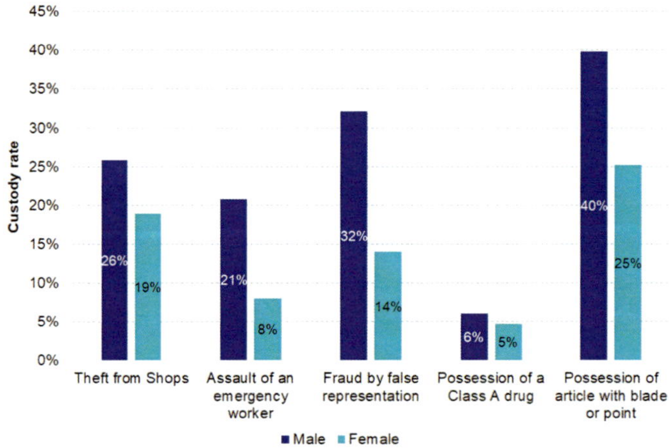

Figure 2.1. *Proportions of males and females throughout the criminal justice system (CJS), 2019.*

Source: GOV.UK (2020).

Below are some key observations.

1. **Crime Categories:** Women exhibit lower rates of criminal activity compared to men across all crime categories. When analyzing major, violent crimes such as robbery or murder, it is evident that men tend to be the primary perpetrators, while women are less inclined to engage in such acts. One interesting exception to note is that the male-driven prostitution industry has been found to result in a higher number of arrests of women.
2. **Offense Severity:** Crimes committed by women generally result in less severe consequences. When we examine the data, we can observe that female offenders tend to cause fewer injuries in their violent offenses, and the financial impact of their property crimes is generally lower in terms of lost money or damaged property.
3. **Context is Important:** It is necessary to take institutional injustices, cultural norms, and the social context into account in order to comprehend gender variances. Women's criminal behavior can be shaped by various factors, including societal norms, familial responsibilities, and socioeconomic conditions.

Generally, the differences in criminal behavior between genders highlight the need for specific approaches in law enforcement, punishment, and rehabilitation. Recognizing these differences can lead to fairer criminal justice systems and more efficient approaches. In this chapter, we will delve into various aspects related to gender disparities in crime rates. We will explore biological explanations, socialization, and gendered expectations for behavior, the influence of masculinity on criminality, female pathways to crime, gendered patterns of victimization and offending, the role of substance abuse in women's criminal behavior, gender and violent crime, the relationship between gender and white-collar crime, gender and cybercrime, and finally, the intersection of race, gender, and crime.

2.1. BIOLOGICAL EXPLANATIONS FOR GENDER DISPARITIES IN CRIME RATES

Sex disparities in crime refer to the differences observed between men and women in terms of their involvement as criminals or victims of crime. These can be classified as feminist studies, sociobiology (which seeks to establish a causal relationship between biological factors, such as biological sex, and human behaviors), or criminology (the scientific study of criminal behavior). Examining crime statistics can provide insights into the relationship between gender inequalities, although they can be challenging to comprehend. Crime rates between men and women can vary due to a range of factors. These include biological elements such as testosterone, sociobiological theories, undetected crimes, and social and cultural influences. It is important to consider the type or motive of the crime itself as a factor (Carrabine et al., 2020).

In a study conducted by Terrie Moffitt and Avshalom Caspi in 2001, they compared male and female characters who displayed antisocial behavior during childhood and adolescence. The study aimed to analyze the childhood risk variables that contribute to deviant behavior in individuals. Childhood delinquency has been found to be associated with various factors such as temperament and behavior problems, neurocognitive difficulties, and insufficient parenting. On the other hand, it is worth noting that individuals who engaged in delinquent behavior during their adolescence did not necessarily experience the same childhood challenges. Based on this study, it has been found that there is a significant difference in the male-to-female ratio for delinquents, depending on whether their offenses began in childhood or adolescence. Specifically, the ratio is 10:1 for those whose offenses started in childhood and 15:1 for those whose offenses started in adolescence. According to Moffitt and Caspi, the development of antisocial behavior can be traced back to early childhood, where a combination of challenging behavior in a high-risk child and a high-risk social environment can worsen the situation. In the realm of adolescent development, there is a phenomenon referred to as the maturity gap. This occurs during the transitional period between puberty and the attainment of adult privileges and responsibilities. It is during this time that otherwise well-adjusted young individuals may experience dysphoria, leading to the emergence of antisocial behavior. This concept was first introduced by Moffitt and Caspi in 2001. The taxonomy theory is examined, which suggests that gender inequalities in crime rates can be attributed to sex differences in the risk variables for life-course-persistent antisocial conduct. Research suggests that there is a lower likelihood for girls to experience learning disabilities, temperamental difficulties, late maturation in verbal and motor development, nervous system dysfunctions, and behavioral issues in early life (Moffitt & Caspi, 2001).

Psychological and biological factors have been used to explain the relationship between gender and criminality. In contemporary sociological theories, there is a growing focus on the impact of gender variations on criminal behavior. Brezina's research centers around the examination of the "general strain theory" and its implications for understanding the variations in crime rates among males and females (Brezina, 2017). There is a theory that suggests a connection between the gender disparity in crime and the unique stresses and experiences that men and women face. Each family has its own unique dynamics, with distinct lives, relationships, socialization patterns, and life experiences.

According to studies, it has been found that there is a more pronounced correlation between crime and delinquency in males. According to Brezina, there are several factors that contribute to a higher likelihood of boys engaging in criminal behavior. These include experiencing homelessness, facing strict parental discipline during their formative years, having negative educational experiences, and lacking adequate support systems. According to Brezina (2017), there is a tendency among certain boys and men to perceive crime as acceptable due to their adherence to certain masculine values that they have internalized.

2.2. SOCIALIZATION AND GENDERED EXPECTATIONS FOR BEHAVIOR

Sex is the term used to describe the biological traits that differentiate males and females. Gender refers to the socially constructed traits that are assigned to the sexes. In every culture, social expectations, customs, and behaviors play a significant role in shaping the definitions of masculinity and femininity. Gender socialization refers to the process of instructing individuals on how to conform to the societal expectations and behaviors associated with their gender. Gender socialization involves the teaching of gender stereotypes. There are certain attitudes and behaviors that are commonly associated with individuals based on gender stereotypes. One example of gender stereotyping is the notion that males are inherently aggressive while females are naturally submissive. According to research conducted by Leaper and Friedman in 2007, it has been observed that by the age of three, children begin to acquire knowledge about gender stereotypes.

2.2.1. Agents of Gender Socialization

During the early years of a child's life, their parents and school play a crucial role in shaping their understanding of gender norms and expectations. It could potentially have its origins in more distant locations, such as the media.

Parents play a crucial role in shaping children's understanding of gender norms from an early age. Parents play a crucial role in shaping their children's lives. Sons often look up to their fathers as role models, while daughters often find inspiration in their mothers. It is commonly believed by parents that there will be variations in personality traits and abilities between boys and girls due to their gender. Parents play a significant role in perpetuating gender-specific norms, as highlighted by Leaper & Friedman (2007).

One effective way for parents to educate their children about gender norms is through play. One example of this is their choice of toys. As an example, it is common for girls to receive dolls and kitchen sets, while boys often receive sports equipment and toy automobiles. There is a common perception that girls' play tends to be more passive, while boys' play is often seen as more active. As an example, it is often expected that boys will engage in play that involves battles, while girls will engage in play that involves tea parties (Leaper & Friedman, 2007).

One approach that parents often employ to reinforce gender norms is assigning housework to their children. Traditionally, girls have often been assigned household tasks such as dishwashing and laundry. According to Leaper & Friedman (2007), boys are often given tasks that require more physical exertion, such as taking out the trash or mowing the lawn. Parents often impart gender norms to their children through the choice of clothing they dress them in and the design of their bedrooms. In the past, parents have held certain expectations regarding the future paths of their children based on gender. As an example, it was commonly expected that girls would pursue roles as homemakers and mothers, while boys were encouraged to prepare for providing for their future families.

Over the past five decades, there has been a notable transformation in family dynamics. It is evident that the structure of families has evolved over time, with the traditional model of a stay-at-home mother and a working father becoming less common in modern society. There is a noticeable difference in the expectations that parents have for their sons compared to their daughters. While some parents still hold traditional and strict standards for their sons, others have more progressive and egalitarian expectations for their daughters.

2.2.2. The Impact of Socialization Based on Gender

Gender is a crucial aspect when it comes to health and wellbeing. Gender socialization can have a profound impact on the lives of both men and women. It affects them in various ways:

1. **Life Decisions:** The gender indoctrination that individuals receive has a profound impact on the trajectory of their lives. One important aspect to consider is the impact it has on an individual's career choices and their perception of their own abilities. Throughout history, there has been a prevailing notion that girls have been socialized to believe that boys are not interested in intelligent women. Consequently, a significant number of young women have opted for occupations that align with traditional gender roles, thereby suppressing their enthusiasm for mathematics and science. It is worth noting that boys often make decisions in life based on gender norms, as highlighted by Leaper and Friedman in their research conducted in 2007. As we delve into history, we come across the notion that boys have traditionally been instructed to perceive an inclination towards the arts as a characteristic more commonly associated with women. Due to this particular rationale, numerous individuals opt not to pursue careers in dance or theater, instead choosing professions that are perceived to align more closely with traditional masculine norms.
2. **Health of Women:** Gender norms can have detrimental impacts on women's physical and mental well-being due to their inherent inequity. Women are often found in roles that have historically been associated with less power compared to their male counterparts. This is a result of traditional gender roles that have been ingrained in society. According to Leaper & Friedman (2007), there has been a concerning decrease in women's control over and access to healthcare due to the persistent gender wage and power inequality. One important factor that contributes to the prevalence of violence against women is the unequal treatment of genders. Marital rape was not considered illegal until 1976 (Leaper & Friedman, 2007). In the

past, women were seen as belonging to their husbands in terms of their sexuality. In contemporary society, it is unfortunately common for rape victims to be unfairly blamed for the assault based on their behavior or statements.

2.3. THE INFLUENCE OF MASCULINITY ON CRIMINALITY

In the last decade, there has been a notable increase in academic focus on the topic of masculine identity and its correlation with criminal behavior. One interesting aspect of criminology's historical focus has been its exploration of topics related to masculinity, albeit indirectly (Tomsen, 2008).

Over the past few decades, there has been significant growth in the field of masculinity studies. This field explores various theoretical perspectives that examine the influence of masculine dominance and the construction of gender identities in society. There is a certain allure to the rush of adrenaline, the nervous excitement, and the sense of fulfillment that certain individuals find in acts of violence. These experiences often seem to be linked to notions of masculinity and are influenced by various social, cultural, and economic factors that reflect the complexities of contemporary society. However, it is important to note that societal and economic factors do not always drive young men towards criminal behavior (Tomsen, 2008).

Engaging in improper behavior can often hold a certain allure and provide a thrilling experience. Furthermore, it is intricately linked to one's sense of identity and the pursuit of social status.

According to Tomsen (2008), the male social networks of the lower classes are often the channels through which the fascination with violence and enjoyment of crime are expressed.

There is an increasing challenge in distinguishing criminological theories on lower-class masculinities from the ongoing debates surrounding the urban underclass and its connection to the global economy. Throughout history, there has been a clear connection between the economy and the formation of lower-class masculinities. This relationship has persisted for generations.

The decline of mutual relationships and traditional communities has led to a growing tension on social cohesion and social capital. This is particularly evident as traditional male occupations in factories, shipyards, steel mills, and mines undergo significant transformations. Additionally, social identities are now more commonly formed around consumption and leisure rather than production and work (Tomsen, 2008). In the present day, there are several factors that contribute to the challenges faced by lower-class males. These include reliance on welfare, inadequate health conditions, and a high rate of imprisonment, which in turn affects tax revenue.

According to Tomsen (2008), there is a perception that they are responsible for a significantly higher rate of crime, specifically violent crime, which contributes to increased social anxiety. Furthermore, they are often blamed for the decline of the traditional nuclear family, the social problems that arise from the increase in single-parent households, and various other issues. Most of their actions or lack thereof can be traced back to the increasing influence of market-oriented neoliberalism, which is linked to the rising tendency to stigmatize and exclude certain identities and groups (Tomsen, 2008).

However, there are numerous legitimate concerns regarding the construction of underclass masculinities by society. Exclusion from the formal economy has a profound impact on shaping identities, which can be detrimental to our society that is characterized by anxiety and sterility. Society's intention becomes evident when practical or financial anchors are removed from individuals' lives. This deliberate act aims to exclude troublesome groups, leaving these men without the support of social control institutions and with limited opportunities to reintegrate into the new norms of the market and consumption. Given the absence of family, employment, and full-time education among these young individuals, their behavior is not as constrained or regulated as it would be otherwise.

2.4. EXAMINING FEMALE PATHWAYS TO CRIME

Due to the gendered circumstances surrounding female criminality, a distinct path into criminal behavior exists for one gender. However, it is important to note that not all female criminals follow a gendered trajectory in the same manner. In other words, it is important to note that there are variations in female criminality not only between genders but also within females (Reisig et al., 2006).

Male offenders may experience similar conditions that contribute to criminal behavior, such as childhood maltreatment. However, it is important to note that the impact of these adverse life experiences may vary among female offenders. Research findings have shown a correlation between instances of sexual and physical abuse experienced by women and their subsequent involvement in criminal activities. There are various factors that contribute to women engaging in criminal activity, such as economic marginalization, arrest records, spousal violence, cultural and societal norms, and marital issues. These pathways have been recognized as significant influences in women's involvement in crime.

There is a significant difference in financial power between female and male offenders, with the former facing a disadvantage. According to Schwartz et al., (2015), there is a noticeable disparity between men and women when it comes to prior full-time employment experience before incarceration. Upon being incarcerated, women face significant challenges in securing employment, both on a full-time and part-time basis, due to the presence of their criminal records. This situation further compounds the challenges experienced by women who bear the responsibility of providing for their families independently, particularly in South Africa where women often find themselves as the sole breadwinners in certain households. There is a concern that these women may become involved in financially motivated crimes (Schwartz et al., 2015).

Reisig et al. (2006) found that there is a notable difference in the level of violence employed in criminal behavior between men and women. This difference becomes more evident in more serious crimes compared to less severe ones. The authors discuss a gender disparity in firearm usage, noting that men tend to employ weapons against their victims, while women often utilize guns when committing crimes alongside male accomplices. When it comes to committing crimes, there are different approaches employed by individuals. While men often resort to weapons and physical force, women may opt for alternative methods such as utilizing their sexuality and confrontational tactics instead of relying on firearms.

There exists a distinct contextual disparity when it comes to male and female offenders in the victim-offender dynamic. It is interesting to note that male criminals often target victims whom they have no personal connection with, whereas female offenders tend to victimize individuals whom they are familiar with, such as intimate partners, friends, or family members (Schwartz et al., 2015). One way to observe the disparities in criminal activity between men and women is by examining the frequency of using force.

As women age, they may experience a decrease in this particular aspect. In contrast, as women age, they tend to engage in fewer violent crimes compared to men.

Gender disparities in stealing arise due to distinct motivations between men and women when it comes to engaging in this criminal behavior. According to research conducted by Reisig et al. (2006), there is a difference in the motivations behind financial crimes committed by males and females. The study suggests that males may engage in such crimes to maintain their social status, whereas females may do so to provide financial support for their friends and families. The gendered pathways theory offers a deeper understanding of how women's criminal behavior is influenced by gender.

2.5. GENDERED PATTERNS OF VICTIMIZATION AND OFFENDING

When we examine the data, it becomes evident that the rate of criminal activity among women is significantly lower than that of men. It is a widely accepted fact that most crimes exhibit certain patterns, although there are variations in the extent of women's involvement in different types of criminal activities (Heidensohn, 2012). In addition, due to the relatively low number of crimes committed by women, even a slight increase in the overall figures could lead to a disproportionately significant surge. Heidensohn's research indicates that the percentage of women involved in criminal proceedings in several European nations ranged from 10% to 20%.

Based on historical research, it has been found that this share does not vary significantly from current levels, except for a few rare cases. According to Burman & McIvor (2004), the rate of women's crime remained relatively stable or even experienced a slight decline throughout the 20th century, despite the overall increase in crime rates. Contrary to popular belief, studies on delinquency have shown that a higher number of females compared to males are hesitant to admit their involvement in criminal activities (Burman & McIvor, 2004). Based on the findings, it can be concluded that there is a reduced gender gap, especially in relation to juvenile delinquency.

Furthermore, the increase in the number of women being arrested, convicted, and incarcerated, especially for drug- and assault-related crimes, indicates a growing level of aggression among them (Figure 2.2).

Figure 2.2. *Number of women in jail rising faster than men.*

Source: Bruinius (2016).

When examining the characteristics of female criminal behavior, it becomes apparent that women tend to engage in less severe offenses compared to men.

These include minor motoring offenses, drug offenses, prostitution, fraud, and handling stolen items. In addition, it is worth noting that a significant number of women who engage in criminal activities do so for the first time. There is a limited number of women who can be categorized as professional offenders. It is worth noting that there is a correlation between the gender of offenders and victims of violent crimes.

Statistics show that males tend to be the most frequent perpetrators of such crimes, which in turn explains why they are also more likely to be the victims of violent crimes. It is important to note that the occurrence of violent crime can vary, as highlighted by Burman & McIvor in 2004. It is worth noting that the number of male homicide victims surpasses that of female victims. The relationship between the attacker and the victim can differ significantly. In many cases, women are tragically more likely to be killed by someone they know intimately, either a current or former partner. On the other hand, men tend to face a higher risk of being killed by someone they are not familiar with, such as a stranger or acquaintance. "Women are more prone to experiencing certain forms of victimization, such as rape and domestic abuse, compared to men."

In order to fully understand victimization, it is crucial to consider various factors beyond just gender. Elements like ethnicity and class play a significant role in determining the likelihood of becoming a victim. Furthermore, it is crucial to consider societal standards, broader social, political, and economic contexts, and variations in victimization rates within nations (Burman & McIvor, 2004). Scholars often direct their attention towards the court's punitive policy, examining it through the lens of gender. There is a debate among scholars regarding the treatment of women compared to men. One perspective highlights the lower incidence of major crimes, including violent offenses, committed by women. One possible explanation for this potential difference is that they have a lower likelihood of reoffending. It is worth noting that in some countries, there has been a significant increase in the proportion of women in jails over the past few decades, although the overall proportion of women incarcerated has remained relatively constant (Burman & McIvor, 2004).

Each of these challenges holds great importance for policymakers. The analysis of victimization and criminal offending highlights the importance of understanding these experiences in relation to class and ethnicity, as revealed by Burman & McIvor in 2004. Criminology is a field that offers valuable insights into various aspects of crime and victimization. It helps us understand the true extent of crime, the influence of gender, victimization patterns that may not be addressed by the criminal code, and the impact on victims. These are all important areas that criminology helps us explore and comprehend (Burman & McIvor, 2004). Policymakers should utilize this knowledge to effectively prevent crime, develop gender-sensitive criminal law legislation, and implement legal norms in the real world.

2.6. THE ROLE OF SUBSTANCE ABUSE IN WOMEN'S CRIMINAL BEHAVIOR

Drug use is a significant factor that contributes to the involvement of women in the criminal court system. The prevalence of drug usage among female criminals is quite high, and research has consistently shown a strong correlation between drug use and repeated encounters with the criminal justice system. Based on national statistics, it has been found that a significant proportion of women in federal and state prisons meet the criteria for drug addiction or dependency (Tuchman, 2014). Research on drug misuse and criminal activity reveals an interesting finding: prior to their involvement with the criminal justice system, female prisoners tended to have a higher frequency of drug experimentation compared to their male counterparts (Figure 2.3).

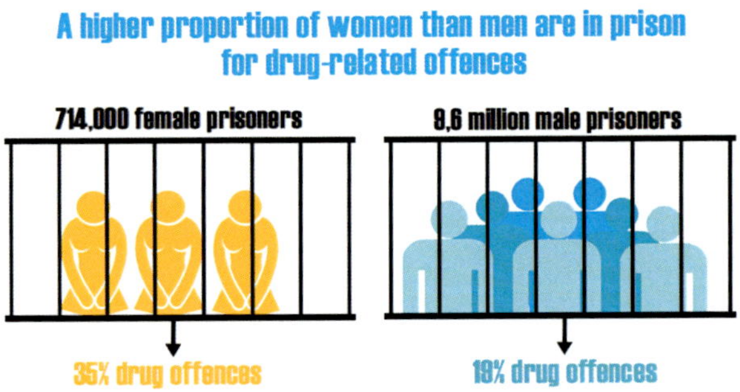

Figure 2.3. *Men and women in prison for drug-related offences.*

Source: UNODC (2024).

Violent crimes have been observed to be the primary pathway for males to become involved in the criminal justice system. However, it is worth noting that drug-related offenses and drug use also play a significant role in men's interactions with the legal system. It has been suggested that there may be a potential link between women's drug usage and their experiences of interpersonal violence (Tuchman, 2014).

There is a viewpoint that suggests that while men may express their anger outwardly when faced with a negative experience, women are more inclined to turn to drugs as a way to cope with internalized feelings of shame, often stemming from past instances of abuse. Previous research has found that men tend to be the main contributors to drug use among women (Tuchman,

2014). Female offenders have reported that drug misuse can be traced back to a previous incident of physical abuse, where drugs were used as a way to establish a connection with men. Prisoned wComen have also emphasized the ways in which their romantic partners manipulated the criminal justice system and how they became involved in drug trafficking. Studies on female drug dealers and traffickers challenge this assertion, demonstrating that men do not always play a central role in women's involvement in drug use and the drug market economy. According to Tuchman (2014), women involved in the drug market have demonstrated a level of independence and decision-making in their choice to participate, challenging the perception of them as mere victims.

In qualitative research, a pathway perspective is often used to develop additional typological categories or pathways that highlight important characteristics or events leading to women's involvement in criminal activities. In Tuchman's analysis, the focus was on women who found themselves entangled in the court system, exploring the various factors that contributed to their disadvantaged circumstances such as poverty, limited education, and other forms of marginalization. Another perspective to consider is that of individuals commonly referred to as "street women." These individuals may have come from abusive homes and found themselves caught in the criminal justice system due to engaging in activities such as theft, drug misuse, drug dealing, or prostitution. It is important to note that these survival strategies are considered illegal. Finally, the pathway known as "battered women" connects various cases of abuse, drug abuse, and criminal behavior to relationships where abuse is prevalent (Tuchman, 2014). According to Tuchman (2014), it is often observed that women who find themselves in the criminal justice system have a history of childhood maltreatment. This unfortunate experience is often followed by drug abuse, which eventually leads to their involvement with the system.

2.7. GENDER AND VIOLENT CRIME

For decades, the topic of why men commit more crimes than women has captivated sociologists, psychologists, and criminologists. Crime statistics worldwide consistently highlight a significant gender disparity, with men being overrepresented as both victims and offenders. In order to gain a comprehensive understanding of this issue, we will delve into the different aspects that play a role in it.

2.7.1. The Global Difference in Crime Rates by Gender

According to global crime statistics, there is a clear trend indicating that men are consistently involved in a higher number of criminal activities compared to women. This pattern is evident across various categories such as property crimes, violent crimes, and white-collar offenses. Crime rates globally show a significant overrepresentation of males, as indicated by data from the and other international crime databases (Steffensmeier et al., 2006).

1. **Male Involvement in Violent Crimes:** It is worth noting that there is a disparity in crime rates between males and females, with males being more likely to commit crimes. However, it is also impoHGJJrtant to acknowledge that males also experience higher rates of victimization. Based on data provided by the World Health Organization (WHO), it has been observed that a significant majority of homicide victims across the globe are men.
2. **Property Crimes:** Men are more likely than women to commit property crimes, such as theft and burglary. Research conducted by the Federal Bureau of Investigation (FBI) and other similar organizations worldwide consistently reveals a pattern where men tend to be more inclined towards committing property crimes compared to women (Steffensmeier et al., 2006).
3. **White-Collar Crimes:** When examining the gender distribution of white-collar crimes, it is evident that although there has been some balance historically, men continue to be overrepresented in these cases. According to the Association of Certified Fraud Examiners (ACFE), research has shown that a higher percentage of individuals involved in corporate fraud are male.

Understanding the gender gap in crime rates requires a comprehensive examination of various factors, including biological and evolutionary features, social impacts, and psychological predispositions.

2.7.2. Perspectives From a Biological and Evolutionary Framework

1. **Testosterone Levels:** It has been suggested that higher testosterone levels in men may be related to the biological distinctions between men and women. Testosterone, a hormone more prevalent in men, has been linked to a greater likelihood of engaging in criminal behavior. This hormone is associated with traits such as assertiveness and dominance.
2. **Evolutionary Psychology:** From an evolutionary perspective, aggressive behaviors may have emerged as advantageous strategies for survival and reproduction. From a scholarly perspective, one can view male aggression as an evolutionary trait that has historically provided advantages in the competition for mates and resources.

2.7.3. Social Factors

1. **Gender-Specific Behaviors:** This arise from the distinct socialization that boys and girls receive. Research suggests that there is a correlation between a boy's upbringing in environments that tolerate or encourage violence and their increased likelihood of engaging in criminal behavior.
2. **Gender Roles and Expectations:** Criminal behavior can be influenced by gender roles and societal expectations. Emphasizing the importance of strength and dominance in societal expectations of masculinity can potentially lead men to engage in more risky behaviors, sometimes leading to criminal actions.
3. **Socioeconomic Factors:** A major influence on criminal conduct is economics. It is a common observation that men, often facing higher levels of unemployment and economic instability, may resort to engaging in criminal behavior in order to meet their financial needs.
4. **Income Disparity:** Research from around the world indicates a link between crime rates and income disparity. Income inequality can have a significant impact on crime rates within a nation. This issue tends to affect men more due to their social and economic status.

2.7.4. Psychological Aspects

1. **Disparities in Traits:** Men may exhibit higher levels of impulsivity and risk-taking, two psychological traits linked to criminal activity. According to Steffensmeier et al. (2006), the likelihood of engaging in criminal behavior is influenced by a combination of environmental and biological factors. These factors contribute to the development of certain characteristics associated with criminal activity.
2. **Neurological Disparities:** Research indicates that there could be variations in the structure and functionality of the brains between men and women, which could impact impulsive and decision-making behaviors.
3. **Substance Misuse:** Substance misuse is more common among men and is closely associated with criminal activity. Substance abuse has the potential to result in a decrease in inhibitions, impaired decision-making abilities, and an increased likelihood of engaging in criminal behavior.
4. **Mental Health Disorders:** There is a complicated relationship between criminal activity and mental health disorders. Research has shown that there may be a disparity between males and females

when it comes to seeking mental health treatment. This disparity could potentially worsen the connection between mental illness and criminal behavior.

2.7.5. Men's Affection From Criminological Perspectives

1. **The Cultural Construction of Masculinity:** In the realm of masculinity studies, there is a concept called "hegemonic masculinity" that emphasizes how cultural influences play a significant role in shaping the idealized behavior associated with being a man. It has been observed that societal expectations of toughness, power, and risk-taking can exert significant pressure on men, potentially leading them to engage in criminal behavior as a means of affirming their masculinity (Steffensmeier et al., 2006).
2. **Exploring Risks and Illicit Behavior:** There is a strong correlation between engaging in risk-taking behaviors and criminality, aligning with traditional perceptions of masculinity. Research has shown that there is a correlation between men's engagement in risky behaviors and their tendency to feel compelled to demonstrate bravery and aggression.
3. **Crimes Typically Associated with Males:** Crimes such as assaults are often perceived by society as predominantly committed by men. From a scholarly standpoint, it is worth noting that societal expectations can exert a significant influence on males, potentially leading them to engage in criminal activities that align with stereotypical notions of masculinity.
4. **Crisis of Masculinity:** A crisis of masculinity may result from societal changes, such as shifting gender roles and economic upheavals. According to Steffensmeier et al. (2006), when faced with challenges to traditional gender norms, men sometimes respond by engaging in criminal behavior as a way to regain a sense of lost masculinity.

2.7.6. Various Viewpoints Within Criminological Feminism

1. **Patriarchal Society Structures:** Gendered crime patterns are believed to be a direct consequence of the societal structures that favor patriarchal norms, as feminist criminology suggests. Placing a heavy emphasis on male authority within hierarchies can result in detrimental consequences for women, potentially impacting their involvement in criminal behavior.

2. **Economic Inequality:** From a feminist perspective, it is argued that criminal behavior is greatly impacted by disparities in economic circumstances. Financial pressures can sometimes lead individuals, particularly those in higher social positions, to resort to criminal activities. However, women may face unique challenges within institutional systems.

There are multiple factors that contribute to the higher crime rates among men compared to women. These factors encompass sociological, psychological, and biological aspects. Global crime data often reveal disparities in crime rates between genders, necessitating a comprehensive examination of the factors contributing to these differences. A holistic approach is necessary to address this discrepancy, considering the complex interplay between biology, socialization, and individual psychology. In order to achieve a more just and equitable future with a significant reduction in crime, it is crucial for societies to adopt gender-responsive policies, implement educational initiatives, and prioritize targeted economic and social programs (Steffensmeier et al., 2006).

Understanding the gender gap in crime rates requires a thorough examination of feminist and masculinity theories in criminology. These frameworks provide a comprehensive understanding of how gendered crime trends are shaped by power dynamics, cultural expectations, and structural disparities. To develop more fair and effective strategies for addressing the root causes of criminal behavior in both genders, it is crucial for researchers and legislators to consider these different perspectives.

2.8. THE RELATIONSHIP BETWEEN GENDER AND WHITE-COLLAR CRIME

It is worth noting that the higher representation of men in the corporate world does contribute to a higher likelihood of white-collar crimes being committed. However, it is important to recognize that this correlation does not imply causation, and it would be inaccurate to make sweeping generalizations. There is no denying the potential for women to become engaged (Chowdhury & Gibson, 2019).

Research on gender and white-collar crime reveals intriguing connections. Both men and women participate in criminal activity, but their involvement differs significantly. It is crucial to note the following observations:

1. Men are typically the ones responsible for serious, violent white-collar crimes such as fraud and embezzlement. However, it is worth noting that women often engage in these criminal activities at a comparable or even higher rate than men. It is worth mentioning that

when it comes to crimes related to reproductive medicine, women are more likely to be involved than men.

2. When women do commit crimes, the consequences are typically less dire. When we examine the behavior of female offenders in comparison to their male counterparts, we find that their violent offenses tend to result in fewer injuries, and their property crimes generally lead to less financial loss or damage to property.

Scholars disagree as to whether women's low incidence of white-collar crime is more likely a result of opportunities lost than of socialization against crime. There is an ongoing debate regarding the likelihood of women engaging in embezzlement. Some argue that women are just as likely as men to commit this crime, while others emphasize the influence of identity risks and gender socialization as important factors in determining the likelihood of women engaging in embezzlement (Chowdhury & Gibson, 2019).

Some of the most infamous examples of white-collar crimes include the cases involving Martha Stewart, Enron, and Bernie Madoff. Bernie Madoff orchestrated the largest Ponzi scheme in American history. He convinced individuals to invest with him as a finance and investment counselor by promising exceptionally high returns in a brief timeframe. However, the funds he was promising to those who joined him in investing turned out to be the very funds he was persuading new investors to contribute. This business plan may seem acceptable in the short term, but it is important to consider the long-term consequences. If the funds from new investors are not enough to sustain the returns promised to previous investors, the entire strategy will eventually crumble. At the time of his arrest in 2009, Bernie Madoff had managed to deceive investors and swindle an astonishing amount of over $65 billion.

A significant number of individuals who placed their trust in Madoff's financial management and invested their funds with him experienced a complete loss of their assets. Madoff was sentenced to a 150-year jail term after pleading guilty to 11 counts of various financial offenses. Based on the documents, it was determined by medical professionals in September 2019 that the patient is suffering from a terminal illness and has a limited life expectancy. According to Chowdhury & Gibson (2019), his current desire remains unfulfilled.

To fully understand the role that gender plays in white-collar crime, it is crucial to consider factors such as socialization and opportunity. These elements play a significant role in shaping the dynamics of this issue. It cannot be guaranteed that white-collar crime is influenced by gender. After careful analysis, it becomes apparent that there are several differences when comparing corporate crime and gender among men and women (Chowdhury & Gibson, 2019).

One possible explanation for the higher proportion of males engaged in white-collar crime is the greater number of men in the commercial workforce, coupled with the highly masculine nature of the corporate environment (Chowdhury & Gibson, 2019). It is observed that men tend to exert greater influence over others compared to women, particularly in cases involving low-ranking women who may feel compelled to conform, assist, or engage in white-collar crimes. According to Chowdhury & Gibson (2019), women in lower levels often feel pressured to conform to the prevailing male culture and adopt certain habits to prove their ability to collaborate with their male counterparts.

There is a notable disparity in the involvement of men and women in corporate crimes. This can be attributed, in part, to the fact that men often do not feel compelled to offer psychological justifications for their actions before engaging in such illicit activities. According to Chowdhury & Gibson (2019), there is a tendency for women to provide explanations or justifications for their choices before engaging in unethical activities, as opposed to men. Financial demands from families, which women perceived as reasonable, played a significant role in justifying women's participation in white-collar crime. Men may have a tendency to engage in white-collar crimes without much consideration for validation or consequences, as they often fail to justify their actions. There is a notable disparity in the types of white-collar crimes committed by individuals of different genders. Research suggests that women may be more likely to engage in less serious white-collar crimes in business environments due to differences in their positions within the company. This finding highlights the influence of the male-dominated nature of these environments. It is worth noting that a significant number of women are not in executive board positions or in roles that are deemed significant enough for dishonest behavior to be classified as a serious white-collar crime.

2.9. GENDER AND CYBERCRIME

Gender plays a significant role in the realm of cybercrime. Here are a few notable observations:

1. **Online Behavior:** Gender plays a significant role in shaping and influencing people's behavior. The way individuals engage with the online world has a profound impact on their interactions, decision-making processes, and propensity for taking risks.
2. **Vulnerability:** Gender is an important aspect to consider when discussing vulnerability. Women and men may find themselves in different risk categories due to factors such as their social networks, online behaviors, and susceptibility to cyberthreats.

3. **Justice Access:** For victims of cybercrimes, gender affects their ability to obtain justice. Women, particularly those from marginalized backgrounds, may encounter additional challenges when seeking legal remedies.
4. **Reinforcing Inequalities:** Gender dynamics in the online sphere frequently perpetuate offline gender disparities. In order to promote equity and fairness in cyberspace, it is crucial to acknowledge and tackle these underlying dynamics.

Throughout the globe, women face a disproportionate amount of online abuse, especially if they are part of specific religious, racial, or ethnic communities, have a particular sexual orientation, are economically disadvantaged, or are disabled. According to a study conducted by Amnesty International, a significant number of women surveyed in multiple countries reported instances of cyberharassment and online abuse.

Specifically, approximately 25% of the 4,000 women polled in the United States, the United Kingdom, Denmark, Sweden, Spain, Italy, and Poland indicated that they had encountered such forms of mistreatment at least once (Myers Jr. & Radhakrishna, 2018).

In addition, it is concerning that 41% of these women who experienced online harassment expressed genuine concern for their personal safety due to the abuse they endured. Various forms of inappropriate content, including explicit text messages, emails, photos, videos, and threats of violence, have unfortunately been transmitted to women through various online platforms such as chat rooms, instant messaging, social media, and dating websites (Myers Jr. & Radhakrishna, 2018).

Instances of cyberharassment and cyberstalking have been observed targeting feminists, feminist groups, women's rights activists, and organizations across the globe.

Instances of sexual abuse, harassment, and stalking targeting members of Mujeres Insumisas, a feminist organization in Colombia, have been extensively documented in various online and offline settings (Myers Jr. & Radhakrishna, 2018). Research findings have revealed that when a woman occupies a prominent position in the public eye, she becomes susceptible to receiving derogatory comments and facing alarming threats of physical and sexual violence. As an example, it is worth noting that when UK Labor MP Jess Phillips advocated for the identification of Internet trolls, she unfortunately faced an alarming number of over 600 rape threats in just one night, alongside numerous other threats and derogatory comments (Myers Jr. & Radhakrishna, 2018).

2.10. THE INTERSECTION OF RACE, GENDER, AND CRIME

The intersection of race, gender, and criminality is a significant area of study that aims to elucidate the complex relationships between these variables (Burgess, 2006). In recent decades, there has been a significant increase in scholarly research on this topic, which has greatly enhanced our understanding. Early feminist criminologists advocated for the use of gender-specific theoretical frameworks and empirical research, while also critiquing masculinist perspectives on crime. These efforts to protect women and girls from abuse led to the implementation of new laws that mandate the arrest of individuals who engage in domestic abuse (Burgess, 2006). Intersectionality emphasizes how an individual's experiences are influenced by the overlapping factors of gender, race, and class. This perspective considers the convergence of gender, race, and justice, rather than solely focusing on the intersections of gender, race, and crime, which often center around criminal behavior. Researchers examine disparities in the implementation of legal proceedings and the manner in which systemic aggression affects the vulnerability of women belonging to racial minority groups to various forms of violence and punitive actions.

Emerging research, including intersectional and Black feminist studies, compels us to transcend binary conceptions of gender and scrutinize the broader framework. By engaging in this activity, we can enhance our understanding of the complexities associated with criminal behavior and the impact of intersecting identities. Recognizing these intricate connections is crucial for formulating equitable legislation, addressing systemic biases, and promoting justice for all individuals within the criminal justice system. This ongoing investigation challenges individuals to engage with the intricate matters of crime and justice (Burgess, 2006).

2.10.1. The Relationship Between Gender and Criminal Behavior

1. **Gender Inequalities:** Females constitute a smaller proportion of arrests compared to males across most criminal categories. However, their level of involvement varies depending on the type of offense.
2. **Crime Types:** Women are less frequently involved in serious and violent crimes, such as robbery and murder. Instead, they are commonly linked to offenses such as prostitution, fraud, and theft.
3. **Severity:** The repercussions are generally less significant when women engage in criminal activities. According to Burgess (2006),

their acts of violence result in fewer casualties, and their property crimes incur lower financial costs.

2.10.2. The Relationship Between Race and Crime

1. **Racial Disparities in Treatment and Crime:** Adult Blacks are almost five times more likely than Adult Whites to report that they have been stopped by the police unjustly because of their race or ethnicity. Black men report a significantly higher frequency of unfair stops.
2. **Structural Inequalities:** The criminal justice system continues to exhibit racial disparities. Historically, Black or African American individuals have faced a greater likelihood of being victimized and arrested.
3. **Intersectionality:** The confluence of gender and race complicates encounters with the criminal justice system. Women of color may face specific vulnerabilities due to systemic disparities.

2.10.3. Vulnerability and Structural Violence

Multiple perspectives from different intersecting identities: Feminist criminologists highlight the intersection of justice, racism, and gender. The study examines the impact of systemic violence on women of color's vulnerability to violence and punitive actions, as well as disparities in the implementation of justice.

Gender perspectives beyond binary: Academics advocate surpassing the limitations of gender binary thinking. Analyzing the broader framework aids in comprehending the complexities associated with criminal behavior and its consequences for disadvantaged communities.

Ultimately, achieving equitable policies, addressing institutional prejudices, and promoting justice for all individuals within the criminal justice system necessitate a comprehensive comprehension of the intricate connections between gender, race, and crime. This continuous investigation challenges individuals to engage with the intricate matters of crime and justice (Burgess, 2006).

CHAPTER 3

WOMEN IN THE CRIMINAL JUSTICE SYSTEM

Contents

According to recent research by Niau (2021), it has been found that women who are engaged in the criminal justice system face a higher risk of becoming victims of violent crimes, particularly in terms of frequency. In addition, it is important to note that there is an increase in violence against women, particularly during periods of economic hardship, despite the overall decrease in violence. There is a significant disparity between men and women when it comes to owning a secure and comfortable home, having a dependable source of income or support, and having access to emergency housing options. Women face a higher risk of sexualized exploitation as a result of concerns about homelessness, increased aggression, threats, or financial need. Additionally, they often take on the role of primary caregivers for children or other individuals in their immediate surroundings.

It is important to consider the various challenges that women may encounter following their release from incarceration. These challenges include housing instability, limited access to family assistance, economic hardships, difficulties in maintaining relationships with their children, strained social networks, and barriers to employment. According to Niau (2021), minor offenses lead to swift criminalization and severe punishment. It is important to note that individuals who watch television without a license and receive unpaid fines are not subject to a higher rate of imprisonment. In this chapter, we will delve into various aspects of the criminal justice system that pertain to women. We will explore the roles of women as both offenders and victims, as well as the presence of gender bias in law enforcement. Additionally, we will examine how women are treated within the legal system and their experiences in correctional facilities. Furthermore, we will discuss the effects of incarceration on women and their families, the challenges they face upon reentry into society, and the importance of gender-responsive programming in the criminal justice system. Lastly, we will highlight the role of advocacy organizations in supporting women and share some promising practices for achieving gender-responsive justice.

3.1. WOMEN AS OFFENDERS

It is worth noting that there is a significant disparity between the number of men and women convicted of crimes. According to a recent study by Niau (2021), men constitute the overwhelming majority of those convicted, while women account for approximately one in six of those convicted. Convictions among males have experienced a decline over the past decade, and a similar trend has been observed among females. Research suggests that women tend to receive admonishments rather than jail sentences more frequently than men when facing punishment. It is observed that sentences for women tend to be shorter compared to sentences for men. Women, on average, have been found to have a lower reconviction rate compared to men. However, it is worth noting that this gap has been closing in recent times. It is worth noting that the number of female inmates is significantly lower compared to their male counterparts, who constitute the overwhelming majority. According to recent research by Niau (2021), it has been found that less than 20% of violent offenses are committed by women. It is worth noting that approximately one in six cases of domestic abuse involve a female accused party, while the majority of cases involve a male accused party. Over the past five years, just over 10% of homicides have had a female accused, while the vast majority of accused individuals have been male (Figure 3.1).

Figure 3.1. *Women offenders.*

Source: BBC (2020).

As an example, in the year of 2019–2020:

- Women made up 17% of those found guilty of a crime.
- Women made up 9% of those sentenced to prison.
- Women made up 7% of those serving any length of time in jail.
- On average, 5% of inmates were female.

In the realm of domestic violence incidents during the period of 2020–2021, it is worth noting that men were implicated in the overwhelming majority (82%) of cases, at least in instances where their gender was identifiable. A small percentage of these cases involved male victims, while the majority, around 80%, had female victims. The percentage of instances involving female accused is comparatively lower. According to data from 2020–2021, there were instances of domestic abuse where the accused was female and the victim was male, accounting for 16% of the cases. Additionally, there were instances where the accused and the victim were both females, making up 2% of the cases.

According to recent data from Niau (2021), approximately 18% of domestic abuse cases involved female perpetrators.

3.1.1. Prisons, Reconvictions, and Convictions

During the fiscal year 2019–2020, it was observed that 17% of all convictions were attributed to women, while the remaining 83% were attributed to men. When it comes to criminal behavior, there are notable differences between men and women. It is worth noting that certain types of offenses, such as "fraud" (34%), "drunkenness and other disorderly conduct" (32%), and "cruelty to and unnatural treatment of children" (71%), have a higher percentage of convictions compared to others. These particular offenses seem to be more commonly associated with a specific group, accounting for 17% of all convictions. Statistical data from Niau (2021) indicates that there is a higher likelihood of men receiving jail sentences compared to women. It is worth noting that in 2019–2020, the majority of individuals found guilty were men, comprising 83% of the total. Similarly, men constituted a significant majority of those serving prison sentences, accounting for 91%. Out of all the convictions, 17% were attributed to females. Interestingly, females were more prone to receiving "Other sentences," which mainly consisted of admonishments. In fact, 27% of these particular punishments were given to females. When determining a sentence, it is important to consider various factors such as the severity of the offense and the offender's criminal history (Niau, 2021). In addition, it is important to consider the unique circumstances of the offender when deciding on an appropriate form of punishment. In 2019–2020, the most common charges against women placed on remand were attempts at murder and serious assault, ordinary assault, and drug offenses, as reported by Niau in 2021. Among women serving sentences, the most common index offenses include violent assault, attempted murder, and murder. According to Niau (2021), the average daily jail population for men from 2019 to 2022 showed that sexual index offenses accounted for 15% of their population. Interestingly, the number of women incarcerated for similar offenses was found to be significantly lower. It is interesting to note that women tend to be imprisoned more often for offenses related to dishonesty, as opposed to men who are more commonly incarcerated for violent crimes, excluding sexual offenses. It is worth noting that there is still a disparity in the length of sentences given to women compared to men, despite the fact that the frequency of shorter sentences has decreased for both genders. However, it is worth noting that there has been a consistent upward trend in the proportion of women receiving life sentences over the past decade. Specifically, the percentage has risen from 6.7% in 2009–2010 to 12.2% in 2019–2020.

3.2. WOMEN AS VICTIMS

Violence against women and girls is a deeply concerning issue that continues to plague our world on a daily basis. It is a widespread violation of human rights that demands our attention and action (Chinkin & Gormley, 2023). This issue hinders the full and equal participation of women and girls in society and has significant health, economic, and psychological consequences for them, both in the short and long term. The impact of this phenomenon on society as a whole, as well as on the lives of individuals and families, cannot be overstated. Various factors, such as the COVID-19 epidemic, conflicts, and environmental crises, have significantly exacerbated the prevalence of violence against women and girls. These conditions have not only worsened existing issues but have also given birth to new and escalating risks (Chinkin & Gormley, 2023).

3.2.1. Forms of Violence Against Women

1. **Violence between Intimate Partners:** Intimate relationship violence encompasses behavior by an intimate partner or ex-partner that causes physical, sexual, or psychological harm. These behaviors encompass a range of domineering actions, physical aggression, and sexual coercion. Violence against intimate partners is a form of domestic violence. Domestic violence encompasses acts of violence that occur within the confines of a private, domestic environment, typically involving individuals who share familial or close relationships. Domestic abuse is a complex issue that extends beyond the victimization of women. It encompasses the mistreatment of children and the elderly within the confines of their own homes (Figure 3.2).

Figure 3.2. *Violence against women.*

Source: Essentials (2021).

Examples of intimate partner violence include physical acts of violence such as choking, slapping, or burning. Acts of sexual violence encompass instances such as the rape of a spouse. Psychological acts of violence encompass the deliberate use of intimidation or enforced isolation to instill fear. In the realm of economic acts of violence, we find the exercise of absolute control over financial resources, the denial of access to funds, and the prohibition of attendance at work or school (Chinkin & Gormley, 2023).

2. **Sexual Assault:** Sexual violence encompasses any form of hurtful or unwanted sexual behavior imposed upon an individual. The topic covers various types of sexual harassment, such as verbal abuse, threats, exposure, unwanted touching, incest, and forced or attempted sexual actions with a woman without her consent (Chinkin & Gormley, 2023).

Here are a few examples of sexual violence:

i. **Sexual Harassment:** Sexual harassment encompasses a wide range of behaviors, including verbal, nonverbal, physical, written, and electronic messages. Sexual harassment can manifest in various forms, spanning from inappropriate comments and lingering gazes to unwelcome physical contact. Instances of sexual harassment include sharing inappropriate jokes or stories, engaging in unwelcome physical contact, repeatedly asking someone out or pressuring them for sex, and making inappropriate comments about someone's appearance or body (Chinkin & Gormley, 2023).

ii. **Rape:** Non-consensual penetration of another person's body by another person through the vagina, anal, or oral routes with any part of their body or object is considered rape. This can involve the use of physical force or manipulating the victim into giving consent out of fear or inability to refuse. Instances of this phenomenon can manifest in various types of relationships, involving both familiar and unfamiliar individuals, and even during times of armed conflict.

iii. **Corrective Rape:** When an individual is subjected to rape due to their gender identity or sexual orientation, it is referred to as "corrective rape." According to Chinkin & Gormley (2023), the objective is to persuade the individual to embrace a conventional gender identity or heterosexuality.

iv. **Sexual Violence in Conflict:** Acts of violence against women during armed conflict encompass a range of egregious violations, such as systematic sexual assault, forced pregnancy, forced sterilization, coerced, or forced use of contraceptives, female infanticide, and prenatal sex selection. Here, we have a collection of instances where women have experienced human rights violations in the midst of armed conflict.

3. **Femicide:** This refers to the intentional killing of a woman or girl solely based on her gender identity. There are various factors that could contribute to the gender-related motivation behind the killing. These factors may include power imbalances between men and women in society, gender stereotypes, discrimination against women and girls, or a combination of these elements.

Femicide and other gender-related homicides of women and girls represent an extremely severe and brutal manifestation of violence directed towards women. Occurrences can manifest in various settings, encompassing both public and private domains, and encompass a multitude of scenarios involving the connection between the perpetrator and the victim. Instances of this nature include situations where the victim has experienced previous instances of physical, sexual, or psychological abuse or harassment. Additionally, it encompasses cases where the killings occurred within the framework of human trafficking, forced labor, or slavery. Lastly, it encompasses situations where the victim's body was discarded in a public location (Chinkin & Gormley, 2023) (Figure 3.3).

Figure 3.3. *Anti-femicide protest.*

Source: Obudho & Ntonjira (2024).

Honor killings, also known as gender-related killings, involve the tragic act of killing a family member, often a woman or girl, due to the belief that they have brought shame or dishonor to the family. These murders often arise from allegations of sexual purity violations involving female family members.

4. **Trafficking of Persons:** Human trafficking is a serious global issue that revolves around the exploitation of individuals for financial gain (Chinkin & Gormley, 2023). Various tactics are employed

by traffickers to maintain control over their victims. These tactics encompass blackmail, emotional manipulation, physical and sexual abuse, as well as the confiscation of official documentation. Abuse can happen in various locations, including the victim's home country, while they are on a trip, or in a foreign country.

There is a wide range of forms of human trafficking. It is important to note that this crime has a significant impact on individuals of all genders, ages, and backgrounds. However, it is particularly concerning that women are often the primary victims, with girls being especially vulnerable to trafficking for the purpose of sexual exploitation (Chinkin & Gormley, 2023).

3.3. GENDER BIAS IN LAW ENFORCEMENT

Advocates and activists are calling for an end to discriminatory policing practices that target individuals based on their race, gender, sexual orientation, disability, or immigration status. This issue has gained attention and support from various cities and states globally. In Avalos' study from 2020, it was found that… There is an attempt to modify police tactics that have the potential to put lives at risk and undermine the integrity of our legal system.

Gender-based policing, particularly the concerning and unlawful practices employed by law enforcement when dealing with domestic violence and sexual assault cases, demands greater scrutiny during this era of reform. Various organizations, including the U.S. Department of Justice, civil rights advocates, and law enforcement officials, have expressed their concerns about police practices and regulations that rely on damaging gender stereotypes when dealing with victims of violence. Not only does gender-biased policing undermine the equal legal protection and safety of victims of sexual assault and domestic abuse, but it also erodes the trust between law enforcement and the communities they are meant to serve (Avalos, 2020).

Gender-biased policing encompasses tactics employed by law enforcement that rely on gender stereotypes, resulting in discrimination and disproportionate impact on women. This type of policing exposes women and LGBT individuals to abuse, violence, or hostility from police personnel (Avalos, 2020).

Gender-biased policing tends to be most evident in instances of sexual assault and domestic violence. Instances of gender-biased policing can be observed in various scenarios. These include delays in testing sexual assault kits, mishandling or insufficiently investigating domestic violence and sexual assault complaints based on the victim's gender, sexual orientation, clothing, sexual history, criminal history, emotional state, or appearance. Additionally, intimate partner violence against LGBT individuals may be disregarded if it involves a same-sex partner. Transgender individuals, particularly trans women of color, often face harassment due to their gender identity. Furthermore, there are cases where police officers are not held accountable for domestic violence or are allowed to retain positions of authority despite engaging in sexual harassment or assault (Avalos, 2020).

3.3.1. The Frequency of Policing Based on Gender

It is undeniable that a significant portion of police officers in the country perform their duties with meticulousness, professionalism, and unwavering integrity (Campbell & Feeney, 2022). Through various investigations conducted by the Department of Justice, advocates, and other entities, it has been revealed that police departments exhibit persistent and systemic bias patterns when responding to calls for help in cases involving domestic abuse and sexual assault. These biases primarily affect women, although some men are also impacted.

3.4. THE TREATMENT OF WOMEN IN THE LEGAL SYSTEM

Gendered stereotypes, norms, and values are expressed and reinforced by various aspects of society, such as laws, regulations, and institutions. Criminal procedure and legislation are essentially the same. Discriminatory laws can take various forms, such as criminalizing homosexuality or other same-sex intimacy, or even exempting sexual violence against a member of the same sex from being classified as rape or other forms of violence. These examples highlight the significant discrimination faced by individuals based on their gender identity and sexual orientation (Oberwittler, 2019). There are various criminal laws and practices that have been found to exhibit discriminatory tendencies.

3.4.1. Substantive Criminal Codes

- Actions such as prostitution, adultery, and premarital sex are criminalized, even though they may not be penalized as severely when carried out by men.
- Actions that are exclusive to female performance should not be criminalized. Abortion, even when performed for medical reasons, serves as an illustrative example.
- Actions that are considered criminal under international law include stealing, violating dress regulations, and unauthorized fleeing from one's home. It is concerning that certain crimes, such as intimate partner abuse and female genital mutilation/cutting, have not been

made illegal or that appropriate action has not been taken to stop and compensate the victims of these crimes.

- Imprisonment may be a consequence for women who engage in minor offenses and are unable to post bail.

3.4.2. Criminal Procedure Codes

- It is important to consider the potential differences in reactions between men and women when applying the defense of provocation. Failing to take these differences into account could result in a failure to treat women appropriately in such cases.
- Certain laws require longer sentences for individuals, primarily women, who intentionally kill their abusers. However, these laws tend to reduce punishments for individuals, primarily men, who kill in response to provocation caused by their spouses or female relatives.
- Preventing women who have experienced assault from making claims of self-defense. When it comes to sentencing, it is important to consider the psychological impact, especially in cases involving battered woman syndrome.

Based on the available research, it is evident that women are not commonly involved in violent crimes. However, it is worth noting that a significant number of women who have been convicted of murder or manslaughter have committed these acts against their male spouses or family members, often as a result of a history of domestic abuse. Based on the findings of a UNODC Global Study on Homicide, it is evident that women and girls constitute the majority of homicide victims across the globe. Surprisingly, intimate partners or family members are responsible for only a fifth of these homicides (Oberwittler, 2019). When we examine the breakdown of victims and perpetrators, we can observe a notable disparity in the proportions assigned to male and female victims of killings by family members or intimate partners. According to a study conducted by Oberwittler in 2019, there is a significant disparity between the genders when it comes to intimate partner-only homicides. The study found that a staggering 82% of the victims were female, while only 18% were male.

3.5. WOMEN'S EXPERIENCES IN CORRECTIONAL FACILITIES

A significant majority of individuals incarcerated globally are men. The criminal justice system has always treated incarcerated women differently at every stage, from arrest to sentencing and the implementation of punitive measures. The discrepancy in prison populations between men and women can be attributed to real demographic differences in the severity of crimes committed. Additionally, society tends to hold the belief that female offenders are more capable of rehabilitation compared to their male counterparts (Koski & Costanza, 2015).

Harassment issues are prevalent in correctional facilities. There is a concerning issue where some prisoners engage in inappropriate behavior towards newly hired female cops, such as giving them uncomfortable lengthy looks, making lewd comments, and facial movements.

It is a common occurrence for female officers to hesitate in discussing the harassment they face at work due to concerns about the potential repercussions on their work environment or job security. Correctional officers who are women face unique challenges due to the complex dynamics of their role.

The combination of vulnerability and authority can potentially create a situation where the misuse of power becomes more likely. It is important to recognize that they are not only victims, but also capable of engaging in harmful behavior.

It is worth noting that a significant majority of sexual misbehavior cases, specifically 61%, and a notable proportion of staff harassment cases, specifically 21%, involve female correctional officials. Furthermore, the data reveals that a significant majority of incarcerated individuals, specifically 69%, have reported instances of victimization by female staff members within correctional facilities (Koski & Costanza, 2015).

Correctional officials may turn to drugs and alcohol as a temporary coping mechanism for the pressures and challenges they face in their line of work. Although female officers are less prone to substance abuse compared to their male counterparts, they still partake in these activities as a means to alleviate the physical symptoms of burnout that arise from their demanding role as correctional officers (such as headaches, insomnia, and backaches). According to Koski & Costanza (2015), the police employed the use of alcohol and drugs to alleviate these psychosomatic physical symptoms.

In the criminal justice system, substance misuse often arises due to a facility's failure to recognize and value the hard work of its employees, a lack of social support, or the verbal abuse inflicted by other staff members. Unfortunately, these circumstances tend to have a greater impact on women. Engaging in a diverse range of extracurricular activities has been found to reduce the likelihood of women falling into substance abuse, as suggested by the research conducted by Koski & Costanza in 2015.

3.6. THE IMPACT OF INCARCERATION ON WOMEN AND THEIR FAMILIES

It is worth noting that there has been a significant increase in the number of women incarcerated in recent decades. However, there is a lack of knowledge regarding the experiences of these women and the subsequent effects on their families (Kajstura, 2017). Considering the fact that women are significantly more prone than men to assume the role of primary caregivers for young children while they are in prison, the impact of female incarceration on the well-being of these children is a matter of great importance. Based on previous research, it has been found that when a mother is incarcerated, there is an increased chance of her child being placed in foster care. This, in turn, can have a negative impact on the child's overall well-being (Kajstura, 2017).

Children whose mothers are involved in the criminal justice system face numerous challenges and difficulties. These include psychological stress, engaging in antisocial behavior, being suspended, or expelled from school, financial hardships, and potential involvement in criminal activities. Understanding the impact of parental incarceration on children's well-being can be quite challenging. The research on the risk factors for these children is not always consistent, making it difficult to predict how they will fare in such circumstances (Kajstura, 2017). Research findings suggest that a child's ability to overcome challenges and succeed in life is greatly impacted by the quality of the parent-child relationship and the level of social support available to the child and their family. To fully understand the unique dynamics of the family in question and to create a safety net for the child and a successful re-entry for the incarcerated parent, it is crucial for correctional practitioners to establish strong partnerships with law enforcement, public schools, and child welfare agencies.

Estimations indicate that the number of children with incarcerated mothers can vary. Based on a study, it has been found that a significant number of children, estimated to be between 1.7 million and 2.7 million, have experienced the absence of at least one parent due to imprisonment during their formative years. It is concerning to note that approximately 11% of young individuals may be at risk. According to a study conducted by Kajstura in 2017, it was found that approximately 50–75% of individuals who are incarcerated have a minor child. Interestingly, this percentage is similar to the parenting rate in the general population.

Parental incarceration has been found to have a significant impact on various risk factors that children may face. Research has shown that when a parent is incarcerated, children are more likely to experience negative outcomes in areas such as education, mental health, and social development. It is crucial to understand the potential consequences of parental incarceration in order to develop effective interventions and support systems for these vulnerable children.

Extensive research has shown that when a parent is incarcerated, it can have significant impacts on a child's emotional, physical, educational, and economic well-being. It is important to note that each situation is unique, and every child may respond in their own individual way:

1. **Participation of Children in Crime:** A significant concern revolves around the potential consequences of imprisoning a parent, which may trigger a series of criminal behaviors in future generations. Nevertheless, it is important to note that risk factors may not be universally present in every child, and understanding or predicting these behaviors can be challenging. As we examine the data, we find that the rates of incarceration among children of incarcerated women are significantly higher compared to children of jailed fathers. Furthermore, these children tend to experience arrests at an earlier age and with greater frequency. Additional research is required to gain a comprehensive understanding of this correlation. However, it is possible that this difference suggests that, in most cases, the mother is the primary provider of support for the child (Kajstura, 2017).
2. **Psychological Problems and Antisocial Behavior:** Research on violence and depression in children with incarcerated mothers has yielded inconsistent results, largely due to various factors such as gender, age, race, and family status. As evidenced by a study conducted by Kajstura in 2017, it was found that children belonging to the African–American community or those whose parents are both incarcerated exhibited significantly higher rates of depression.

One common result of parental incarceration is often categorized as antisocial behavior, encompassing a variety of actions that go against societal norms, such as persistent dishonesty and engagement in criminal activities. Research shows that children of incarcerated mothers display a higher frequency of antisocial behaviors compared to other factors such as drug use and mental health conditions. This meta-analysis, which examined 40 children, highlights the significance of maternal incarceration in relation to the development of antisocial behaviors in children.

3. **Achieving a High Level of Education:** As an example, a study revealed a significant correlation between externalizing behavioral problems and parental incarceration. According to the researcher, it is likely that the limited follow-up period for data collection is the

reason behind the absence of a corresponding decrease in educational outcomes and other social attainment indicators (Kajstura, 2017). It is interesting to note that the researcher recognized that certain children were able to overcome their externalizing behavior issues and develop resilience prior to facing negative consequences in school. On the other hand, another study revealed a significant rise in the probability of school suspension and expulsion for children whose mothers are incarcerated. Further research is necessary to differentiate the impact of parental incarceration on educational achievement from other potential factors.

4. **Economic Well-Being:** It is important to note that a significant number of children with incarcerated mothers face financial challenges that hinder their ability to thrive. Based on a study conducted by Kajstura in 2017, it was found that the family's income experienced a decrease of 22% during the mothers' incarceration and a further decrease of 15% upon their release.

3.7. CHALLENGES FACED BY WOMEN UPON REENTRY

According to Miller (2021), approximately 2 million women are released from prison each year. During the reentry phase, women encounter unique challenges as they transition from prison back into society. However, it is worth noting that correctional programs aimed at promoting successful reintegration have predominantly focused on men. It is worth noting that programs that take into account gender-specific aspects in their designs have not been allocated the same level of funding. This is despite evidence suggesting that the outcomes of men's reentry programs may not be applicable to women (Miller, 2021).

Below are five key insights regarding women and reentry, supported by comprehensive data and research.

1. At the end of 2021, 1 in 138 women were under correctional supervision, meaning they were either in jail, prison, or on community supervision (Miller, 2021). Unfortunately, there is still a lack of information regarding their characteristics throughout the entire nation.

   According to recent data from Miller (2021), the number of women in prison, jail, or on probation or parole as of December 31, 2021, stood at nearly 1 million, which translates to 720 per 1,00,000. It is worth noting that there has been a 25% decline in the number of females under correctional supervision from 2011 to 2021. Also worth noting is the significant increase of 85,100 women detained in municipal jails, which represents a 22% rise from the previous year. It is worth noting that the representation of women in correctional supervision stands at over 18%. However, there is a significant lack of comprehensive national data on their characteristics, which hinders our ability to analyze factors such as age, race, ethnicity, type of offense, or conviction status. According to current available statistics, there is a disparity in incarceration rates between different racial and ethnic groups of women. Black, Hispanic, and American Indian/Alaska Native women are incarcerated at higher rates compared to white women. However, it remains uncertain how much of this overrepresentation is also reflected in the populations under community supervision (Miller, 2021).

2. Women have different pathways into the criminal justice system than do men. Men and women have distinct pathways into the criminal justice system. Studies have revealed that there are different patterns in the family backgrounds of individuals who have experienced trauma, co-occurring disorders, dysfunction, and substance abuse. These factors have been found to be associated with their engagement with the criminal justice system. There is a significant overrepresentation of women with incarcerated backgrounds among those who have experienced sexual abuse and trauma. Many reentry programs available for women were originally designed for men and fail to consider the distinct ways in which women navigate the criminal justice system (Miller, 2021).

3. The outcomes of gender-responsive programming for women reentering society are encouraging. When women reenter society after being incarcerated, they may face unique challenges compared to men These challenges can include being more vulnerable to becoming victims of crime, facing economic disadvantages, dealing with mental illness, or co-occurring disorders, struggling with drug use, being parents of minors, or experiencing a combination of these difficulties. It is highly likely that these elements are all interconnected with the potential for reoffending, as suggested by Miller (2021).

   Gender-responsive programming involves assessing specific needs and risks related to gender, as well as considering treatment goals like mental health, substance abuse, and family dynamics. Gender-responsive interventions that incorporate parenting training, trauma treatment, mental health components, and childcare have been found to be associated with reduced recidivism and increased treatment retention after release (Miller, 2021). When it comes to women going through reentry, it is recommended to incorporate specialized programs that cater to their needs. These programs may include cognitive behavioral therapy, peer or mutual support, or all-female group sessions (Miller, 2021).

4. Programming that addresses substance use, mental health, or co-occurring disorders before, during, and after supervision can be especially helpful for women.

   It is crucial to provide comprehensive treatment to women involved in the justice system, as they often face challenges such as substance abuse, mental health issues, and co-occurring illnesses (Miller, 2021). Analyses of drug abuse treatment for women have found that certain programs have been particularly successful in reducing recidivism and substance use. These programs prioritize gender responsiveness, provide individualized case management, address co-occurring mental health and substance use issues, and offer transitional support.

5. Reentry programs that take into account the cultural needs of females involved in the judicial system have the potential to enhance their chances of success.

   Based on early research findings, it has been suggested that culturally responsive programs, which consider factors such as a person's color, ethnicity, sexual orientation, and other identities, could potentially yield better results in terms of reducing recidivism rates and increasing program participation compared to traditional programming. It has been suggested that incorporating culturally responsive techniques that consider the unique characteristics of the individual and their intersecting identities could potentially improve the effectiveness of gender-responsive reintegration programs (Miller, 2021).

3.8. GENDER-RESPONSIVE PROGRAMMING IN THE CRIMINAL JUSTICE SYSTEM

One of the significant challenges that the criminal justice system grapples with is the reentry of incarcerated individuals into society. Annually, approximately 6,00,000 people are released from correctional facilities in the United States, posing a considerable hurdle. According to Miller (2021), the number of women in that group is approximately 78,000, which translates to more than 200 women per day (Figure 3.4).

Figure 3.4. *Gender-responsive approach for women in the justice system.*

Source: CSG Justice Center (2022).

It is worth mentioning that a significant proportion of incarcerated women happen to be mothers with children who are below the age of 18. It is worth noting that a significant number of incarcerated mothers have full custody of their children and have every intention of resuming their parental responsibilities once they are released. This stands in stark contrast to the majority of male offenders. According to Miller (2021), the average number of children for a female prisoner is approximately 2.5. Every year, approximately 2,00,000 children in the United States go through the challenging situation of having their primary caregiver incarcerated and subsequently released from prison. In addition, it has been observed that women tend to be more responsive to therapy and have lower rates of relapse, even when participating in similar programs (Miller, 2021).

3.8.1. The Nature of Female Offending and the Rise of Gender-Responsive Programming

To truly grasp the nature of female offending, it is crucial to have a deep understanding of substance usage and addiction. This is because a significant number of women find themselves being arrested for drug-related offenses, including manufacturing, possession, or sale of drugs. Additionally, many women resort to property crimes as a means of obtaining drugs, such as stealing to support their drug habit. Men and women often follow different paths when it comes to addiction, crime, and drug usage, as highlighted by Miller (2021).

Research has shown that there is a higher likelihood of women using drugs and participating in criminal behavior when they are involved in interpersonal relationships. Additionally, their behavior tends to be influenced by the actions of their romantic partners. Research indicates that there is a higher prevalence of co-occurring psychiatric problems, familial dysfunction, negative self-concept, and histories of childhood maltreatment and abuse among female criminals compared to their male counterparts (Miller, 2021). Women involved in the criminal justice system have a higher prevalence of mental health conditions such as depression, anxiety, borderline personality disorder, and notably, post-traumatic stress disorder (PTSD), when compared to the general population. Women tend to have a higher likelihood of reporting past drug use, mental health issues, and co-occurring illnesses compared to men (Miller, 2021). These findings have significant implications for reentry programs, as both of these factors have been shown to be associated with higher rates of recidivism and relapse. Gender-responsive programming in prisoner reentry and rehabilitation has been advocated by practitioners and researchers. This is because there are documented gender differences in etiology, disease progression, motivation for treatment, and self-efficacy. Programming that acknowledges gender sensitivity aims to address the unique challenges faced by incarcerated women, while also utilizing certain characteristics that are conducive to rehabilitation. Research has shown that certain programs have been linked to reduced rates of recurrence and increased treatment retention after release. These programs include those that incorporate mental health components, offer additional services for women, provide trauma treatment, offer aftercare support, and include childcare and parenting classes (Miller, 2021).

3.8.2. Reentry Programming Specifically Designed for Women

Upon reentering society, women who are released from prison face a range of challenges that are both similar to and different from those experienced by men who have been detained. When examining the differences between men and women who are incarcerated, it becomes evident that women face a higher likelihood of experiencing violence and mistreatment, enduring economic disadvantages, and engaging in regular drug use. Parents of small children are more prone to experiencing co-occurring illnesses or mental health issues. Throughout history, reintegration programs have primarily focused on male inmates. Risk assessment tools were originally developed with male offenders in mind, often neglecting gender-specific variables (Miller, 2021).

One crucial aspect of developing gender-responsive programming involves carefully assessing the individual risks and needs of each person. Consideration is given to various factors specific to women in prison, including parent-child relationships, family reunification, substance abuse, and mental and physical health issues. When considering programming for women involved in the criminal justice system, it is recommended to incorporate cognitive behavioral therapy, all-female group sessions, and mutual support groups (Miller, 2021). It is crucial to ensure that women who engage in criminal activities are properly evaluated and assessed for their likelihood of reoffending, their criminogenic needs (factors that contribute to criminal behavior), and their readiness for treatment, just as we do for all individuals involved in criminal behavior. However, it has been suggested by several studies that risk assessment tools designed for male criminals may not be as suitable for females. In addition, several instruments have been developed to categorize and address the specific needs of women. These include the Women's Risk and Needs Assessment (WRNA), the Gender Informed Needs Assessment (GINA), the COMPAS for Women, and the Service Planning Instrument for Women (SPIn-W).

3.9. THE ROLE OF ADVOCACY ORGANIZATIONS IN SUPPORTING WOMEN

Women's groups, feminists, proponents of gender parity, and the women's movement actively contributed to the creation of the Sustainable Development Goals (SDGs) from the outset. Without the consistent leadership and involvement of women, particularly through the lobbying efforts of the Women's Major Group, the SDGs would not possess the same potential for revolution. The process of creating the SDGs was a truly transformative journey, filled with excitement, challenges, and moments of frustration. The world is currently confronted with the task of initiating an implementation process that upholds the human rights of every individual. It is also crucial to establish a system of evaluation and monitoring that holds all responsible parties, such as governments, the private sector, and international financial institutions, accountable for their contributions towards achieving the goals (Rivas et al., 2016).

3.9.1. The Major Group of Women

The Women's Major Group is one of the nine major groups recognized by the United Nations Rio Earth Summit in 1992's Agenda 21. Alongside trade unions, children & youth, NGOs, Indigenous peoples, local authorities, business, science & technology, and farmers, the Women's Major Group plays a crucial role in facilitating UN processes on Sustainable Development. The WMG is a coalition of more than 600 member organizations, networks, and individuals who work together to advance women's human rights, women's empowerment, and gender equality. They are dedicated to promoting sustainable development through active participation in intergovernmental negotiations on the environment and sustainable development (Rivas et al., 2016).

The WMG has a significant impact on policy by ensuring and promoting the meaningful involvement of women's groups, other organizations, and social movements that work towards gender equality, gender justice, and sustainable development in UN policy settings. The WMG actively engages with decision-makers and utilizes media platforms to advocate for various policy issues. Its aim is to ensure that civil society is given a formal and institutional role in UN discussions, to raise awareness about women's demands, and to hold governments accountable for their actions (Rivas et al., 2016). The extensive influence of the positions developed by the reputable and diversified global membership of the WMG is undeniable.

Advocacy groups play a crucial role in promoting gender equality and women's rights. These organizations play a crucial role by making significant contributions in the following ways:

1. **UN Women:** It collaborates with governments, civil society organizations, and member states to develop and implement laws, policies, and services that are advantageous to women. Their primary areas of focus include sustainable peacebuilding, economic autonomy, women's participation in governance, and violence prevention.
2. **Women's Rights in Development Association (AWID):** They promote the implementation of policies and practices that are responsive to gender issues, facilitate discussions, and provide assistance to movements advocating for gender justice. AWID fosters collaboration among activists, facilitates the sharing of knowledge, and coordinates collective endeavors in support of feminism.
3. **Womankind Worldwide:** By advocating for women's rights, their aim is to bring about transformative changes in the lives of women. They collaborate with various organizations in Ethiopia, Kenya, Nepal, Uganda, and Zimbabwe to promote and protect women's rights.
4. **Amnesty International:** This organization works against violence and promotes gender equality, while it is not just focused on women. The Stop Violence Against Women program places a significant focus on implementing legislation to ensure that victims of violence have access to justice.

These organizations strive to enhance the well-being of women and girls globally through their efforts in shaping legislation, securing funding, and raising awareness (Rivas et al., 2016). Their efforts play a vital role in constructing a society that is fair and just for all, irrespective of gender.

3.10. Promising Practices for Gender-Responsive Justice

To effectively address the unique needs and experiences of women in the criminal justice system, it is important to consider the following constructive approaches for gender-responsive justice:

1. **Create and Put into Effect Rules That Specifically Take Gender Disparities into Account:** It is imperative that these laws take into account the impact of trauma, specific risk factors, and the various pathways that contribute to women's involvement in criminal activities. Offering programs in correctional facilities that prioritize gender-responsive approaches and focus on mental health, drug abuse treatment, vocational training, and rehabilitation has been highlighted by Treskon & Bright (2017).
2. **Understanding Trauma-Informed Approaches:** It is important to recognize that many women who are part of the legal system have experienced significant trauma in their lives, including instances of sexual assault, domestic abuse, or childhood neglect.

It is important for employees to be trained in implementing trauma-informed procedures that prioritize empowerment, safety, and trust. This can greatly benefit the overall well-being of individuals affected by trauma.

3. **Exploring Alternatives to Incarceration:** Consider alternative approaches for minor infractions. Diversion, restorative justice, and community-based initiatives have proven to be less harmful and more effective. Consider the impact of incarceration on families, especially when women are the primary caregivers.
4. **Health and Reproductive Rights:** Make sure that everyone has access to family planning, mental health treatments, and prenatal care. It is important to address the specific medical needs of women in custody who are pregnant or postpartum, as highlighted by Treskon & Bright (2017).
5. **Child Welfare and Parenting:** Encourage family reunification initiatives and good parenting practices. Strengthen the connections that separate incarcerated mothers from their children. In order to support women in maintaining strong relationships with their families, it is beneficial to provide them with parenting education and resources.

6. **Staff Training with a Focus on Gender Responsiveness:** Provide correctional employees with valuable knowledge on de-escalation tactics, effective communication strategies, and the unique challenges related to gender. It is crucial for correctional facilities to cultivate an atmosphere that is empathetic and respectful.
7. **Economic Empowerment:** To improve economic stability after release, provide education, job placement services, and vocational training. It is important to promote financial independence among women by focusing on enhancing their financial literacy.
8. **Cooperation with Community Organizations:** Collaborate with community-based organizations to provide assistance for women's services, such as housing, jobs, and mental health support.

It is important to understand that the pursuit of gender-responsive justice requires ongoing effort, collaboration, thorough examination, and progress. Implementing these strategies can lead to a more equitable and streamlined criminal justice system for women (Treskon & Bright, 2017).

Women's interactions with the criminal justice system are complex and diverse. Several significant patterns emerge when examining their roles as perpetrators, victims, and experts. It is important to recognize the impact of gender-specific pathways to criminal behavior, as highlighted by Treskon & Bright (2017). It is worth noting that women tend to have a higher likelihood of encountering certain risk factors. These include trauma histories, economic vulnerabilities, and family responsibilities. Furthermore, it is crucial for the criminal justice system to implement gender-responsive policies and practices. It is important to consider the specific needs of women, which include support for parenting and financial independence, as well as access to healthcare and reproductive rights. Furthermore, it is crucial for community organizations and correctional facilities to collaborate closely.

One way to enhance women's chances of successfully reintegrating into society is by equipping them with the necessary resources, education, and vocational training. Ultimately, a gender-responsive strategy ensures that justice is fair and impartial, considering the intricacies of women's lives within the context of the criminal justice system (Treskon & Bright, 2017).

CHAPTER 4

GENDER-BASED VIOLENCE (GBV)

Contents

Gender-based violence (GBV) is a significant peril to an individual's well-being and security and constitutes a serious infringement of human rights. Individuals who flee their residences often face heightened susceptibility to physical, sexual, and psychological mistreatment, encompassing coerced prostitution, sexual violation, and sexual aggression. Individuals of male, female, and female youth gender are all prone to experiencing violence solely due to their gender or biological sex, however, women and girls are especially susceptible (Figure 4.1).

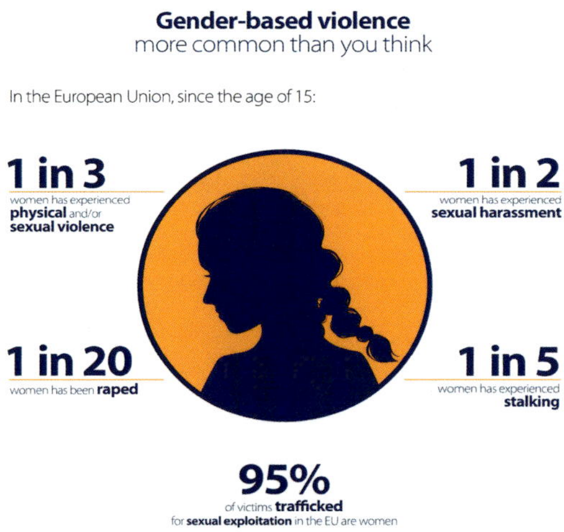

Figure 4.1. *Gender-based violence and violence against women.*

Source: European Institute for Gender Equality (2024).

Approximately 33% of women are projected to experience physical or sexual abuse at some stage in their lives. This chapter will provide a comprehensive examination of the prevalence of gender-based violence, including intimate partner violence, sexual assault, and rape, stalking and harassment, trafficking, and exploitation of women. It will also explore the intersection of gender-based violence and technology, as well as the cultural and religious factors that contribute to gender-based violence. Additionally, it will discuss legal responses to gender-based violence and present prevention and intervention strategies. Finally, it will analyze the impacts of gender-based violence on women's health and wellbeing.

4.1. GENDER-BASED VIOLENCE PREVALENCE

The United Nations defines gender-based violence as actions that cause physical, mental, or sexual harm or suffering, as well as threats of such actions, coercion, and other restrictions on personal freedom (Djamba & Kimuna, 2015). The problem of gender-based violence is pervasive and reaches epidemic proportions. During her lifetime, approximately one out of every three women will encounter this phenomenon. Violence against women and girls is a global issue that affects individuals regardless of their race, social status, or income level.

Gender-based violence, as defined by Djamba & Kimuna (2015), refers to the traditional belief that women are considered inferior to men. Additionally, they encompass conventional roles that reinforce prevalent aggressive or forceful behaviors, such as mistreatment and aggression within families. Furthermore, UN Women enumerates female genital mutilation, acid attacks, coerced matrimony, and dowry-related fatalities (Djamba & Kimuna, 2015) (Figure 4.2).

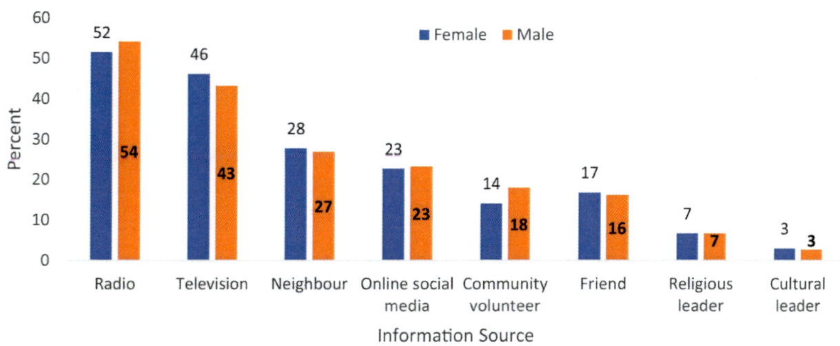

Figure 4.2. *Source of information on GBV during COVID-19 by sex.*

Source: Bukuluki et al. (2023).

4.1.1. Statistics, Outcomes, and Empirical Data Related to Gender-Based Violence

Violence against women and girls is a widespread violation of human rights that occurs all over the world.

- Global projections indicate that approximately 33% of women will encounter gender-based violence at some point in their lives. Gender-based violence may endanger individuals' personal security, independence, self-respect, and overall welfare.
- According to the World Bank: Approximately 35% of women worldwide experience intimate partner violence, including physical or sexual abuse, as well as non-partner sexual assault.
- Globally, 7% of women acknowledge being victims of non-partner sexual assault.

- Intimate partners are responsible for up to 38% of female homicides globally.
- According to UN Women, in 2018, approximately 13% of women aged 15 to 49 reported experiencing physical or sexual abuse by their husband's intimate partner in the past year. In the same year, there were 10 recorded victims of human trafficking worldwide, including approximately five adult women and two girls.
- Women make up 92% of the identified victims of trafficking for sexual exploitation. A total of 81,000 women and girls perished globally in the year 2020. Out of the total number of women mentioned, 47,000, or 58%, were victims of homicide committed by either their boyfriend or a close family member.
- Approximately 736 million women globally, accounting for nearly one-third of the female population aged 15 and above, have encountered intimate partner violence, non-partner sexual assault, or both on at least one occasion in their lives (30% prevalence).
- A minimum of 158 countries have implemented laws against domestic abuse, while 141 countries have done so for sexual harassment in the workplace. Global child marriage rates have declined over the past decade. The prevalence of early marriage among young women aged 20 to 24 has decreased by 15%, declining from nearly 25% in 2010 to 20% in 2020.
- As of 2019, there are approximately 3.7 billion women and girls worldwide. It is estimated that 1 billion females in this generation may experience some form of impact. This encompasses the entire population residing on the African continent.

Violence perpetrated against women knows no limits. Every woman or girl, regardless of her location or circumstances, can be affected. Nevertheless, the problem may be particularly grave in regions where women possess limited social and economic influence or where legislation safeguarding their rights is not effectively implemented. Instability, poverty, and illiteracy are all factors that can contribute to the continuation of gender-based violence.

Underdeveloped countries may exhibit the highest occurrence of these components. Recent estimates indicate that approximately 700 million girls worldwide were married before reaching the age of 18, with many of these marriages being forced against their will. Young girls who are married at a young age are often vulnerable to experiencing physical or sexual abuse (Djamba & Kimuna, 2015).

4.2. VIOLENCE AMONG INTIMATE PARTNERS

Intimate partner violence (IPV) is a significant public health problem that affects women globally, regardless of their age, socioeconomic status, race, religion, ethnicity, sexual orientation, or educational level. Victims of IPV may endure enduring consequences that can last a lifetime, including psychological anguish, lasting physical harm, ongoing health problems, and potentially even mortality. Intimate partner violence (IPV) impacts women across all age groups, but it is particularly prevalent among women who are of reproductive age. Intimate partner violence (IPV) is associated with gynecological complications, difficulties during pregnancy, unintended pregnancies, and sexually transmitted diseases (STDs), including HIV (Chamberlain & Levenson, 2010).

Intimate partner violence, or IPV, refers to a recurring pattern of aggressive and coercive behavior that encompasses physical harm, psychological abuse, sexual assault, gradual isolation, stalking, deprivation, intimidation, and coercion related to reproduction. These behaviors, known as tactics of dominance, are enacted by individuals who are currently, previously, or desiring to be in a romantic or intimate relationship with an adult or teenager, with the aim of exerting control over their partner. It has the potential to impact individuals of both genders in any given community, irrespective of their age, socioeconomic status, race, religion, ethnicity, sexual orientation, or educational attainment. It can also impact both heterosexual and same-sex relationships. Victims of IPV may endure enduring consequences that can last a lifetime, including psychological anguish, irreversible physical harm, ongoing health problems, and potentially even death (Chamberlain & Levenson, 2010).

4.2.1. Patterns of Intimate Partner Violence

Intimate relationship violence encompasses various forms of harm, including sexual violence, psychological abuse, physical abuse, and coercion to procreate. Physical abuse encompasses actions such as hurling objects, shoving, kicking, biting, slapping, strangling, striking, beating, intimidating with a weapon, and employing a weapon. Psychological abuse, encompassing behaviors such as name-calling, denigration, blaming, threats, stalking, and seclusion, undermines a woman's self-esteem and self-value. The perpetrator often systematically alienates themselves from the victim's relatives and acquaintances and may refuse to provide her with provisions, money, transportation, and healthcare. Sexual violence encompasses a variety of sexual acts, including rape, coercion, and non-consensual kissing, touching, or fondling. Reproductive coercion refers to actions within a relationship that involve controlling or manipulating someone's ability to reproduce. It can occur independently of any physical or sexual abuse (Chamberlain & Levenson, 2010). A partner can impede contraceptive efforts, decline to engage in safe sexual practices, deliberately expose a partner to HIV or STIs, manipulate the progression of a pregnancy (by coercing the woman to have an abortion, carry the pregnancy to full term, or harm herself to induce a miscarriage), forbid sterilization, or limit access to other reproductive health services (Figure 4.3).

Figure 4.3. *Intimate partner violence statistics on a global scale.*

Source: Law Journal for Social Justice (2023).

Approximately 20% of women who have experienced abuse and sought assistance from family planning clinics disclosed being forced into becoming pregnant, while 15% reported instances of intentional interference with their use of birth control methods. In addition to the risk of unintended pregnancy, there are other dangers involved in disclosing a sexually transmitted infection to a partner. These concerns should be taken into account, especially in the context of expedited partner therapy.

According to Chamberlain & Levenson (2010), women who have been physically or sexually abused are more prone to feeling afraid when they inform their partners about having a sexually transmitted infection (STI). According to a study, clients who are exposed to intimate partner violence (IPV) are more inclined to have partners who deny responsibility for sexually transmitted infections (STIs) or accuses them of being unfaithful.

4.2.2. Consequences of Violence Towards Intimate Partners

Some women who experience intimate partner violence (IPAV) may have acute injuries to the head, face, breasts, abdomen, genitalia, or reproductive system. Other non-acute symptoms include persistent headaches, irregular eating and sleep patterns, palpitations, persistent pelvic pain, frequent or urgent urination, irritable bowel syndrome, sexual dysfunction, abdominal pain, and recurrent vaginal infections (Chamberlain & Levenson, 2010). These non-acute symptoms often serve as clinical signs of internalized stress, which is also referred to as somatization. Posttraumatic stress disorder (PTSD), often associated with depression, anxiety disorders, substance addiction, and suicide, can be caused by this stress. Research confirms the long-lasting physical and psychological consequences of past or ongoing acts of aggression (Chamberlain & Levenson, 2010).

Intimate Partner Violence has substantial adverse societal and economic consequences. Annually, approximately 2,50,000 hospital visits are attributed to IPV. The annual expenditure on direct medical and mental health care services, as well as lost productivity from paid employment and household tasks, due to intimate partner rape, physical violence, and stalking, along with the treatment of alcoholism, suicidal thoughts and attempts, mental health problems, pregnancy, and pediatric issues resulting from co-occurring child abuse and witnessing of abuse, amounts to over $8.3 billion (Chamberlain & Levenson, 2010). Examples of intangible costs include the decreased self-esteem of women, untreated depression, and a lower quality of life.

4.3. SEXUAL ASSAULT AND RAPE

Sexual assault encompasses a range of different forms, but it is important to note that the victim is never responsible for the occurrence of such acts.

1. **Sexual Assault: What is it?:** Sexual assault is defined as any sexual activity or interaction that occurs without the explicit consent of the victim. There are several types of sexual assault, including:

- Unwanted sexual contact or fondling refers to any non-consensual physical contact of a sexual nature.
- Forcing a victim to engage in sexual activity includes acts such as oral sex or penetration of the offender's body.
- Rape. Although sexual assault encompasses various forms, rape is a specific category within it. Sexual penetration without consent is specifically encompassed within the legal definition of "rape." The FBI defines rape as the act of penetrating the vagina or anus with any body part or object or engaging in oral penetration with another person's sex organ, without the consent of the victim.

2. **Force: What is it?:** Not all manifestations of force are directly linked to physical coercion. Perpetrators may utilize psychological coercion, emotional manipulation, or pressure to compel a victim into engaging in non-consensual sexual activity (Kruttschnitt et al.,

2014). Certain perpetrators may utilize intimidation tactics or make threats of harm towards the victim or their family with the intention of compelling the victim to comply.

3. **Who are the Perpetrators?:** The majority of individuals who perpetrate these offenses are acquaintances of the victim. Intimate partner sexual violence and acquaintance rape represent two instances of the majority (eight out of ten) of sexual assaults perpetrated by individuals known to the victim.

Instances of sexual assault perpetrated by individuals known to the victim are sometimes labeled as "date rape." Acquaintance rapists can assume various roles, such as a classmate, neighbor, friend's partner, or any other individual, in addition to their role as a potential date. It is essential to remember that consent for increased or continued sexual contact does not originate from dating, previous intimate encounters, or other actions such as kissing (Kruttschnitt et al., 2014).

Occasionally, the victim may be unaware of the identity of the perpetrator. This type of sexual assault is commonly referred to as "stranger rape." Stranger rape can occur through a variety of means (Figure 4.4):

1. **Blitz Sexual Assault:** This is the act of a perpetrator attacking a victim suddenly and aggressively, typically taking place at night in a public location.

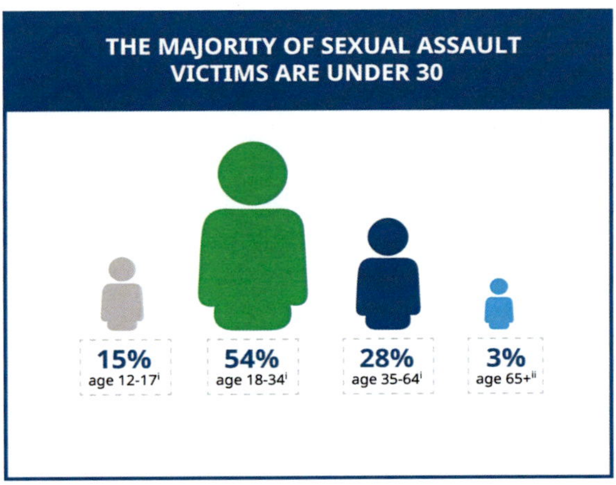

Figure 4.4. *Victims of sexual violence.*

Source: Victims of Sexual Violence: Statistics | RAINN (n.d.).

2. **Sexual Assault by Touch:** This refers to the act of an assailant making physical contact with the victim with the intention of gaining their trust through flirting or other manipulative tactics. The

assailant then coerces the victim into a situation where the sexual assault can occur.

3. **Home Intrusion Sexual Assault:** This is the act of an unauthorized individual entering the victim's residence.

Both survivors of stranger and acquaintance rape often blame themselves for inadvertently provoking the assailant through their behavior. It is crucial to remember that the actions of a perpetrator are never the responsibility of the victim (Kruttschnitt et al., 2014).

4.4. STALKING AND HARASSMENT

Stalking or harassment refers to the persistent behavior of someone that consistently instills fear, distress, or intimidation in another person. Stalking or harassment can affect anyone, as it manifests in various ways. The Protection from Harassment Act of 1997 categorizes harassment and stalking as criminal offenses (Catalano, 2012).

1. **Mistreatment:** The individual causing annoyance could be an unfamiliar person, a resident nearby, or an acquaintance within your local community. Mistreatment can encompass various behaviors, such as:

- Workplace or school bullying;
- The act of cyberstalking, which involves the online harassment of someone;
- Asocial behavior;
- Engaging in the act of sending text messages that are offensive in nature;
- Sending gifts that are unnecessary or unwanted.

Making unwanted visits, sending unwanted emails or letters, or making unwanted phone calls.

Repetitive occurrence of undesirable behavior qualifies as harassment.

2. **Sexual Harassment:** Sexual harassment, which is a form of discrimination, is explicitly forbidden by the Equality Act of 2010 (Catalano, 2012). As per the Act, any behavior that is unwelcome and of a sexual nature is considered sexual harassment.

Here are some examples of sexual harassment. Sexual harassment encompasses a range of inappropriate behaviors, such as:

- Making sexual jokes, comments, or gestures;
- Using derogatory terms like "slut" or "whore;"

- Staring or leering at someone's body;
- Sharing explicit images or videos;
- Touching or groping someone who is exposing themselves;
- Coercing or bribing someone into engaging in sexual activity (Catalano, 2012).

3. **Stalking:** Harassment and stalking share similarities, however, stalking tends to involve a higher degree of violence. The individual who will be the focus of the stalker's obsession is the target. An individual whom you are acquainted with, such as a friend, a previous romantic partner, or even an unfamiliar person, may be engaging in the act of monitoring your movements and activities. Regardless of the victim's familiarity or past relationship with the perpetrator, stalking remains unlawful and should never be supported or tolerated (Catalano, 2012).

Examples of stalking include consistently trailing someone, entering their residence without consent, monitoring someone's online activities, lingering in places they know the person frequents, tampering with their belongings, covertly observing or surveilling someone, and engaging in identity theft by making purchases or signing up for services using another person's identity.

If the behavior that is not desired has happened on multiple occasions, it is classified as stalking (Catalano, 2012).

There are four indicators that are commonly associated with stalking. If the behavior, you are experiencing is:

- Fixated;
- Obsessive;
- Unwanted; and
- Repeated.

4. **Cyberstalking and Intimidation:** Cyberstalking and cyberbullying are prevalent phenomena on various online platforms such as social networking sites, chat rooms, gaming sites, and other forums (Catalano, 2012). As an example:

- To engage in communication (via phone calls, text messages, emails, social media platforms, or the establishment of fabricated accounts) with the purpose of obtaining personal information.
- Engaging in activities such as spreading computer viruses, cyberbullying, or jeopardizing personal identity by sharing private photos, chats, or confidential information can damage one's reputation.

4.5. THE ISSUE OF TRAFFICKING AND EXPLOITATION OF WOMEN

July 30th has been designated by the United Nations as the World Day Against Trafficking in Persons. This important initiative aims to increase awareness about the pervasive problem of modern slavery (Deshpande & Nour, 2013). Trafficking is a grave violation of human rights that preys upon the most vulnerable individuals in our society. Individuals who possess preexisting vulnerabilities are at a heightened risk of falling victim to trafficking during times of crises and conflicts, ultimately becoming subject to the dehumanizing acts of being bought, sold, and traded as mere commodities.

According to Deshpande & Nour (2013), women and girls are often victims of trafficking and are subjected to various forms of exploitation, such as sexual slavery, forced labor, or forced marriage. There is a disturbing pattern of human rights violations, particularly towards women and girls, who often become the victims of abuse and violence. Living under the constant threat and authority of criminal networks is a harsh reality for many individuals. These networks exploit their vulnerabilities and limited opportunitics, leaving them in a vulnerable position (Deshpande & Nour, 2013).

There are multiple factors that can make women vulnerable to becoming victims of human trafficking. Various societal issues such as poverty, social inequality, disputes, barriers to education and work, and discrimination play a significant role. Often, individuals are lured by appealing offers of improved opportunities and lives abroad, only to discover themselves trapped in a harsh reality where they are treated as mere commodities. Women and girls from marginalized communities, including immigrants, refugees, and indigenous peoples, are particularly vulnerable to human trafficking, as studies have shown (Deshpande & Nour, 2013).

Trafficking has severe consequences that extend well beyond the realms of exploitation, encompassing both sexual and physical harm. Exposure to it can lead to significant psychological, physical, and emotional damage. Individuals in this situation are constantly burdened by the pervasive threat of violence, which poses a constant danger to both themselves and their loved ones. Due to the harsh conditions they endure, a significant number of individuals experience ongoing health problems, including chronic illnesses and sexually transmitted diseases. According to Deshpande & Nour (2013), individuals experience a significant decline in their confidence and sense of self-worth, leading to a loss of faith in others.

In order to effectively combat human trafficking, it is crucial to establish strong international partnerships and continue to make progress in this area. It is crucial to enhance the criminal justice institutions and ensure that individuals who engage in criminal activities are held accountable. It is crucial that legislation addressing human trafficking is consistently enforced, fair, and open to scrutiny. Addressing poverty, increasing job and education opportunities, and promoting women's empowerment and gender equality are additional measures to combat human trafficking. It is of utmost importance to address the issue of women and girls being trafficked in order to minimize the associated risks.

As an illustration, the Roma Women's Initiative in North Macedonia, which is a partner organization of The Kvinna until Kvinna Foundation, is dedicated to combating human trafficking among Roma women, who belong to a marginalized community (Deshpande & Nour, 2013).

In addition, it is crucial to provide extensive support and safeguards for women and girls who have fallen prey to the heinous crime of human trafficking. This comprehensive program encompasses a range of essential services, such as secure housing, access to quality healthcare, professional psychological support, and dedicated assistance to facilitate their successful reintegration into society. It is essential to provide access to services that are based on rights and to ensure the preservation of the integrity and dignity of individuals who have been exposed. These elements play a crucial role in the rehabilitation process.

Most importantly, it is crucial to actively address the root cause and raise public awareness of the issue. According to Deshpande & Nour (2013), the issue of trafficking in women will continue as long as there are individuals who exploit them by engaging in the buying and selling of their bodies. Understanding and tackling the vulnerabilities faced by women in relation to human trafficking requires the collective involvement of governments, non-governmental organizations, civil society, and private citizens.

Trafficking is a grave violation of human rights and a global crisis that demands immediate and resolute measures. Through collective efforts, individuals have the power to transform the world and create a future where women and girls are free from the constant threat of human trafficking.

4.6. THE INTERSECTION OF GENDER-BASED VIOLENCE AND TECHNOLOGY

Tech-facilitated gender-based violence refers to the misuse of technology to perpetrate acts of harassment and violence against individuals based on their gender. These abstract aims to highlight the growing concern surrounding various forms of violence in the Indian context, specifically focusing on revenge porn, sextortion, and online grooming (Organization, 2023). In order to effectively develop preventative and intervention techniques, it is crucial to have a deep understanding of the intricate relationship between violence and technology. In recent years, technology has facilitated the rise of harmful activities that specifically target, and exploit individuals based on their gender. The non-consensual sharing of intimate photos or films, commonly known as revenge porn, has become a significant issue that inflicts severe mental distress, societal stigma, and damage to one's reputation (Organization, 2023).

Sextortion, the act of coercing individuals into providing explicit material or engaging in sexual activities through threats, has emerged as a significant concern. In the online realm, individuals have unfortunately found it more convenient to partake in the disturbing act of online grooming. This deplorable practice involves offenders manipulating and exploiting vulnerable individuals, particularly children, for their own sexual motives.

Digital technology plays a vital role in global development, offering immense potential to advance women's rights, gender equality, and health outcomes, particularly in the realm of sexual and reproductive health (SRH). ICTs are being utilized in various ways to address access challenges and enhance the provision of SRH services.

Technology, on the other hand, presents us with both opportunities and challenges. One of the most alarming issues today is the rise in technology-facilitated gender-based violence (TFGBV). Gender-based violence (GBV) that occurs through the use of ICTs, such as smartphones, mobile phones, the internet, social media, or other digital platforms or tools, is commonly referred to as TFGBV. It is also known as cyber violence, online violence, or digital violence (Organization, 2023).

1. **TFGBV: What is it?:** TFGBV includes both offline violence that is carried out using technology and violence that occurs in virtual environments. The range of behaviors encompassed by this issue is quite extensive. These actions can involve hate speech, stalking, online harassment, the unauthorized sharing of private photos (commonly referred to as revenge porn), sextortion (which entails the dissemination of sexual information online or coercing someone into prostitution through threats or blackmail), as well as threats made through digital channels. Furthermore, it is important to acknowledge that technology can be utilized to instigate or escalate acts of violence against women and girls in the physical world. As an example, to exert control and instill fear in their victims, intimate partner abusers often employ tools such as GPS, tracking devices, and cell phones. One interesting example involves the utilization of technology by sex traffickers to identify, entice, subjugate, and control their victims, as highlighted by Organization (2023).

2. **Who is at Risk?:** TFGBV poses a significant threat to women worldwide, regardless of their access to digital technology. Some women may be more likely to experience it based on their individual characteristics or behaviors. Reports indicate that women who identify with various intersecting aspects of their identity, such as color, ethnicity, ability, caste, sexual orientation, or gender identity, are unfortunately more prone to experiencing online harassment and attacks (Organization, 2023). Adolescent girls and young women are particularly vulnerable to instances of sexual harassment, abuse, and exploitation that occur via mobile phones and social media platforms. Age is considered to be a significant risk factor for TFGBV.

Based on a comprehensive global study conducted in 32 countries by Plan International, it was found that a significant 58% of teenage girls have unfortunately experienced the distressing reality of being subjected to harassment on social media platforms.

Based on the findings of the study, it was observed that a significant proportion of girls and young women who identify as LGBTI, disabled, or members of an ethnic minority have reported instances of online harassment related to their sexual orientation (Organization, 2023). TFGBV, often preceding physical violence, is a commonly employed tactic to instill fear in female human rights advocates.

According to Organization (2023), it is concerning that an increasing number of women and girls are at risk of experiencing violence through the use of technology. This includes acts committed by individuals such as friends, strangers, and even former partners.

One of the reasons behind this trend is the increasing availability of cell phones and internet access for women and girls across the globe. Based on a comprehensive investigation conducted by the Economist Intelligence Unit, it has been found that adult women in 51 countries who have engaged in TFGBV have provided the following reports:

- A significant percentage of women, specifically 38%, have experienced instances of internet violence firsthand.
- Women between the ages of 18 and 30 have reported a significant incidence of online aggression, with a rate of 45%.
- A significant majority of respondents, specifically 65%, reported that they were aware of other women who had experienced cyber targeting.
- A significant majority of respondents, specifically 85%, reported witnessing instances of women being subjected to online abuse.

4.7. CULTURAL AND RELIGIOUS FACTORS IN GENDER-BASED VIOLENCE

Cultural identities are formed through the collective experiences of a community, encompassing their traditions, challenges, achievements, and triumphs (Initiative, 2013). Cultures play a crucial role in nurturing a strong sense of pride, resilience, community, intersectional identities, and a feeling of belonging. In many societies, customs and traditional beliefs are used to justify gender-based violence and inequality, which is a concerning issue. There are various movements that seek to question the cultural constructs that dictate where power dynamics and gender norms are established. Just as individual DNA varies from generation to generation, cultural DNA also undergoes changes. It is important to recognize that certain customs and explanations may have an expiration date.

There are three interconnected cultural domains that contribute to the perpetuation of gender-based violence. The culture of misogyny and gender-based violence not only devalues women, girls, and LGBTQ people, but it also has the harmful effect of normalizing or downplaying abuse, disregarding sexism, promoting aggressive or toxic masculinity, and using men's achievements to excuse, rationalize, or deny the repercussions of their behavior (Initiative, 2013).

Within ethnic and identity-specific communities, deviations from cultural norms are seen as transgressions. These communities use various methods to ensure conformity, such as violence, coercion, pressure, rejection, or what one gay survivor described as a slow and painful process. They also closely monitor and enforce the boundaries of what they consider culturally acceptable (Initiative, 2013).

Systems' cultures can present challenges to accessing resources and services, which can disproportionately affect individuals from marginalized communities, including people of color and gender. The perception of gender violence is heavily influenced by cultural factors. In some societies, it may be disregarded as an unintentional problem, used as a convenient excuse by certain communities, or linked to stereotyping by various institutions.

It is worth noting that religious beliefs often play a significant role in shaping people's lives. Therefore, it is understandable that many women find solace in religious teachings and affiliations when discussing their experiences of abuse (Pertek et al., 2023). Religious societies and institutions impart values and belief systems to their members through various means such as texts, traditions, teachings, and doctrine. In addition, members often have personal counseling or support connections with religious leaders, who can provide guidance and instruction. Religious texts and teachings can serve as valuable resources in assisting victims of abuse in finding safety and initiating the healing journey. On the other hand, religion can be manipulated to justify or validate harmful behaviors. Communities and religious beliefs will undoubtedly have a significant impact on the issue of violence against women.

Religious and secular leaders face two important tasks. Firstly, they must recognize that religious texts, beliefs, and teachings can both support and hinder victims of violence. Secondly, they should delve deeper into religious texts and teachings, exploring alternative interpretations to minimize obstacles and maximize opportunities for women (Pertek et al., 2023). It is unacceptable for any individual to be forced to make a decision between their personal beliefs or cultural background and their own well-being. It is important for her to have access to a range of services that can provide both faith-based assistance and guidance, as well as community-based advocacy and refuge (Pertek et al., 2023). In order to effectively address the needs of rape victims and battered women, it is crucial for clergy members to acquire knowledge about violence against women and establish strong connections with nonreligious advocates and services. In order to effectively support victims, it is crucial for secular advocates and counselors to recognize the significance of women's religious backgrounds. Establishing connections with clergy and religious organizations can provide valuable resources to address their needs. Community leaders who hold positions of influence, such as religious leaders, have the ability to greatly influence the conversation surrounding violence against women.

Research has demonstrated the intricate relationship between culture, religion, and the potential negative impact on women. It is important to recognize that religion serves as an identity marker that intersects with cultural and societal norms. There has been criticism regarding the influence of cultural interpretations of religious beliefs on gender roles. This influence has been linked to issues such as intimate partner violence and the promotion of societal tolerance towards violence (Pertek et al., 2023). Research has shown that women in certain cultural contexts have faced pressure to remain in abusive relationships due to the influence of authoritative figures, such as religious leaders.

Religious scriptures have unfortunately been misinterpreted, leading to the manipulation of these misunderstandings to incite violence against religious minorities. This has been particularly evident in situations of forced displacement, where tensions are heightened, and symbolic violence becomes prevalent in resettlement environments. Religion has the potential to incite violence, persecution, and discrimination. Survivors of ethnic minority groups may experience heightened levels of discrimination if their religious identity is prominently displayed. There is substantial evidence indicating significant levels of violence and discrimination against religious minorities, including instances of anti-Muslim prejudice in countries with immigrant populations (Pertek et al., 2023).

4.8. LEGAL RESPONSES TO GENDER-BASED VIOLENCE

Gender-based violence against women and girls has a far-reaching impact, transcending national boundaries and socioeconomic differences. It is a staggering reality that a significant number of women, nearly one in three globally, experience intimate partner violence, including physical or sexual abuse, or non-partner sexual violence, at some stage in their lives. Women and girls experience various types of gender-based violence, including intimate partner economic and psychological abuse, technology-enabled violence, sexual exploitation abuse and harassment (SEAH), human trafficking, female genital mutilation (FGM), and forced marriage (Cretsinger et al., 2023).

In recent years, member nations of the OECD have significantly increased their efforts to raise awareness, prioritize, and advocate for the prevention of gender-based violence against women. Gender-based violence (GBV) remains a pervasive issue that impacts societies worldwide, despite efforts in legislation, investment, planning, and policy coordination. During the COVID-19 pandemic, GBV gained significant attention and was referred to as a "shadow pandemic." Effective government mechanisms are crucial in addressing gender-based violence. In order to effectively address the issue at hand, it is crucial to consider a range of factors. These factors encompass the implementation of comprehensive policies, adoption of holistic approaches, coordination of government activities, allocation of sufficient financing and resources, collection of accurate data, establishment of thorough laws, and efficient enforcement of said laws (Cretsinger et al., 2023).

It is crucial to emphasize the importance of enhancing efforts in collecting data on gender-based violence (GBV). Understanding the complex and far-reaching impact of gender-based violence, it is crucial to develop policies that are informed by a thorough understanding of the specific political and socioeconomic contexts of each nation. For a comprehensive understanding, it is crucial to have a substantial body of evidence. One effective way to enhance gender sensitivity is by integrating high-quality data and evidence, especially gender-disaggregated data, into the policy-making process (Cretsinger et al., 2023). In order to develop effective prevention and risk management strategies for gender-based violence, it is crucial to have a comprehensive grasp of the prevalence, incidence rates, and relevant demographics of GBV within a nation. It is important to consider the distinct characteristics of each type of GBV when conducting data gathering initiatives. In order to address the issue of femicides, it is crucial to gain a deep understanding of the underlying factors that contribute to the heightened risk of gender-related mortality faced by women and girls, particularly at the hands of their intimate partners (Cretsinger et al., 2023).

To comprehensively tackle GBV, it is essential to employ a range of data collection techniques and instruments, both quantitative and qualitative in nature. There are various sources that can provide valuable information, such as survivors' and victims' testimonies, government agents' and service providers' accounts, population-based surveys, and administrative data gathered by the government and other service providers. Having access to this type of data is crucial for developing appropriate responses and informing policy decisions.

In order to obtain results that are comparable and provide a comprehensive analysis of the issue and its progression, it is essential to conduct data collection activities consistently over a prolonged duration. As an example, Spain has been conducting a "Macro Survey on Violence Against Women" every four years since 1999. This survey covers various forms of abuse against women, including economic, sexual, psychological, and physical abuse. In 2006 and 2014, the national statistics office of Italy conducted a comprehensive survey on violence against women. The survey encompassed various aspects, such as the prevalence of physical, sexual, and psychological abuse experienced by women over time. In June 2022, the Italian parliament enacted a law that mandates the collection of statistics on gender-based violence. This measure aims to provide valuable data for the formulation of policies and the implementation of effective GBV surveillance systems (Cretsinger et al., 2023).

It is widely recognized that there is a need for more statistics on GBV. However, data gathering poses challenges for all nations. There are several factors that play a role in the official estimates of gender-based violence (GBV) presenting lower numbers than the actual prevalence of violence. These factors include the presence of stigma, underreporting and non-disclosure due to fear of retaliation or further violence, as well as a lack of understanding and confidence in the police and justice systems. Comparing data over time and across nations can be challenging due to variations in survey techniques, questions, and terminology. Consistency gaps can be observed in administrative data when different levels of government, sectors, and geographies are involved in their collection. This is due to the involvement of various actors in the data collection process. One challenge faced by many nations is the limited capacity of their national statistical agencies when it comes to data collection, particularly in the area of gathering data on gender-based violence (Cretsinger et al., 2023).

In addition, it is crucial to monitor and assess initiatives and policies in order to gather valuable data on ongoing requirements, gaps, and new challenges in the eradication of GBV. It is crucial to regularly evaluate and monitor the effectiveness of institutional controls, procedures, and initiatives implemented to prevent and address gender-based violence. In recent years, the OECD DAC Members have made significant strides in strengthening their monitoring and evaluation system for SEAH response and prevention. When examining policy responses, support, and follow-up, it is important to utilize various techniques such as evaluations, independent progress and impact assessments, and review mechanisms to analyze best practices, lessons learned, and standard definitions. An effective evaluation of response efforts should involve the active participation of victim/survivor groups, local actors involved in development and humanitarian initiatives, and the communities they serve (Cretsinger et al., 2023).

4.9. PREVENTION AND INTERVENTION STRATEGIES

Gender-based violence can be prevented, despite its persistent threat to the safety and well-being of women and girls in their everyday lives. Here are a few examples:

1. **Empowering Women and Girls is Crucial for Their Development and Progress:** It involves ensuring that girls have access to education and encouraging their continued attendance in school. Additionally, it entails providing women with economic opportunities and resources to enhance their empowerment. Furthermore, addressing gender inequalities, particularly within the family, requires adopting feminist approaches that challenge and dismantle existing barriers.
2. **Creating Safe Spaces for Women and Girls:** This involves several important strategies. Firstly, providing financial assistance to women can help empower them and give them the resources they need to thrive. Secondly, interacting with male allies is crucial in promoting gender equality and fostering a supportive environment. Additionally, including women in leadership decision-making is essential for ensuring their voices are heard and their perspectives are taken into account. Lastly, assisting regional organizations for women's rights that are led by women can have a significant impact in advancing gender equality (Morrison et al., 2007).
3. **During Times of Crisis, it is Crucial to Establish Comprehensive GBV Services Promptly:** This will help safeguard the well-being of women and girls, reduce their vulnerability to violence, and enhance

their ability to bounce back and recover. When developing programs for individuals impacted by crises, it is crucial for humanitarian organizations to embrace a perspective that takes into account the imbalances in power between genders.

Despite our knowledge of the severity of GBV, its devastating consequences, and our capacity to address it, humanitarian interventions continue to overlook the urgency it demands. Only 28% of the financing requirements for GBV were met in 2021, a decrease from the 32% in 2020 and the lowest percentage recorded in the past four years.

Although there has been an increase in programs targeting gender-based violence (GBV), particularly sexual violence against women and girls, among refugee populations, there remains a lack of information regarding the effectiveness of these programs in preventing various forms of GBV. Additionally, there has been limited assessment of programs that do not specifically address sexual violence (Morrison et al., 2007).

Review articles have extensively explored the effectiveness of GBV prevention initiatives. However, there is a notable gap in the literature when it comes to examining these initiatives in the context of refugee situations. In such circumstances, the risks faced by women and girls may be even more pronounced. As an example, a comprehensive analysis was conducted on GBV prevention strategies globally.

However, the focus of the study was primarily on initiatives implemented in high-income countries, where the majority of evaluations have been carried out. The initiatives aimed at preventing gender-based violence among populations of refugees were not included. A different study examined interventions in areas affected by armed conflict, including refugee populations. The authors, however, specifically concentrated on sexual violence, which is just one form of gender-based violence that women and girls may face (Morrison et al., 2007).

Recent assessments of humanitarian initiatives have highlighted the importance of having data on successful GBV preventive tactics. There is a lack of practical guidance on how to include GBV prevention programming in different humanitarian sectors, such as health, water and sanitation, education, and livelihood programs.

While there have been general statements about the importance of involving various actors in prevention and response efforts, there is a need for more specific guidance on implementation. It is clear from a recent evaluation conducted in Syria on the implementation of the Inter-Agency Standing Committee (IASC) Guidelines for Gender-Based Violence Interventions in Humanitarian Settings (Morrison et al., 2007).

4.10. EXAMINING THE EFFECTS OF GENDER-BASED VIOLENCE ON WOMEN'S HEALTH AND WELLBEING

Extensive research has been conducted over the years to examine the detrimental impact of various forms of gender violence, including sexual abuse and harassment, on individuals' physical and mental well-being. Research has shown that sexual harassment can have significant impacts on mental health, including increased levels of anxiety, depressive symptoms, and feelings of humiliation, shame, and self-blame (Sanjel, 2013). In addition, there has been a significant finding that links sexual harassment in the workplace to cases of suicide and attempted suicide. In addition, research conducted in different work settings has shown that women who are subjected to sexual harassment often suffer from psychological distress. This condition is characterized by the presence of negative thoughts and emotions related to anxiety, fear, or depression. It often requires additional treatment such as psychotherapy or medication. In addition, the workplace can be affected by various factors such as stress, burnout, and job disengagement, which can be attributed to instances of sexual harassment. A study conducted on the impact of physical health has revealed various implications related to the gastrointestinal tract, such as appetite loss, nausea, gastritis, headache, exhaustion, and menstrual disorders (Sanjel, 2013).

Sexual harassment is unfortunately a prevalent issue that can occur within the campuses and colleges of universities. Sexual harassment is a prevalent issue within universities, with men, including students, faculty, and other staff members, being identified as potential perpetrators (Sanjel, 2013). There are several manifestations of this behavior, which can include both physical and psychological abuse, as well as sexual aggression. It also involves coercing individuals to stay in relationships, giving unwanted sexual attention, and using bribes or threats to maintain romantic relationships. According to Sanjel (2013), there is a perception among students who have experienced sexual harassment that the school lacks support and that the environment is permissive. Through a careful examination of narratives, it became evident that a male professor stood out as the sole individual who firmly addressed the issue of a male student engaging in sexual harassment towards two female students in a master's program. In the realm of emerging alternative masculinities, there is a notable movement that actively opposes gender-based violence by offering support to its victims.

Gender violence continues to persist in university settings, fueled by the power dynamics and abuse within academic institutions, as well as the normalization of violence and perpetuation of sexist stereotypes. These factors contribute to the perpetuation of this issue. Rejecting certain proposals from teachers can have serious consequences for victims of sexual harassment at university. It not only affects their productivity, but also hinders their academic success (Sanjel, 2013). Embarrassment is a common psychological response experienced by individuals who have been subjected to sexual harassment.

Child sexual abuse is a form of sexual violence that is categorized under gender-based violence. Research has also explored the lasting health consequences of childhood and teenage sexual abuse. Child sexual abuse, as it is commonly known, is referred to as such by international organizations and the scientific community.

According to the CSA, it is clearly stated that when another individual engages in sexual relations with a child or minor who is unable to give consent, it is considered abuse. CSA can occur solely for the purpose of an individual's sexual pleasure, without involving any form of exchange. Abuse can manifest itself even without the explicit use of force. Instead, it relies on various elements such as manipulation, authority, or power. Coercing children into engaging in sexual activity can have detrimental effects on their well-being, even if they are not fully aware of the consequences (Sanjel, 2013). This is essentially how the wide category of child sexual exploitation (CSA) is defined.

CHAPTER 5

GENDER, RACE, AND CRIME

Contents

The correlation between gender, race, and crime is intricate and captivating within the realm of criminology. These three factors, namely crime rates, geographical locations, and people's perception of the criminal justice system, have a mutual influence on each other (Barak et al., 2010).

1. **The Relationship between Gender and Criminal Behavior:** The correlation between gender dynamics and criminal behavior is significant. Historically, criminological theories often disregarded the unique trajectories that contribute to criminal behavior in women, instead prioritizing the study of male offenders.

   However, studies are increasingly recognizing the significance of gender. Women's participation in criminal activities encompasses a wide range of behaviors, often linked to circumstances such as interpersonal relationships, substance abuse, or financial necessity (Barak et al., 2010).

   Research on female criminality has elucidated the complexities of victimization, agency, and the impact of social expectations.

2. **The Intersection of Criminal Justice and Race:** The criminal justice system continues to demonstrate racial disparities. Black and Indigenous individuals, in particular, face a significantly higher likelihood of being arrested, convicted, and receiving severe sentences compared to other groups.

   These disparities arise from discriminatory laws, prejudiced implementation, and systemic racism. Racial minorities are overrepresented in correctional facilities, indicating the presence of systemic injustices.

   Scholars engage in discussions regarding topics such as subconscious prejudice, racial discrimination based on appearance, and the impact of historical wrongdoings on the outcomes of the contemporary criminal justice system.

3. **Intersectionality and Beyond:** The analysis becomes significantly more intricate when examining the intersection of gender and race. Black women face unique challenges as they are often subjected to discrimination due to both their gender and race.

   Intersectionality theory posits that identities interact in complex ways to shape experiences, surpassing mere additive effects. The statement prompts us to examine how victimization and criminal behavior are shaped by the intersections of race, gender, class, and other variables (Barak et al., 2010). Exploring further, individuals uncover disparities, adaptability, advocacy, and the potential for transformative progress. In order to establish a criminal justice system that is fair and unbiased, it is crucial to fully understand the connections between gender, race, and criminal behavior. This chapter examines various subsections, such as intersectionality and multiple marginalization, the criminalization of black women, Latinas in the criminal justice system, indigenous women and the legal system, Asian American women and crime, middle eastern women and criminal justice, intersectional feminist approaches to crime, the impact of immigration policies on women, racial profiling, and gender, and building solidarity across gender and racial lines in the fight against injustice.

5.1. INTERSECTIONALITY AND MULTIPLE MARGINALIZATION

The theoretical framework of intersectionality highlights how individual experiences are shaped by the overlapping power dynamics of racism, sexism, heterosexism, and classism. This particularly applies to individuals who experience marginalization in multiple aspects, such as their racial/ethnic background and their sexual and gender minority status (Creek & Dunn, 2014). Relationality, one of the six core principles of intersectionality, highlights the interconnectedness and mutual influence of social positions that were previously considered separate and independent.

Intersectionality refers to the intricate connections, interdependence, and inseparability that exist among different identities, "isms," and social-structural elements. There are numerous social aspects that exhibit overlap, intertwining, and occasionally indistinguishability. An in-depth comprehension of power, marginalization, and oppression can be achieved by examining the intricate connections between these concepts. For example, the concepts of gender and race/ethnicity can become closely intertwined, resulting in a form of racism that is specifically based on gender. In other words, the concept of gendered racism cannot be fully understood by simply combining gender with race/ethnicity in a simplistic manner, as stated by Creek & Dunn (2014). Intersectionality is an academic field that examines how different forms of privilege and oppression are interconnected and influenced by various social constructs, such as gender, race/ethnicity, sexual orientation, nationality, economic status, and spirituality (Creek & Dunn, 2014).

The concept of intersectionality originated from the scholarly work, activism, and legal thinking of Black feminists. They emphasized the limitations of addressing racial and gender discrimination as separate matters, and instead emphasized the importance of considering how these forms of discrimination intersect with other structural factors that influence one's experiences and identity (Creek & Dunn, 2014). Women of color who were critical of early feminism observed that it often centered around the experiences of white, middle-class women. These women tended to view their own experiences with gender oppression as a template for understanding the various forms of oppression faced by other groups of women (Creek & Dunn, 2014). This perspective led to the neglect of women's distinctions and the excessive emphasis on their commonalities. Moreover, it was proposed that the experiences of white women were considered representative for all individuals, thereby diminishing, or disregarding the importance of intersecting factors.

When exploring the complex landscape of social justice, it becomes clear that intersectionality is an essential framework that allows us to understand the diverse viewpoints of marginalized individuals. Endorsed by Kimberlé Crenshaw, this concept recognizes that identities intersect to create unique and often compounded forms of disadvantage (Creek & Dunn, 2014).

5.2. THE LEGAL CLASSIFICATION OF BLACK WOMEN AS CRIMINALS

A significant number of Black women and girls have been subjected to criminalization following their victimization by gender-based abuse. A remarkably high proportion of Black women experience gender-based violence, including domestic abuse (Sears, 2023). More than 50% of Black women have experienced rape, physical abuse, or stalking by an intimate partner at some stage in their lives. Approximately half of African American women disclose experiencing sexual assault at some point in their lifetimes. Black women face a twofold higher risk of being fatally shot by a romantic partner in comparison to white women. Black women aged 18 to 34 are three times more likely to be shot and killed by an intimate partner compared to white women of the same age group (Sears, 2023).

The interpretation of self-defense laws is more permissive when it comes to white men who perceive men of color as a threat, but it is much more restrictive when it involves women and gender non-conforming individuals defending themselves against sexual assault and domestic abuse. The exclusion of black women from definitions of "respectable" and/or "proper" womanhood, sexuality, and attractiveness has had an impact on their perceived entitlement to agency and physical autonomy (Sears, 2023).

Gender-based violence disproportionately exposes Black women and girls to the risk of being criminalized and incarcerated.

- Black women who neglect to safeguard their children from their abuser are subject to criminal charges and substantial prison terms. As an example, Kerry King intervened when she became aware that her partner was mistreating her daughter. Not only did her boyfriend cause harm to Kerry, but he also prevented her and her daughter from departing. Both Kerry's boyfriend and I were apprehended by the authorities once they arrived. Following a conviction for child abuse, her partner was sentenced to 18 years in prison, along with seven years of probation. Kerry was sentenced to 30 years in prison after it was discovered that he had not stopped his abusive behavior.
- Black females who engage in behaviors such as running away, using drugs, or skipping school are often treated as criminals due to their responses to trauma or abuse. As an illustration, Bresha Meadow endured years of physical and verbal abuse from her father, who repeatedly made threats to harm her and her family. Bresha committed patricide at the age of 14. At the age of 16, she was ultimately released after being incarcerated in a juvenile detention facility and receiving treatment at a psychiatric hospital.
- Black women who protect themselves from their assailants are subjected to criminalization and imprisonment. Consider this example, Erica Sheppard, a Black woman, is currently imprisoned and has endured instances of sexual assault, intimate partner violence, and child abuse. Her pleas for help were ignored, and the safety protocols implemented to protect her proved ineffective—much like they do for numerous other incarcerated Black women. She contacted the police for help a month prior to the crime, for which she was sentenced to death, because her partner had been subjecting her to severe physical abuse, including pointing a gun at her and making death threats. No action was taken by the law enforcement officers. Subsequently, a male perpetrator compelled a female victim to participate in the robbery, resulting in her demise. The prosecutor argued for the execution of Erica, despite her lifelong experience of trauma and injury. The jury that sentenced Erica to death was never informed about her previous traumas. For the past 27 years, she has been incarcerated on death row in Texas.

According to Sears (2023), a significant majority of girls in the legal system, specifically 84%, have experienced abuse or violence from their families prior to being incarcerated. Additionally, a substantial proportion of women in prison, ranging from 70 to 80%, have endured violence from their intimate partners. The magnitude of the consequences of gender-based violence on incarcerated

Black women and girls is significant, considering their disproportionate representation in jails, prisons, and detention centers, as well as the lack of reporting on instances of abuse and sexual violence (Sears, 2023).

5.3. LATINAS IN THE CRIMINAL JUSTICE SYSTEM

The precise figure for the total count of Latinos who are arrested, incarcerated, under probation, or on parole remains undisclosed (Lopez & Pasko, 2017). An analysis of state criminal justice statistics revealed that only 15 states recorded ethnicity in arrest records, while 40 states provided information on race, such as "white," "black," or "other" (Figure 5.1).

Figure 5.1. *Black women are three times more likely to be incarcerated than white women.*

Source: Maule (2016).

Although the United States is home to various ethnic groups, Latinos are projected to account for 28.6% of the population by 2060. Unfortunately, they are the group that is most adversely affected by state policies that fail to consider ethnicity. The evidence indicates significant racial disparities within our criminal justice system. Insufficient data prevents the accurate documentation of ethnic disparities, hindering politicians, community members, and advocates from comprehending the precise impact of mass incarceration on Latinos (Lopez & Pasko, 2017).

The neglect of gathering and disclosing ethnicity data not only affects Latinos, but also has an impact on the entire criminal justice system. States that categorize individuals solely as "black" or "white" likely classify the majority of their Latino inmate population as "white," thereby inflating the number of "white" inmates and obscuring the disparity between the white and black populations within the criminal justice system.

Most criminal justice data in several states does not encompass Latinos. This is according to data on the racial and ethnic makeup in five categories, namely prison population, prison population by offense, arrests, probation population, and parole population. The data was collected from publicly accessible and user-friendly online sources. Regular reports have been provided on arrests and the populations of individuals in jail, probation, and parole. However, only one state, Alaska, has consistently included data on Latinos (Lopez & Pasko, 2017). The poll exclusively considered data that states publicly disclosed, despite the likelihood that other governments routinely gathered such data. According to Lopez & Pasko (2017), only 39% of states provided data categorized by ethnicity for two or more of our five measures. In contrast, 75% of states regularly and recently reported data for at least one of our five measures.

States employ multiple agencies to collect statistics on criminal justice, and these institutions may not always collaborate effectively. States must ensure that all pertinent agencies, including law enforcement, the department of prisons, and the parole board, uniformly gather ethnicity data to ensure equitable representation of Latinos across the criminal justice system. The assessment of the system's impact on Latinos is hindered by the absence of accurate and thorough data collection across all agencies (Lopez & Pasko, 2017).

States that have a significant number of Latino residents do not automatically possess superior data. According to Lopez & Pasko (2017), only 10 states contain 75% of the entire Latino population in the country. Although these states have a significant number of Latino residents, there are significant discrepancies in the reported ethnicity data for these populations. California, Florida, and New Mexico all provided ethnicity data in fewer categories compared to the average state. Given the higher concentration of Latinos residing in these states, their increased involvement in the criminal justice system makes accurate data reporting in these states especially vital. In regions where government agencies do not furnish data on ethnicity, the general public and political leaders may lack awareness of the impact of criminal justice policies on the Latino population (Lopez & Pasko, 2017).

5.4. INDIGENOUS WOMEN WITHIN THE LEGAL SYSTEM

According to a study conducted by Baldry & Cunneen (2014), the percentage of Indigenous people who reported experiencing victimization in the preceding year was 28%, compared to 18% among non-Indigenous Canadians. When we examine the data, we find that Indigenous people have a significantly higher rate of violent victimization compared to non-Indigenous people. The rate stands at 163 incidences per 1,000 people for Indigenous individuals, while it is only 74 incidents per 1,000 people for non-Indigenous individuals (Figure 5.2).

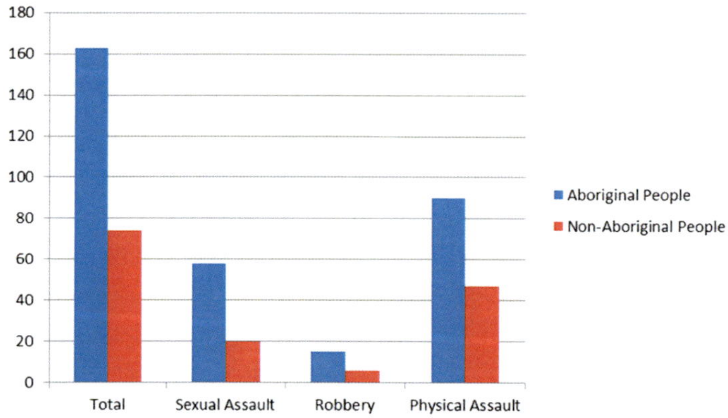

Figure 5.2. *Violent victimization incidents reported by indigenous (aboriginal) people and non-indigenous (aboriginal) people.*

Source: Evaluation of the Family Violence Prevention Program (2019).

The rate of violent victimization among Indigenous women was significantly higher compared to non-Indigenous women and Indigenous men. In fact, it was approximately three times higher than the rate for non-Indigenous women and double that of Indigenous men. According to the data from 2014, there was a significant disparity in the number of violent events experienced by Indigenous women compared to Indigenous men. Specifically, for every 1,000 Indigenous women who were victims, there were 220 violent events, while for Indigenous men, the number was 110. According to a study conducted by Baldry and Cunneen in 2014, it was found that non-Indigenous women reported 81 cases of violent victimization per 1,000 individuals, whereas non-Indigenous men reported 66 cases. It was found that Indigenous women reported 115 incidences of sexual assault per 1,000 people, a significantly higher number compared to the 35 incidences per 1,000 reported by non-Indigenous women.

Researchers can utilize an analysis strategy to investigate particular risk factors associated with victimization. According to Baldry & Cunneen (2014), when considering various risk factors, there is no evidence to suggest that Indigenous people are more prone to violent victimization compared to non-Indigenous individuals. On the contrary, the higher victimization rates among Indigenous people appear to be linked to a range of other risk factors. These include a history of childhood abuse, perceiving social disorder in one's neighborhood, experiencing homelessness, substance abuse, and varying levels of mental health. Nevertheless, it is important to note that victimization risk variables alone do not provide a comprehensive explanation for the disproportionately high incidence of victimization experienced by Indigenous women.

Research has shown that Indigenous identity can be considered a risk factor for the violent victimization of Indigenous women, even when other risk factors are taken into account. It is worth mentioning that Indigenous women, in comparison to their male counterparts, have a higher likelihood of reporting experiences of childhood sexual and physical abuse. Mistreatment during infancy can significantly increase the likelihood of victimization.

It is worth noting that there is a significant disparity in the representation of Native Americans as both murder suspects and victims of homicide. As an illustration, it is worth noting that although Indigenous people accounted for approximately 4.9% of the Canadian population in 2017, a significant 24% of all homicide victims were from this community (Baldry & Cunneen, 2014). In contrast to non-Indigenous individuals, whose homicide rate stood at 1.42 per 1,00,000, the homicide rate among Indigenous people was significantly higher at 8.76 per 1,00,000, representing a six-fold increase. There was an 8% increase in the homicide rate among Indigenous people in 2017 compared to 2016.

Throughout history, Native American women have faced numerous challenges when it comes to navigating the complexities of the legal system. The experiences of individuals are shaped by a variety of factors, including legal loopholes, institutionalized prejudice, and historical injustices.

1. **Legal Loopholes and Missed Justice:** Tribal nations in the United States have been unjustly denied the right to prosecute non-Native Americans for crimes committed on their territory for nearly half a century. This flaw has significant implications.

   One group that experiences a particularly significant impact is violence against women of Indigenous descent. When we examine the rates of violence among women of different races, we find that their rates are significantly higher, reaching two to three times the average. This alarming trend can be described as nothing short of an epidemic.

   It is worth noting that crimes are seldom prosecuted by tribal nations, even when their law enforcement officers have the authority to detain individuals on tribal grounds (Baldry & Cunneen, 2014).

2. **The Ruling of the Supreme Court and the Push for Reform:** In a recent ruling, the Supreme Court affirmed the law enforcement authority of tribes. It remains challenging to prosecute non-Native American offenders.

The reauthorization of the Violence against Women Act (VAWA) is currently being discussed in Congress. The proposed revisions aim to grant tribal governments the legal capacity to independently prosecute offenses, including sexual assault and domestic abuse, without relying on federal prosecutors.

3. **Intersectionality and Accountability:** These are crucial aspects to consider when examining the treatment of Indigenous women within justice systems. It is evident that both indigenous and non-indigenous justice systems perpetuate systematic prejudice against Indigenous women. According to Baldry & Cunneen (2014), individuals become more vulnerable due to uncertainties and gaps in the law.

   Intersectionality is a concept that recognizes how different identities can combine to create specific forms of disadvantages. It is important to acknowledge the multiple forms of marginalization that Indigenous women often experience.

   In order to achieve progress in promoting equality for Indigenous women, it is crucial to acknowledge and rectify the historical injustices they have faced. Additionally, it is imperative to provide support and education to legal professionals, enabling them to develop a deeper understanding and appreciation for different cultures and perspectives (Baldry & Cunneen, 2014).

5.5. ASIAN AMERICAN WOMEN AND CRIME

The issue at hand is the complex intertwining of racism faced by Asian Americans as a whole and the specific racialized misogyny experienced by Asian American women, particularly since the onset of the pandemic. Nevertheless, even after two years, Asian American women continue to share accounts of violent and harassing incidents. In the recently released surveillance footage, a man can be seen viciously attacking a woman in New York, subjecting her to a barrage of punches to her head and face. Shockingly, he proceeds to stomp on her seven times, displaying a disturbing level of violence. The ongoing complaints provide compelling evidence of the widespread presence of racism and misogyny that is specifically targeted at Asian American women.

Determining the true extent of harassment and violence against Asian American women has proven to be a challenging task. Statistics from the advocacy group Stop AAPI Hate indicate that an increase in anti-Asian hate events seems to have a disproportionate impact on women. It is important to note that the organization's data is self-reported, crowdsourced, and not independently confirmed. In addition, it is challenging to determine the full scope of anti-Asian bias in previous years. This is primarily due to scholars initiating data collection efforts after the pandemic, particularly in response to what they perceived as inadequate information from law enforcement agencies and government entities.

However, it is widely known that the data on bias incidents and hate crimes reported by law enforcement agencies is notoriously incomplete and underreported. It is worth noting that there has been a significant rise in attacks driven by prejudice against Asians, with a staggering 73% increase between 2019 and 2020, as reported by the FBI's annual report on hate crimes. Research from Cal State San Bernardino reveals a significant increase in hate crimes against Asians in the first quarter of 2021, as compared to the same period in 2020. In 24 of the country's largest cities and counties, these crimes have surged by 189%. Although specific data on hate crimes against Asian American women is not provided, it is crucial to consider the conclusions drawn by community groups.

5.5.1. The Attacks Do Not Exhibit a Discernible Pattern

Recent attacks on Asian American women have brought to light several significant questions: One important aspect to consider is the root causes of the violence and the potential strategies that could have been implemented to prevent it from occurring.

When examining the attacks, it becomes apparent that there is no discernible pattern beyond the victims' gender and color. Consequently, finding answers to these inquiries has proven to be quite challenging. There are individuals whose motivations may not be easily discernible.

According to authorities, there is no evidence that suggests a connection between the high-profile crimes committed by Christina Yuna Lee and Michelle Go and racism. (Later, New York City Mayor Eric Adams criticized law enforcement for dismissing that notion too quickly.) The directors of the NYPD's Special Victims Division and Hate Crime Task Force were promptly reassigned as part of a routine reshuffling, according to WABC. There was no mention of any racial slurs being uttered by any of the suspects, and it did not appear that they had a documented history of anti-Asian prejudice. Once the signs were absent, the focus of the conversation turned towards the backgrounds of the suspects.

Assamad Nash, the individual believed to be responsible for the tragic death of Christina Yuna Lee, is facing charges for other offenses in addition to being homeless. Based on official reports, Martial Simon, the individual believed to be responsible for the tragic death of Michelle Go, was without a permanent residence and had encountered legal issues on multiple occasions in relation to his mental well-being. As reported by The New York Times, he has had a tumultuous journey, frequently transitioning between jails, hospitals, outpatient mental health clinics, and the streets.

It has been argued by some that taking into account their previous criminal records, the suspects should not have been allowed to roam freely. The bail reform rules in New York, allowing certain defendants to be released from jail before their trial without having to pay bail, received criticism from both Republicans and a majority of Democrats. Others have raised concerns about the impact of progressives' restorative justice responses to crime on public safety. It has been suggested by certain individuals that the continued existence of Lee and Go could have been ensured had they been incarcerated.

Upon careful examination of Nash's records, The New York Daily News made a significant discovery. It became evident that the implementation of progressive prosecution strategies and bail reform rules alone were not enough to explain how Nash ended up on the streets. According to the Daily News, Manhattan judges still had the authority to impose bail in Nash's previous cases, despite the implementation of bail reforms.

One of these cases involved an alleged incident where Nash reportedly punched a stranger at a subway turnstile. Nevertheless, they made the decision not to do so, as is typically the case for misdemeanor offenses, even prior to the implementation of bail reforms, as stated by the Center for Court Innovation. It is worth noting that the argument attributing blame to bail reforms is weakened by the observation that many areas with rising crime rates have chosen to maintain cash bail systems.

Previous discussions have highlighted the importance of enhancing mental health and housing services as a means to prevent acts of violence. On the other hand, mental health professionals and racial justice activists have raised objections to the notion that homeless individuals with mental illnesses are a significant contributor to violent crimes, including violence and harassment targeting Asian American women.

There are numerous other situations in which individuals are not experiencing homelessness. Contrary to popular belief, it is not classified as a mental illness. It is unfortunate that a significant number of individuals are engaging in hate crimes and events without any apparent hindrances. However, it is important to note that many Asian American women often feel a sense of fear while navigating their daily routines. Furthermore, they are strongly encouraging their authorities to take action.

5.6. MIDDLE EASTERN WOMEN AND CRIMINAL JUSTICE

Wars and conflicts have had a significant impact on women and gender in the Middle East, as noted by Dalacoura (2019). The civil wars and subsequent relocations in Yemen, Libya, and Syria have had a significant negative impact on women. Furthermore, it is important to note that the emergence of the Islamic State (IS) has led to a distressing increase in incidents of sexual assault against young girls and women, particularly in Syria and Iraq (Dudouet, 2014) (Figure 5.3).

Figure 5.3. *Syrian Kurdish women demonstrate in the north-eastern Syrian city of Qamishli.*

Source: Dima (2023).

According to a study by Dalacoura in 2019, it has been reported that the 'Arab Spring' had a significant impact on the life expectancies of women in Yemen and Syria. The study suggests that in Yemen, life expectancies dropped from 85 to 75 years, while in Syria, they remained unchanged at 66 years. In addition, it is worth noting that women have often been exploited as symbols to reinforce national and sectarian collective identities. This has resulted in the emphasis on "traditional" gender roles. Wars and conflicts had a significant impact on specific women groups, such as the female Arab population in Israel and the Kurdish women of Turkey. This impact was intensified by the complex interplay between gender and other identities. According to Dudouet (2014), women from the Middle East have played a crucial role in resisting tyranny imposed by official governmental institutions and organizations, and this continues to be the case. Based on Dudouet's categorization of reactions to oppression, it is interesting to note that Palestinian women engage in various forms of resistance. These include non-traditional methods such as cultural resistance, as well as more direct forms like armed or non-peaceful resistance. On the other hand, Iraqi women tend to express their resistance through more conventional actions and widespread civil society activism that extends beyond the national level. Kurdish women in Turkey employ nonviolent methods of resistance against the repressive Turkish state. They choose to join the Kurdistan Workers' Party (PKK) and assume leadership positions or engage in active combat (Dudouet, 2014).

In addition to subjecting Palestinian women to sexual assault and cruel abuse in jails and detention centers, the Israeli police also restrict their freedom of movement. These women, unfortunately, do not have access to healthcare and other essential services. According to Dalacoura (2019), pregnant Palestinian women sometimes found themselves in the unfortunate situation of having to deliver their babies near the checkpoints, without any access to medical assistance.

There are certain locations that ambulances are unable to access, possibly due to restrictions at checkpoints. In addition, it should be noted that Israeli forces have created significant obstacles for women in accessing their daily necessities, including in areas like Al Khalayleh and Azzun Almeh. In addition, it is worth noting that Palestinians face significant limitations when it comes to accessing public transportation. This unfortunate reality only serves to further isolate them and exacerbate the challenges faced by Palestinian women in obtaining basic supplies. As time goes on, the increased barriers, roadblocks, and curfews have a negative effect on women (Dalacoura, 2019).

Some Palestinian women perceive these acts of victimization as a form of non-peaceful resistance. On the other hand, there are those who feel powerless to protect themselves when detained or at checkpoints. Additionally, some families encourage their daughters to leave school, further exacerbating the situation. Through challenging the prevailing stereotypes of Middle Eastern women, oppressive behaviors serve to empower Palestinian women instead of dehumanizing them. According to Dalacoura (2019), the anxieties experienced by Palestinian women play a significant role in their resistance, alongside their nationalist motivations.

Ultimately, this leads to a rejection of the dominant Western narrative that depicts women, both in general and Middle Eastern women in particular, as helpless victims (Dalacoura, 2019).

5.7. INTERSECTIONAL FEMINIST APPROACHES TO CRIME

Feminist viewpoints in criminology encompass a diverse array of theories that aim to address the historical oversight of women in traditional criminological theories. The viewpoints presented in this analysis consider various factors such as patriarchy, power dynamics, capitalism, gender inequality, and the concept of intersectionality when examining the roles of female offenders and victims. Winterdyk (2020) has thoroughly explored these aspects. Here is a brief overview of the six main feminist perspectives.

5.7.1. Liberal Feminism

The objective of liberal feminism is to achieve gender equality within society. According to liberal feminists, sexism and injustice permeate all aspects of society, ranging from the criminal justice system to the workplace and educational institutions. Outlawing discriminatory laws and practices is crucial for the establishment of a fair and just society. According to liberal feminists, it is crucial for women to have equal opportunities in terms of jobs and education, as argued from a criminological perspective. As an example, it can be argued by a liberal feminist that incarcerated women should be granted equal access to the same programs as their male counterparts, in order to address the specific needs of female offenders. One aspect that needs to be considered is the failure of the liberal feminist perspective to acknowledge the diverse demands and risk factors that women face, distinct from those experienced by men (Winterdyk, 2020).

5.7.2. Radical Feminism

Radical feminism views the current social system as patriarchal. According to Winterdyk (2020), society is organized in a gendered social framework in order to maintain control over women. Violence against women is employed by men as a means of exerting control and perpetuating their oppression. It is worth noting that men sometimes utilize the criminal justice system as a means of exerting control over women. One crucial step in addressing violence against women is to challenge and deconstruct the existing patriarchal societal structure (Winterdyk, 2020).

5.7.3. Marxist Feminism

Marxist feminists view society as a source of oppression for women, similar to the perspective of radical feminists. There is a distinction between the two perspectives. Marxist feminists argue that the oppression of women is primarily rooted in the capitalist system. Women are often subject to exploitation within a capitalist and classist economy. Exploitation in a capitalist society often results in women having limited options when it comes to the workforce, often being confined to low-paying positions. It is worth noting that there is a significant disparity in the involvement of women in property crime and sex work, which can be attributed to the unequal access they face. According to Winterdyk (2020), the liberation of women can only be achieved through the dismantling of capitalism and the subsequent restructuring of society, aligning with the perspectives of other Marxist thinkers.

5.7.4. Socialist Feminism

Social feminists combine Marxist and radical ideologies. It is believed by some that women face oppression within the current societal system. Instead of solely attributing these unequal power dynamics to patriarchy, it is important to recognize that the combination of capitalism and patriarchy is responsible for them (Winterdyk, 2020). Addressing unequal power structures requires the removal of gender inequality and the capitalist culture. According to socialist feminists, the existence of gendered inequalities in crime rates can be attributed to disparities in class and power. This is particularly evident in the fact that men tend to commit more violent crimes than women.

5.7.5. Post-Modern Feminism

Unlike the other perspectives discussed earlier, postmodern feminists argue that there isn't a single "reality" of feminism. Instead, they believe that when studying how gender, crime, and deviance influence our understanding of the world, it is crucial to highlight the wide range of experiences among women. Postmodern feminists acknowledge the power dynamics that exist in society, particularly in relation to gendered distinctions. They focus on how these constructed differences influence the prevailing gender discourses. An important area of study involves analyzing the language and other forms of communication that shape society's perception of women and the accepted 'truth' about them. It is noteworthy to acknowledge that postmodern feminism recognizes the profound influence of various factors, including color, sexual orientation, and class, on women's lived experiences (Winterdyk, 2020).

5.7.6. Intersectional Feminism

It is important to consider how gender intersects with other forms of inequality, such as race, class, ethnicity, ability, gender identities, and sexual orientation. Intersectional feminists have developed solutions to address these complexities (Winterdyk, 2020). Intersectional approaches acknowledge that women can experience various forms of discrimination. However, certain theories attempt to present the lived experiences of all women as being on an equal footing. Understanding the intricate dynamics between these disparities is crucial in determining how they influence a woman's vulnerability as a victim or her potential involvement as an offender. Indigenous feminism has emerged as a significant discourse within feminist theory. One must consider the complex dynamics at play when examining the experiences of Indigenous women, including the ways in which race, gender, and historical power structures have been utilized to oppress them (Winterdyk, 2020).

5.8. THE IMPACT OF IMMIGRATION POLICIES ON WOMEN

Due to the dynamic nature of the political landscape, Congress has yet to approve and enact comprehensive immigration reform (CIR). In recent years, there has been a noticeable increase in the number of laws being passed by states and municipalities that specifically target undocumented immigrants. These policies have had a detrimental impact on entire communities, as highlighted by Passel and D'Vera Cohn in their research. Immigrant communities across the nation are often left waiting for much-needed reforms to address the shortcomings of the immigration system. Unfortunately, amidst this wait, immigrant women are often overlooked and disregarded (Passel & D'Vera Cohn, 2009).

When we consider the situation of women, particularly those without legal status, it becomes evident that they often face greater vulnerability and limited economic opportunities compared to men. As evidenced by research conducted by Passel and D'Vera Cohn in 2011, one possible explanation for the lower salaries observed among immigrant women is their limited access to higher education. According to a study conducted in 2008, immigrant women had a median annual income of $21,182. This was $3,259 lower than the income of native-born women and $8,351 lower than the income of men who were born abroad. It is important to recognize that women who are immigrants face a higher risk of exploitation in various contexts, such as when traveling across borders, seeking employment, and even within their own homes. Immigrant women, unfortunately, bear the brunt of the flawed immigration system, often without receiving the attention they deserve.

It is important for legislators to consider the specific changes needed to ensure that Comprehensive Immigration Reform (CIR) does not inadvertently create additional barriers and unattainable eligibility requirements for certain immigrant women. This is particularly crucial as many immigrant women endure hardships without voicing their struggles. As part of a comprehensive immigration reform package, it is crucial to acknowledge the valuable contributions of immigrant women who work part-time and informally. This path to legalization should be included, as highlighted by Passel & D'Vera Cohn in 2009.

It is important to recognize that women need independent means to seek legal recognition, rather than depending solely on their spouses or fathers. It is important to consider that a significant portion of immigrant women, who make valuable contributions to the workforce, have had limited opportunities for employment and education. It is important to consider the roles of women in immigrant families and their status as the primary beneficiaries of the system, as highlighted by CIR.

In order to ensure the protection of the most vulnerable immigrants and prevent them from falling victim once more, it is imperative that we make necessary changes to our enforcement procedures. According to Passel & D'Vera Cohn (2009), the absence of immigration reforms will continue to subject a significant number of immigrant women to exploitation, criminal activity, family separation, and limited economic prospects.

5.8.1. Legal Obstacles to Achieving Equality in Contemporary Immigration Law

Women immigrants from their native nation come to the United States in search of safety, economic opportunity, and family reunification. Women's migration is often driven by the disparity in gender opportunities within their home countries (Passel & D'Vera Cohn, 2009). Many immigrant women are forced to flee their home countries due to political unrest and violence, leaving them particularly vulnerable to being targeted. In addition, it is worth noting that individuals from certain societies may face limitations in terms of women's economic opportunities. According to Passel & D'Vera Cohn (2009), individuals may choose to travel to the US in order to be with their families, as they may not wish to raise their children alone. Women are often faced with external pressures that often compel them to migrate to another country. However, upon their arrival, women frequently encounter challenges in attaining the economic opportunities and safety they desire.

From the very beginning of the migration process, women often face various disadvantages. Given the current criteria for employment-based immigration, which take into account factors such as education, specialized occupational needs, and economic opportunity, it appears that women may face greater challenges in meeting the requirements for employer sponsorship compared to men. It is worth noting that family sponsorship is a frequently chosen avenue for women to immigrate, as opposed to employment-based immigration. As an illustration, in Fiscal Year (FY, 2009), a total of 1,12,694 females and 99,165 males were granted legal permanent resident (LPR) status under family-based "preference" categories. It is worth noting that the number of males who obtained LPR status through employment-based visas was 74,563, while the corresponding figure for women was 69,471. It is interesting to observe that a significant portion of these women were descendants of the primary male visa holder. It is important to note that the family immigration procedure can present certain challenges and delays, resulting in families being separated for extended periods of time. For instance, according to Passel & D'Vera Cohn (2009), backlogs and other difficulties in the process can lead to separations lasting over 20 years.

When it comes to women who are seeking to be reunited with their sponsoring family member, unfortunately, they are currently facing a significant delay in their native countries due to the existing backlogs. In certain countries, women often find themselves in a challenging situation when they are separated, as they may not have equal opportunities as men in terms of employment and economic prospects. According to Passel & D'Vera Cohn (2009), the backlogs in immigration processing can have significant financial and emotional implications for women and their families, despite eventually leading to reunification.

5.9. RACIAL PROFILING AND GENDER

Victims of racial discrimination and related intolerance often face a multitude of injustices, such as segregation, limited job opportunities, and widespread poverty. It is widely acknowledged that women face numerous challenges in societies worldwide, such as unequal pay for comparable work, high illiteracy rates, and limited healthcare access (Welch, 2007). It is important to note that inequality can be influenced by both race and gender, and these factors are not mutually exclusive. It is worth noting that there is a significant overlap between these two issues, resulting in the occurrence of compounded or double discrimination (Welch, 2007).

For many women, social identity-related characteristics such as race, color, ethnicity, and country of origin can become significant factors that shape their experiences. According to Welch (2007), certain groups of women may experience specific issues or be disproportionately affected by certain factors.

Consider the various social challenges that a Roma woman residing in Eastern Europe would encounter. She faces constant animosity and has a limited number of allies due to her Romani background. She faces marginalization in both her family and community due to her gender and minority status. It is important to note that the aforementioned statement holds true for various groups of women across different regions. For instance, women who are indigenous to Australia, Dalit women in India, and female asylum seekers in England, among others, face similar challenges and experiences. These women exist at the intersection of gender and racial discrimination.

Based on the available data, it is evident that women, regardless of their race, have a significant journey ahead of them in order to achieve true equality with men. According to a recent report from the United Nations Development Fund for Women (UNIFEM) (Welch, 2007), women continue to fall behind in several important indicators that measure gender equality and women's empowerment.

The global literacy rates for women and men stand at 71.4% and 83.7%, respectively. According to Welch (2007), it is worth noting that a significant majority, specifically two thirds, of the 960 million adults who currently lack literacy skills are female. According to Welch (2007), there is a significant gender pay gap in the industry and services sectors, with women typically earning only 78% of what men make in the same field. In the 1990s, the proportion of women in decision-making roles saw a significant increase in only 28 nations. In addition, it is worth noting that out of the 1.3 billion individuals who are currently living in poverty, a significant 70% of them are women (Welch, 2007).

When considering a woman's race, it becomes evident how she faces the dual challenges of racial and gender discrimination, along with the accompanying intolerance. The topics that require special attention are racialized violence against women, trafficking in women, and the challenges faced by minority women in the workforce.

Violence against women motivated by race or ethnicity is widely recognized as a clear example of intersectional discrimination. The occurrence of rape incidents in Rwanda, Burundi, Bosnia, and Kosovo highlights the disturbing reality of women being specifically targeted based on their race, resulting in gender-based violations. This is evident from the research conducted by Welch in 2007. One consequence of ethnic conflict is the significant number of female refugees, who unfortunately encounter challenges related to gender and sexual violence. It is important to note that the International Criminal Tribunals for Yugoslavia and Rwanda have acknowledged the use of rape as a weapon of war, specifically targeting women based on their ethnic or religious background. These tribunals are actively pursuing legal action against individuals involved in such cases, in line with this recognition.

5.10. BUILDING SOLIDARITY ACROSS GENDER AND RACIAL LINES IN THE FIGHT AGAINST INJUSTICE

Establishing solidarity among individuals of diverse genders and races is of utmost importance in the ongoing battle against injustice. Intersectionality is a crucial concept that plays a significant role in supporting this collective effort. It is important to thoroughly analyze its significance.

1. **Approach and a Mindset:** This concept was pioneered by Kimberlé Crenshaw. It was introduced by this esteemed black feminist and critical race academic. The acknowledgement is made that various social characteristics, such as race, gender, class, sexual orientation, disability, and nationality, have an impact on oppressions and that these phenomena are interconnected. Women of color and indigenous feminists have long been at the forefront of developing this idea, highlighting the significance of addressing various aspects of identity.
2. **Dilution and Challenges:** As intersectionality gains popularity, there is a concern that it may be appropriated or diluted. It has the potential to be misunderstood and oversimplified in the context of culture wars and academic discussions. Understanding the lineage of a subject helps us appreciate its theoretical and practical significance, while also preventing misunderstandings.
3. **Practical Applications:** Policymaking and advocacy are influenced by intersectionality. Youth organizing organizations at the grassroots level provide education to their members on intersectional frameworks and equip them with the skills to be effective allies. Government programs prioritize the rights and well-being of Native American women, emphasizing the interconnectedness of race and gender. Activists worldwide employ intersectionality as a means to advocate for fairness and equality, transcending the limitations of individual identities.
4. **Acts of Solidarity:** Coalitions are formed by successful initiatives.

- It is crucial to acknowledge and honor the diverse groups within society while actively resisting and challenging oppressive systems.
- Provide education to allies: Offer individuals the necessary intersectional frameworks to foster a sense of unity.
- It is crucial to prioritize the voices of those who have been marginalized. Expand your experiences beyond mere one-dimensional assessments.

- It is crucial to acknowledge and honor the wide range of human experiences in our pursuit of justice. By working together across racial, gender, and other barriers, we can strive to create a society that is more equitable and fairer.

Ultimately, the intricate dynamics between gender, crime, and race play a significant role in shaping individuals' perceptions of injustice and fairness. Addressing inequities requires recognizing the interconnectedness of various dimensions and the disproportionate impact they often have on marginalized communities. Transitioning to a fairer and more equal society is facilitated by promoting open discussion, advocating for policy reforms, and cultivating compassion.

CHAPTER 6

WOMEN IN LEADERSHIP ROLES IN THE CRIMINAL JUSTICE FIELD

Contents

It is crucial that women occupy leadership roles within the criminal justice system. Despite the presence of advancements, issues persist. In order to establish a justice system that is both more inclusive and efficient, it is crucial to recognize and appreciate the unique perspectives and capabilities that women contribute to these roles.

According to the Bureau of Justice Statistics, the global average for female police officers in county and local departments is approximately 13%. State police organizations struggle to maintain even half of that percentage (Salisbury & Van Voorhis, 2009). Since the mid-1980s, police agencies have made little effort to augment this figure, especially in terms of the inclusion of women in leadership positions. Since the 1970s, multiple studies have shown that diverse and representative police units are better for both the communities they serve and their own effectiveness.

Due to the underrepresentation of women in leadership positions in law enforcement, the responsibility of addressing this highlighted issue has primarily fallen on their male counterparts. When addressing this problem, nearly all organizations have faced significant challenges, and there is a substantial amount of work that needs to be completed in order for their departments to genuinely reflect the diversity of the communities they serve. The gravity of the issue is heightened by the potential stagnation of initiatives aimed at promoting diversity within law enforcement. The underrepresentation of women in law enforcement can be attributed to various factors. Women are often summoned to the field for various personal and professional reasons that differ from those of their male counterparts, even though their male colleagues are carrying out the same tasks.

Both men and women value job security, but women prioritize a positive work environment, job enrichment, family-friendly policies, assignment choice, and social involvement to a greater extent (Salisbury & Van Voorhis, 2009).

The generational gap further hinders the connection between the command staff and the young women they are attempting to recruit for their departments. The effectiveness of the message intended to recruit female officers is likely to diminish if women are not included in the process of creating the messaging. The problem extends beyond the recruitment of women for law enforcement positions. Female police officers also face challenges in terms of retention.

It is commonly believed, based on anecdotal evidence, that challenges in achieving work-life balance, lack of representation, and limited opportunities for leadership are factors that lead women to leave the police force. Comprehensive evaluations are necessary to determine the accuracy of these assumptions. To address the significant underrepresentation of female officers in a particular field, it is crucial to acknowledge the unique skills and capabilities that women can bring to the work. For instance, female officers have demonstrated greater effectiveness in de-escalating confrontations compared to their male counterparts. In order to increase the representation of female officers, it is crucial to provide women with the necessary resources and empower them to establish focused recruitment, mentorship, and leadership development initiatives for both new recruits and existing officers. By doing so, we can foster a culture that will gradually enhance the proportion of women in law enforcement (Salisbury & Van Voorhis, 2009).

6.1. THE HISTORICAL BACKGROUND OF WOMEN IN LAW ENFORCEMENT

The narrative of women's involvement in the workforce, including their participation in American law enforcement, is a constantly evolving one. Throughout the history of law enforcement, women have exerted a significant influence, dating back to the early inclusion of matrons in jails.

1. **Origins:** In the 1800s, when the first police agencies were established in New York City, women began working as matrons in the city's jails. These initial roles were often associated with social work and the criminal justice system, specifically involving the provision of assistance to women and children.
2. **Pioneering Officers:** In 1905, Lola Baldwin became the first female police officer in Portland, Oregon. Prior to being granted the authority to make arrests, she initially focused on social work. Alice Wells, the founder of the International Association of Policewomen, joined the Los Angeles Police Department in 1910, becoming the first female police officer. Margaret Adams was designated as the inaugural female deputy sheriff of the Los Angeles County Sheriff's Department in 1912 (Greene, 2000).
3. **Obstacles and Advancements:** During the 1930s and 1940s, women in law enforcement faced limited opportunities as a result of the Great Depression and World War II. Despite this, women persisted in working in auxiliary roles such as dispatch and administrative support. In the 1950s, there was a significant shift in the status quo as women began actively vying for promotions and taking on positions that were previously predominantly held by men. The International Association of Women Police was founded in 1956 with the objective of advancing the development of female police officers (Greene, 2000).

4. **Recent Accomplishments:** Lola Baldwin assumed the role of Portland, Oregon's inaugural female police officer in the new millennium. In 1972, after changes in employment law that prohibited gender discrimination, Tanya Padgett, Martha Parks, and Tommie Stewart became full police officers in Ann Arbor, Michigan.
5. **Anticipated Challenges:** Despite the progress made, as of 2018, women constituted only 12.6% of the total number of sworn police officers in the United States. Further efforts are required to promote diversity, eradicate gender disparity, and recognize the unique contributions made by female officers. Women play a crucial role in law enforcement, contributing to the development of a fairer justice system and safer communities, as highlighted by Greene (2000) in the context of ongoing progress.

6.2. FEMALE REPRESENTATION IN THE JUDICIAL SYSTEM

Historically, women were deemed unsuitable for the legal profession. Currently, women have begun to pursue careers in this particular field due to the progress and developments that have taken place over time. However, the representation of women in the judiciary, particularly in the higher courts, is significantly inadequate. It is necessary to change this way of thinking. Judges play a crucial role in the administration of justice and the formation of judgments due to their profound and extensive impact on social structures, social order, and systemic inequalities within the system (Peresie, 2004) (Figure 6.1).

Figure 6.1. *To achieve justice, we need more women in justice.*

Source: United Nations: Office on Drugs and Crime (2024).

The judges' rationale and findings when interpreting and implementing the law offer insight into their perspectives and cognitive processes. In order for judicial decisions to be fair and suitable, these opinions must, at a minimum, reflect the characteristics of the judges. It is imperative to bear in mind that the presence of women in the judiciary encompasses more than simply ensuring their perspectives are considered in cases pertaining to women. That is not the entirety of what it is. The objective is to ensure that women receive equal recognition and that the gender perspective is fully incorporated (Peresie, 2004).

Integrating and making the gender perspective visible is necessary for constructing a narrative. Women contribute a gender perspective to the judiciary. An alternative approach, a distinct mindset, and a shifted emphasis. With the aim of upholding the principle of legal governance, judges, regardless of their gender, make decisions in accordance with the law. Through this approach, individuals can reach a shared conclusion regarding a specific dataset, albeit with differing rationales and varying degrees of importance assigned to the relevant information. Their circumstances, surroundings, and personal experiences all influence them. The importance of considering the gender perspective stems from the fact that female judges possess a unique set of experiences and influences that affect their decision-making and reasoning. When the bench includes a variety of viewpoints and arguments, it better represents society as a whole, which increases the public's trust and belief in it (Peresie, 2004). It encompasses a diverse range of social environments and encounters that need to be recognized, encompassed, and, most importantly, appreciated.

Employing gender-neutral language, which is particularly attentive to gendered terminology, roles, and the portrayal of women, is an additional method to enhance the gender perspective for the purpose of inclusivity and visibility. The selection of words, or the absence of it, holds significant importance not only in everyday conversations but especially in making judgments, as language possesses the ability to perpetuate bias (Peresie, 2004). For example, the notion that men have a significant presence in society can be supported by the frequent use of the pronoun "he." Gender bias, whether it is intentional or unintentional, is often hidden in language and can become deeply rooted in the system due to repeated assumptions and presumptions, particularly when it comes to women. While language can perpetuate these biases, it also possesses the capacity to gradually and methodically facilitate the necessary positive transformation. The influence of language on human cognition and its potential to instigate transformative actions has been demonstrated.

Using gender-neutral language is crucial for promoting inclusivity and increasing awareness. Furthermore, it is imperative because it possesses the ability to rectify the disparity and actively endorse a narrative regarding women that is more comprehensive and considerate. Ultimately, language serves as a medium for expressing alternative perspectives, facilitating the development of a more comprehensive and equitable process of logical thinking. When there is a fair representation of women on the bench, all of this becomes possible (Peresie, 2004).

6.3. WOMEN IN THE ROLES OF PROSECUTORS AND DEFENSE ATTORNEYS

Female attorneys face gender roles and prejudices that put them at a disadvantage compared to their male colleagues. However, it is important to emphasize that gender does not affect their talent or competence as prosecutors. The jurors will perceive them as hostile or irrational, leading them to label them as "shrill." Male attorneys rarely face this problem as our culture generally accepts and even praises anger as a characteristic of masculinity. Unlike males, who can appear professional simply by wearing a suit, women attorneys must also meticulously consider their attire (Ramsey, 2002) (Figure 6.2).

Figure 6.2. *Female lawyers still suffer significant gender bias at work.*

Source: Elsesser (2018).

The fight for women's rights, especially within the legal field, has been a persistent struggle. The tireless efforts of dedicated female legal professionals have been instrumental in achieving milestones such as equal representation, the right to work, suffrage, and gender equality. Below is a discussion on transformative impact of five women in the legal profession through their innovative contributions and unwavering commitment to justice and prosperity.

1. **Michelle Obama:** Upon completing her studies at Harvard Law School in 1988, subsequently became the inaugural African American first lady of the United States and emerged as one of the most prominent female figures in American history. While employed

as an intellectual property law specialist at Sidley & Austin, she encountered her future spouse, Barack Obama. During her time as first lady, she initiated the Let's Move campaign, which aimed to eradicate childhood obesity. She spearheaded efforts to enhance the accessibility of nutritious food for disadvantaged individuals and to broaden the range of nutrient-rich food choices in educational institutions. *Jackson Ketanji Brown:* Ketanji Brown Jackson completed her bachelor's and Juris Doctor degrees at Harvard University, earning distinction. Subsequently, she served a two-year tenure at the U.S. Sentencing Commission, followed by another two years working for the federal government in Washington, D.C., and subsequently spent three years in private practice. Subsequently, she assumed the role of vice chairwoman and commissioner for the U.S. Sentencing Commission from 2010 to 2014. In 2021, President Joe Biden appointed her to the D.C. Circuit U.S. Court of Appeals. In 2022, he recommended her for the position of Associate Justice of the U.S. Supreme Court. On June 30, 2022, she achieved the historic milestone of becoming the inaugural Black woman to hold the position of Supreme Court justice.

2. **Lynch Loretta:** Upon completing her studies at Harvard Law School, she made history as the inaugural African American woman to assume the role of attorney general. During the administrations of Bill Clinton and Barack Obama, she held the position of attorney general on two separate occasions. During her two terms in office, she supported the prosecution of individuals accountable for the atrocities committed during the Rwandan genocide. Furthermore, she played a significant role in the legal proceedings against the Brooklyn police officers who subjected Abner Louima, a Haitian immigrant, to harassment and physical assault.

3. **Arabella Mansfield:** She holds the distinction of being the inaugural female lawyer in the annals of American legal history. Despite the fact that only males were allowed to participate in the Iowa state bar exam in 1869, she successfully passed the exam with exceptional results. After successfully passing the bar exam, she made history as the inaugural female attorney in the United States when Iowa removed its prohibition on women practicing law. Despite successfully passing the bar exam, she opted to pursue a degree in activism and teaching instead of practicing law. Despite her passing prior to the official granting of women's suffrage, she devoted her entire life to advocating for this cause.

4. **Ruth Bader-Ginsburg:** Who completed her studies at Columbia Law School in 1959, subsequently became one of the pioneering female law instructors at both Rutgers Law School and Columbia Law School. She held the position of director at the ACLU's Women's Rights Project and was a passionate champion for women's rights. In 1980, President Jimmy Carter extended an invitation to her to become a member of the U.S. Court of Appeals for Washington, D.C. She stayed in that position until 1993, at which point she was appointed as a justice on the U.S. Supreme Court. Throughout her term, she advocated for gender parity, labor rights, and civil liberties (Ramsey, 2002).

6.4. WOMEN IN CORRECTIONAL LEADERSHIP

Over the course of time, the roles of women in leadership positions within the correctional industry have undergone significant transformations. Although facing persistent challenges, their endeavors are indispensable in establishing a criminal justice system that is both equitable and enhanced in its efficacy. Consider the following crucial factors (Figure 6.3):

Figure 6.3. *Effective women leader in corrections.*

Source: York (2020).

1. **Diversify Work Experience:** Officers, regardless of gender, often allocate excessive time to a singular task, thereby diminishing their overall skill set. It is important for women to actively seek out a range of experiences, including tasks that require both technical and interpersonal skills. Exploring areas such as defense tactics, firearms, and hostage negotiations can enhance one's leadership potential.
2. **Education and Networking:** It is crucial to actively seek further education and obtain a college degree. Platforms like LinkedIn

enable research on the professional networks and backgrounds of leaders. Understanding the selection process for executive leadership training in the agency is of utmost importance (Collica-Cox & Schulz, 2019).

3. **Communication Skills:** Effective leadership requires proficient communication skills. Public speaking is crucial, especially at more advanced levels. Engaging in organizations like Toastmasters enhances an individual's proficiency in delivering speeches to a public audience.
4. **Social Media Presence:** Keeping up a professional social media presence can be helpful, even though it can be challenging. CEOs often interact with influential thinkers and advocate for issues in the criminal justice system through popular social media platforms such as LinkedIn and Twitter. Strict compliance with the social media guidelines of the agency is of utmost importance.
5. **Encouraging Diversity:** Females in leadership roles possess the capacity to foster inclusivity and diversity. It is crucial to establish an organizational culture that fosters the growth and development of women. Effective leadership necessitates the incorporation of collaboration, empathy, and communication as crucial elements.

6.4.1. Distinct Obstacles Encountered by Women in Positions of Authority within the Correctional System

Women in leadership positions in corrections encounter several distinct challenges that require careful attention. Several significant areas of concern include:

1. **Stereotypes and Gender Bias:** Women often face preconceived notions about their abilities, especially in male-dominated industries such as prisons. Overcoming gender bias and showcasing one's competence can be challenging as time progresses (Collica-Cox & Schulz, 2019).
2. **Balancing Work and Family:** Leadership roles in corrections demand extended work hours, rotating shifts, and significant levels of stress. Women often face challenges in managing the demands of their work and family responsibilities.
3. **Establishing Credibility and Esteem:** Obtaining respect and authority from both employees and inmates can present a formidable challenge. Women may experience resistance or distrust as a result of adhering to traditional gender roles.

4. **Navigating Male-Dominated Environments:** The majority of employees in correctional facilities are predominantly male. It is imperative for female leaders to assert themselves, assume control, and establish alliances.
5. **Addressing Gender-Specific Needs:** Female offenders have specific needs related to trauma, safety, and health. Leaders in corrections must ensure that policies and programs are designed to address the specific needs and experiences of individuals based on their gender.
6. **Overcoming Gender Barriers:** Women still face significant challenges in reaching top leadership positions. It is crucial to advocate for the promotion of equitable opportunities, advancement in professional skills, and guidance through mentorship.

According to Collica-Cox & Schulz (2019), the presence of women in leadership positions in correctional facilities helps to improve the efficiency and inclusivity of the criminal justice system by successfully overcoming the challenges that arise.

6.5. CHALLENGES FACED BY WOMEN IN LEADERSHIP POSITIONS

Women are exiting the labor force due to a range of factors, including the detrimental impact of work-related burnout on their mental and physical well-being. Female leaders experience higher rates of chronic stress and fatigue compared to their male counterparts. Indeed, 43% of female executives and 31% of male executives reported experiencing burnout. Nevertheless, women in leadership positions face additional challenges apart from the ones mentioned. Presented below are six prominent challenges encountered by female leaders, accompanied by corresponding solutions.

6.5.1. Limited Prospects for Career Progression

MIT Sloan research reveals that despite their superior performance and lower turnover rates, female employees have a 14% lower probability of being promoted compared to their male counterparts. In addition, while women received higher performance evaluations, their potential scores, which reflect their managers' expectations of their future advancement, tended to be lower. Potential is a matter of personal interpretation, which renders it susceptible to bias, leading to discrimination against women. Research suggests that females are less inclined to engage in self-promotion, which consequently hampers their opportunities for career progression. Instead, assess the impact of your contribution and the level of effort you exert. Emphasizing the ways in which your accomplishments correspond with the goals and objectives of the organization will enhance the likelihood of you obtaining salary increases (Kiamba, 2009).

6.5.2. Lack of Flexibility

According to recent LinkedIn data, a majority of women feel that a lack of flexible options at work has compelled them to either resign or contemplate leaving their current job. Some individuals may contemplate sacrificing something in order to attain greater work flexibility. A study conducted by Flex Jobs found that 15% of female participants expressed their willingness to forego employer-matching 401(k) contributions, while 21% of female respondents stated their willingness to give up vacation time in exchange for increased flexibility at work.

Companies must offer a variety of choices to maintain women's interest. Examples of alternative work arrangements include a reduced four-day workweek, flexible scheduling options, and the ability to work remotely or in a hybrid fashion. Ultimately, however, companies must prioritize the viewpoints of their female employees and determine which choices will most effectively assist them.

6.5.3. Inadequate Balance between Work and Personal Life

Working women are more inclined than men to assume household responsibilities and juggle multiple roles. According to a study published in The Lancet Public Health, women are more inclined than men to dedicate twice as much time to caregiving and household chores. When combined with a full-time job, engaging in all of these activities can rapidly lead to burnout for female leaders.

Establishing suitable limits in the workplace is crucial for avoiding burnout. The principles and the context in which you operate will dictate the manner in which you establish limits. Operating a nascent start-up is primarily a mission-oriented environment, wherein it is effortless to obscure the distinctions between professional and personal life. It is crucial to have a clear understanding of your priorities and regularly reassess them.

6.5.4. Lack of Recognition

Female leaders are often undervalued and burdened with excessive workloads. Female CEOs surpass their male counterparts in their efforts to promote diversity, equity, and inclusion (DEI) as well as employee well-being. Nevertheless, most businesses do not officially acknowledge or acknowledge their contributions. Ultimately, women encounter greater challenges in advancing when they dedicate their time and effort to endeavors that are not valued or recognized.

Visibility is crucial for the professional advancement of women in leadership positions. Engage in a discussion with your employer about strategies to enhance your visibility within the company, rather than remaining inconspicuous. For example, seek out challenging tasks that allow you to expand your knowledge and network. Establishing connections and cultivating a network of advocates will enhance the prominence of your endeavor and achievements.

6.5.5. Wage Inequalities

According to a Pew Research Center estimate, women earned approximately 82% of the income earned by males in 2022. One possible reason for this is that, even though there has been a rise in the number of women in higher-ranking positions, they still tend to be overrepresented in lower-paid occupations relative to their overall representation in the labor force. The discrepancy in wages may also be ascribed to gender bias, despite the challenge of quantifying it.

Implementing pay transparency is an effective approach to mitigate the wage gap. According to the National Bureau of Economic Research, the introduction of pay transparency can potentially decrease the gender pay gap by up to 30%. Moreover, it is advisable for companies to conduct regular salary audits to determine if female executives are receiving fair and equal pay. Subsequently, companies can provide salary increases to employees who are earning higher wages in order to narrow the disparity (Kiamba, 2009).

6.5.6. Inadvertent Bias

Women in leadership positions are also impacted by unconscious bias. This situation may lead to insufficient decision-making and unintentional discrimination. Unconscious bias may occur when a hiring team chooses not to consider a woman for an executive position due to the belief that it would be too challenging for her after giving birth. Fortunately, there are methods to increase awareness of unconscious gender bias. Training your personnel is an effective approach to help them identify and address gender bias directly. Categorizing the various types of biases that can exist is another strategy. This strategy aims to increase awareness among individuals about the impact of prejudices on hiring and promotion decisions (Kiamba, 2009).

6.6. GENDER DISCRIMINATION IN CRIMINAL JUSTICE CAREERS

Women may exhibit hesitancy in engaging with law enforcement and reporting criminal activities as a result of their distinct encounters with the criminal justice system. This hesitancy could potentially result in significant consequences, such as the perpetuation of gender disparity and the undermining of core principles of fairness and equal treatment (Helfgott et al., 2018). Unreported crimes are concealed, hindering the administration of justice, and fostering a climate of impunity for perpetrators. Hence, the sensation of detachment and dissociation from the very establishments designed to safeguard and aid the general public has the capacity to reinforce patriarchal norms. These circumstances can also lead women to lose confidence in judicial and governmental systems.

Ultimately, this issue extends beyond the scope of women's avenues to seek legal redress, as it is inherently connected to the autonomy and empowerment of women. Asserting one's rights and seeking justice is a crucial aspect of empowerment, and the various forms of discrimination that women experience significantly impact their capacity to do so. Moreover, women's ability to move around freely may be limited when there are significant concerns about safety and security, and when seeking justice appears to be challenging. This can restrict their ability to engage in social, professional, and educational opportunities, as well as diminish their autonomy in various aspects of life (Helfgott et al., 2018).

Historically, the criminal justice field has been predominantly male, with men serving as experts and responding to male offenders. Consequently, the sector has been primarily controlled and operated by men, catering to the needs of men. The process of achieving gender parity in the criminal justice system is still far from complete, as women working in the police, legal and judicial professions, and corrections continue to encounter various challenges at both individual and institutional levels. The progress in reforming the criminal justice system has been facilitated by the greater diversity in the workforce and the implementation of inclusive practices. These changes were primarily prompted by the growing focus on female involvement in criminal activities (Helfgott et al., 2018).

These challenges have a significant impact on both work-life balance and overall well-being. They extend beyond problems related to entering a profession, staying in it, and the barriers that hinder career progression. Female professionals in the criminal justice field often face paternalistic attitudes, misogyny, and harassment. They also have to deal with gender pay gaps that openly discriminate against them. Moreover, they work in organizational cultures that are predominantly male-dominated and patriarchal in nature (Helfgott et al., 2018). This is because their participation in the traditionally male-dominated field of criminal justice challenges the dominant expectation of what it means to be an ideal woman. The repercussions go beyond the individual and affect the fair and impartial administration of justice, emphasizing the pressing requirement for a decentralized and feminine approach to justice administration.

6.7. THE INFLUENCE OF WOMEN IN LEADERSHIP POSITIONS ON POLICY AND IMPLEMENTATION

It is widely recognized that society as a whole benefit when there is greater gender diversity in leadership positions. Extensive research conducted over the years has consistently shown the significant benefits that women leaders bring to productivity, teamwork, organizational dedication, and justice (Lawson et al., 2022). It is worth noting that a mere 10% of Fortune 500 corporations are led by women, despite the potential advantages that may exist.

A comprehensive psychological study conducted over several decades has conclusively demonstrated that the inclusion of women in leadership positions has the potential to bring about a profound transformation for all individuals involved.

In a significant meta-analysis conducted in 1992, involving 61 research studies led by Eagly, it was discovered that female leaders tend to adopt more powerful transformative leadership approaches. According to a study conducted by Lawson et al., in 2022, it was found that females have a higher tendency to embody the organization's finest attributes and motivate others to rally behind its objectives.

Based on a comprehensive meta-analysis conducted by Eagly in 2020, it has been found that women are now perceived as being equally or even more capable than their male counterparts. The study incorporated data from 16 nationally representative public opinion surveys conducted between 1946 and 2018, with a sample size of over 30,000 American individuals. The researchers analyzed three different types of qualities: competence, agency, and communication. Competence includes intelligence and creativity, while agency encompasses ambition and aggression. Lastly, communication involves compassion and sensitivity. In order to assess the extent to which certain traits were more commonly associated with either men or women, the researchers requested participants to provide ratings.

The findings revealed a significant evolution in competency preconceptions over time. According to a survey conducted in 1946, it was found that only 35% of respondents believed that men and women possessed equal intelligence. Interestingly, among those who did believe in equality, a greater number still considered males to be the more capable gender (Lawson et al., 2022). Based on a survey conducted in 2018, it was found that the majority of respondents, 86%, believed that there was no difference in intellectual capabilities between men and women. A small percentage, 9%, believed that women were actually smarter than men, while an even smaller percentage, 5%, believed the opposite. In addition, over the course of history, societal beliefs regarding women's heightened sensitivity and empathy compared to men have become increasingly entrenched. Based on a study conducted in 2010, it was found that the presence of women in a group has a positive effect on team collaboration. This impact can be attributed to the benefits that women bring to group processes. In two comprehensive studies involving 699 participants, organizational psychologist Anita Williams Woolley, PhD, and her colleagues examined working groups consisting of two to five individuals. It has been found that there is a strong correlation between the presence of women in a group and the collective intelligence of the group. This collective intelligence refers to the group's ability to collaborate effectively and solve a wide range of problems (Lawson et al., 2022). Groups with a higher representation of women showed a greater sense of equality when it came to conversational turn-taking. This, in turn, fostered a more receptive environment where members could fully leverage the collective knowledge and abilities of the group.

According to a nationwide survey conducted by the Pew Research Center in 2008, women outperform or are equal to men in seven out of eight leadership-relevant attributes (Lawson et al., 2022). According to the survey results, there was a difference in opinions regarding the honesty of males and females. Specifically, 20% of the respondents believed that males were more honest, while 50% of the respondents expressed the view that women were more honest than men. According to a recent study conducted by Lawson et al. (2022), the findings regarding IQ are quite interesting. Out of the respondents surveyed, 38% believed that women possessed greater intelligence compared to men, whereas only 14% attributed wisdom to males. In addition, it was found that women received higher ratings in terms of their sociability, creativity, and empathy. Based on a study conducted in 2022 by social psychologist Mansi P. Joshi, PhD, it was found that the mere presence of a female CEO, as compared to a male leader, led people to expect fairer treatment within the company. Additionally, it also increased their expectations of higher wages and status. Research has shown that female leaders, regardless of the industry they are in, play a crucial role in building organizational trust. This is true whether women dominate the industry or not. Moreover, it has been found that female leaders who have held diverse positions within the organizational hierarchy are particularly effective in fostering trust within the organization (Lawson et al., 2022).

6.8. MENTORING AND SUPPORT FOR WOMEN IN THE CRIMINAL JUSTICE SYSTEM

Mentoring refers to the direct and personal interaction between a mentor and a mentee. Matching a mentor and mentee requires expertise. Each mentoring connection is distinct. The Women's Justice Network employs a client-centered approach, wherein the mentee is encouraged to articulate her objectives for engaging with a mentor. Although intentions can vary in their level of specificity, they generally revolve around offering social, emotional, and/or practical assistance (Brown & Ross, 2010). The relationship commences once a suitable mentor is selected following the Women's Justice Network's assessment of the Mentee's motivation and the specific type of support she will require.

This connection is a voluntary agreement between both the mentor and the mentee. Early openness and drive enhance the probability of establishing a mutually advantageous partnership that yields fruitful outcomes (Brown & Ross, 2010). The Mentor, in collaboration with the Women's Justice Network, assists the Mentee in acquiring the necessary knowledge, self-confidence, and guidance to navigate life's difficulties and avoid incarceration, particularly during the crucial adolescent period. A mentoring relationship can be described as a midpoint between a friendship and a professional relationship. Mentees often describe mentors as their primary source of guidance, support, and inspiration. Mentoring involves equipping a Mentee with the necessary resources to independently resolve issues and establish their own networks and social connections. Case management or counseling is not involved (Brown & Ross, 2010).

Mentoring programs offer women and girls the opportunity to acquire coping mechanisms, develop new skills, build confidence, and find direction, thereby enabling them to overcome various challenges and contribute meaningfully to the community without resorting to incarceration. This social support is flexible and specifically tailored to meet the needs of each woman and girl. The primary objective of the Mentoring Program is to enhance the autonomy and well-being of women and girls by enabling them to make informed life choices and adapt their lifestyles accordingly. Additionally, the program aims to facilitate their reintegration into society and promote personal growth through learning from past experiences. The Mentoring Program aims to provide women and girls who have been released from custody or are at risk of entering the criminal justice system with an opportunity to cultivate a sense of community (Brown & Ross, 2010).

This is achieved by facilitating the connection between women who have experience in the criminal justice system and female mentors who have received specialized training. Female mentors are being sought in order to provide women and girls with gender-specific social assistance. The Department of Corrective Services NSW states that the individuals with whom an ex-prisoner associates are the third most reliable indicator of their likelihood to commit another offense. According to Brown & Ross (2010), providing appropriate social assistance and enrolling women leaving prison in a mentorship program reduces the likelihood of their re-incarceration or detention. The mentors are an exceptional group of women, representing diverse age groups, professional and cultural backgrounds, possessing a wide array of interests and abilities, and demonstrating a profound sense of passion and commitment.

Below are several examples of mentoring programs designed specifically for female professionals in the criminal justice field:

1. **The Women in Criminal Justice Mentoring Program at the University of Wisconsin:** Aims to promote women's involvement in criminal justice careers, provide assistance in achieving their educational and professional objectives, and enhance diversity and equality within the criminal justice system. The program pairs students with mentors from local, state, and federal agencies. Professionals from the court, law enforcement, and other criminal justice fields are recognized as mentors.
2. **The Women in Criminal Justice Mentor Program at UW-Platteville:** This is a specialized mentorship program designed specifically for students majoring in criminal justice. It is offered by the University of Wisconsin-Platteville in collaboration with the Wisconsin Department of Justice and the UW-Madison Center for Law, Society, and Justice. The objective is to provide support and guidance to women who aspire to pursue careers in the specified industry (Brown & Ross, 2010).

These programs are essential for promoting the growth of women in the field of criminal justice by providing opportunities for professional development, networking, and empowerment.

6.9. ADVANCING GENDER EQUALITY IN LEADERSHIP

Having a robust change implementation plan and a clearly articulated vision are crucial elements of successful leadership (Dhatt et al., 2017). In relation to gender equality, it involves developing a gender mainstreaming strategy with clear objectives that acknowledge gender concerns as universally accepted and undeniable.

The integration of gender mainstreaming should be included in policies, programs, staff conduct, and training, among other aspects. Every strategy necessitates the allocation of financial and human resources, as well as the unwavering commitment and support of the leadership.

Here are five strategies leaders can employ to promote gender parity, equality, and gender sensitivity.

1. Advocate for gender equality and champion the cause of addressing gender-related issues. Engaging in and actively supporting gender initiatives is a fundamental aspect of being a gender champion. To gain further insight into this topic, it is recommended to read the recent study on gender-inclusive leadership conducted by Professor Elisabeth Kelan at the Cranfield School of Management. Another aspect of being a champion is dedicating time to enlighten others about the importance of these projects for the organization's future. To fulfill this task, it is essential to gather a dedicated team of individuals who actively support and promote gender equality, as well as seek guidance from experienced advisors. Furthermore, it is crucial for you to personally embody the qualities and principles of a gender champion. These roles play a particularly vital role in facilitating organizational change and facilitating the implementation of various plans and initiatives. Surrounding yourself with individuals who have the requisite knowledge and experience will greatly facilitate the promotion of the desired change (Dhatt et al., 2017).
2. Employ gender-inclusive language when engaging in communication. An effective leader sets the tone for the mission and activities of their team. As a leader, it is crucial to ensure that your communication remains consistent across different audiences and platforms, particularly when it pertains to the objectives your company has established for promoting gender equality. Additionally, it is imperative to employ inclusive language in both written and spoken communication. It is unequivocally unacceptable to utilize derogatory or discriminatory language. You demonstrate leadership through your actions.
3. Promote inclusivity and strive for equal representation of different genders and diverse backgrounds. Make continuous efforts to enhance the inclusivity and diversity of work teams, committees, and the entire company by ensuring equal representation of various groups and both genders. Leaders should strive to establish a platform where all perspectives can be expressed simultaneously. This involves placing more emphasis on gendered experiences, such as the dynamics of power and the privileging of certain voices over others. An effective leader is proactive in promoting women's involvement in various roles and ensuring their skills are acknowledged. The authors Dhatt et al. (2017) perceive women and men as equivalent participants in the organization and its activities.

4. Consider gender-specific initiatives. A successful leader acknowledges and addresses the unique needs and experiences of both men and women, taking proactive measures to prevent any negative impact on either group, with particular attention to the well-being of women. Ensuring gender equality in terms of career advancement and promotion is another facet of this issue (Dhatt et al., 2017). In specific cases, this may involve creating customized programs that are designed to address the unique needs and characteristics of women, enabling them to fully realize their capabilities. Some of the most efficient strategies for promoting gender equality in the workplace include mentoring, supporting other women in their career advancement, and enhancing the visibility of women.
5. Expose unjust conduct. This entails advocating for workplace policies and procedures to be more attuned to gender considerations. It is crucial for leaders to prioritize the eradication of discrimination based on gender, especially when it comes to family and caregiving responsibilities (Dhatt et al., 2017). It is crucial to simultaneously recognize and address any potential implicit or explicit gender stereotypes or biases that create hidden obstacles for women.

6.10. THE FUTURE OF WOMEN IN CRIMINAL JUSTICE LEADERSHIP

While both men and women are capable of performing job duties with similar effectiveness, there are unique challenges and support needs that women in the criminal justice field face. These challenges include harassment, discrimination, and disrespect as they work to gain acceptance in a traditionally male-dominated industry.

To address these issues, several professional membership groups have been founded to support and empower women in criminal justice leadership roles. One such organization is the International Association of Women Police (IAWP), which was established in 1915. The IAWP aims to strengthen, unite, and raise the capacity of women in policing internationally. They recognize the outstanding work of female officers, civilians, and male supporters through events, training conferences, and an annual awards program.

Another organization, the National Association of Women Law Enforcement Executives (NAWLEE), was established as the first organization to address the unique needs of women holding senior management positions in law enforcement. NAWLEE offers mentoring opportunities for women and training seminars for female law enforcement executives. Their goal is to encourage women to take on leadership roles and to educate men and women in senior management positions on how to better support and retain women in their organizations. Despite the progress that women have made in the American legal system over the past 150 years, they are still underrepresented in important areas. This is due to the patriarchal culture of the industry and the belief that women are less physically adept than men. However, studies have shown that women are just as effective as their male counterparts in the criminal justice field. In fact, there are clear advantages to hiring women, such as their ability to use linguistic de-escalation tactics and their contribution to minimizing sexual assaults on female inmates.

CHAPTER 7

WOMEN'S ENCOUNTERS WITH JUVENILE JUSTICE

Contents

Women's encounters with juvenile justice have undergone significant transformations over the years. Historically, girls have exhibited a diminished probability compared to boys of becoming entangled in the juvenile court system. There has been progress in addressing their specific needs, as more attention has been given to them. While there is still a lack of female representation, the current situation is an improvement compared to the past. Academics emphasize the importance of implementing strategies that are specifically tailored to address the distinct needs of girls within the system. This chapter will provide a thorough examination of the gender disparities in juvenile delinquency. The topics covered include the pathways that lead girls into the juvenile justice system, the effects of trauma on girls within the system, programs tailored to address the specific needs of female juveniles, the disproportionate criminalization of girls of color, the experiences of LGBTQ+ youth in the juvenile justice system, the influence of families on girls' involvement in crime, restorative justice approaches for female juveniles, advocacy and support for girls within the system, and strategies for preventing girls from entering the justice system.

7.1. GENDER DISPARITIES IN JUVENILE OFFENDING

Gender is a highly influential factor in determining criminal behavior, as men exhibit a higher propensity to engage in criminal activities with greater frequency (Goodkind, 2005). Gender disparities in criminal activity are evident in all major criminological data sources, including self-report, victimization, and official data. However, these distinctions vary significantly depending on the offense and are particularly evident for violent and serious offenses. It is imperative for criminological theory to acknowledge the gender gap in crime, particularly due to the substantial gender disparity in offending.

Goodkind (2005) states that the primary explanations for the gender disparity in criminal activity come from the prevailing theories in criminology regarding learning, control, and strain. Most accounts suggest that the average values of variables derived from these theories differ between males and females, although some argue that these factors have specific effects based on gender. According to learning theories, it is believed that men are more prone than women to come into contact with criminal role models, especially among their peers. These role models promote ideas that support criminal behavior and unjustly encourage engagement in criminal activities. Learning theories suggest that men generally experience reduced levels of direct and indirect supervision, particularly within the family context, which in turn diminishes their capacity for self-control in relation to criminal behavior (Goodkind, 2005). Furthermore, it is asserted that men exhibit lower propensity to vehemently condemn criminal behavior, display reduced commitment to their academic pursuits, and possess weaker emotional bonds with their parents. Strain theories suggest that the gender gap in crime can be explained by the fact that men are more inclined to engage in criminal behavior as a way to cope with stressors, such as being victimized or having negative experiences in school (Goodkind, 2005). Although not explicitly denying these assertions, the present study highlights a factor that mainstream theories have not adequately emphasized in elucidating gender discrepancies in criminal behavior. An overarching theme in the extensive literature on gender, particularly regarding gender socialization, roles, and identity, is that women are taught to prioritize nurturing and caring for others, showing empathy towards others, cultivating strong interpersonal relationships, and adopting a passive/submissive communication style more than men do.

Therefore, it can be inferred that women are less inclined than men to engage in crimes that harm others. This is because women tend to experience a stronger sense of guilt when contemplating the idea of committing a crime. Statistical data suggests that women exhibit a higher susceptibility to experiencing feelings of guilt compared to men, thereby providing some support for this assertion. Nevertheless, criminologists have paid scant attention to guilt as a factor in explaining the gender disparity in crime. This study contributes to the existing research on gender disparity in criminal activity by focusing on the extent to which accounting for anticipated guilt reduces the discrepancy in offending, beyond the factors considered in the most widely accepted hypotheses (Goodkind, 2005).

According to learning theories, interactions with individuals who engage in criminal behavior can lead to the adoption of positive stereotypes about crime and the encouragement of criminal activities, which are considered the primary factors contributing to crime. According to Goodkind (2005), this perspective argues that men have a higher likelihood of engaging in criminal behavior due to their increased exposure to criminals. According to a specific study, males have a higher susceptibility than females to associate with delinquent peers and to adopt beliefs that promote delinquency. Research has also shown that a significant portion of the difference in criminal behavior between genders can be attributed to differences in criminal beliefs and associations with peers. With the exception of a small number of uncommon instances, these studies have failed to sufficiently elucidate the disparity between male and female delinquency (Goodkind, 2005).

7.2. THE ROUTES BY WHICH GIRLS ENTER THE JUVENILE JUSTICE SYSTEM

Girls' pathways into the juvenile justice system are varied and influenced by multiple factors. Historically, females had a lower likelihood of participating in the system compared to males.

However, there has been progress due to increased attention to their specific needs. Girls often become entangled in the system due to trauma, familial discord, and precarious housing situations. In order to develop effective interventions and promote equality in the juvenile justice system, it is crucial to understand these pathways (PCARE, 2017).

1. **Female Apprehension Rates:** The following offenses exhibit the most elevated rates of apprehension:

- Misdemeanors, which refer to minor criminal offenses, while technical probation violations are breaches of the conditions set during probation.
- Survival crimes, which involve acts like stealing clothing or food, breaking into buildings to seek shelter, and providing false information to law enforcement.
- Substance misuse and addiction.
- Girls are detained more frequently than boys for status offenses, such as truancy and running away.
- There has been a rise in arrests for cybercrimes.

2. **Girls of Color:** Girls belonging to ethnic minority groups face a higher likelihood of being arrested, suspended, and incarcerated compared to their counterparts. Girls of color constitute 66% of incarcerated girls, despite comprising only 22% of the total population of young individuals.

   Within the group of students who are currently enrolled, black girls constitute 16% and 37% of the individuals who have been arrested at school, respectively. According to PCARE (2017), black girls constitute 52% of the enrolled students who have been suspended multiple times.

3. **Post-Traumatic Experiences and Instances of Mistreatment:** The occurrence of multiple incidents leading to school suspensions and arrests among girls serves as evidence of the trauma and abuse they have endured. Prior to reaching the age of 18, 25% of females will experience sexual assault, encompassing acts such as rape, relationship violence, and sex trafficking (PCARE, 2017).

According to PCARE (2017), approximately 75% of girls in the juvenile justice system endure physical or sexual abuse, typically perpetrated by their own family members.

Disputes leading to girls' encounters with law enforcement encompass:

- Caregivers such as paternal figures, stepfathers, romantic partners of mothers, and other male family members.
- Peer pressure from other girls can lead to engagement in delinquent behavior. Additionally, experiencing challenges in forming friendships can result in aggressive behavior, conflicts with peers, or social exclusion.
- Interpersonal conflicts that escalate into physical aggression involving both male and female individuals.

There are several concerns regarding the organizational framework of the juvenile justice system as discussed below:

- Not appropriately responding to girls in a manner that aligns with their gender.
- Lack of gender-specific screenings for mental and physical health.
- The lack of resources and counseling for sexual health, treatment for sexually transmitted diseases (STDs), and care for expectant mothers is a significant issue.
- Additionally, there is a lack of gender-responsive training for staff.
- The lack of adequate mental and physical health care provision indicates a deficiency in the system. According to PCARE (2017), there is a lack of adequate resources for mental health, which leads to an inability to identify and address trauma. This can result in traumatization and subsequent episodes of abuse. Additionally, there is a shortage of rehabilitation programs.

These adverse experiences can lead to a range of negative outcomes for female adolescents, including running away from home. Some of the specific causes for female adolescents fleeing their residences include:

1. **Parental Substance Misuse:** When parents or other family members struggle with substance abuse, it can create an unstable and unsafe environment for children. This can lead to feelings of fear, neglect, and a desire to escape from the situation.
2. **Witnessing Violence or Abuse:** Growing up in a household where violence or abuse occurs can have a profound impact on children. Witnessing such behaviors can lead to feelings of fear, trauma, and a desire to escape from the situation.

3. **Neglect:** It refers to the failure of parents or caregivers to provide for a child's basic needs, such as food, shelter, and supervision. When children experience neglect, they may feel unsupported and may seek to find a more stable and caring environment elsewhere.
4. **Family Dysfunction:** This can encompass a range of issues, including poor communication, unresolved conflicts, and inconsistent parenting. When a family is dysfunctional, it can create a chaotic and unpredictable environment for children.

7.3. THE IMPACT OF TRAUMA ON GIRLS IN THE JUVENILE JUSTICE SYSTEM

The number of girls involved in the juvenile justice system has been increasing over the past two decades, surpassing the number of boys. In 2019, girls accounted for more than 30% of juvenile arrests, compared to 18% in 1990. Furthermore, there are over 7,800 girls housed in detention or juvenile penal facilities on any given day. This increase in female arrest rates is particularly notable for violent offenses, with arrest rates for severe crimes such as homicide, sexual assault, and physical assault rising for girls but decreasing for boys (Kerig, 2018) (Figure 7.1).

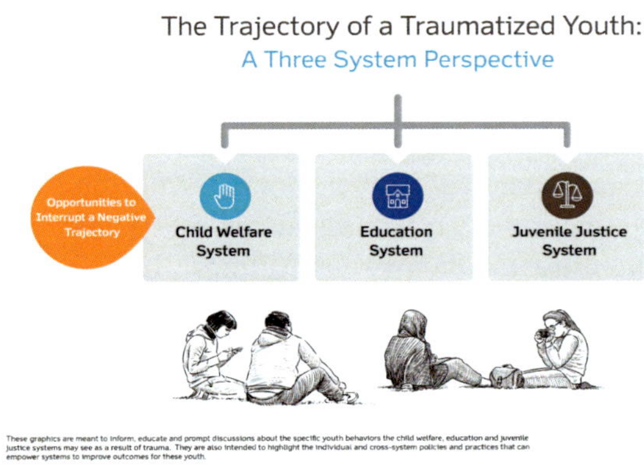

Figure 7.1. *Traumatized youth analyzed through three system perspective.*

Source: Children's Action Corps (2014).

Research has shown that girls involved in the juvenile justice system experience higher levels of psychological trauma, victimization, and mental health issues compared to their male peers (Modrowski et al., 2021). These issues include post-traumatic stress disorder (PTSD), substance abuse, dissociation, depression, and suicidality. The negative effects of traumatic stress and associated mental health issues on girls' development, safety, and well-being throughout adolescence present unique challenges for juvenile justice prevention and intervention programs. Girls in the juvenile justice system have also experienced higher rates of traumatic experiences compared to youth in the community. Rates of psychological trauma exposure among youth in the justice system range from 70% to 96% (Malvaso et al., 2022). Moreover, girls involved in the legal system have been victims at even higher rates than their male counterparts, particularly in cases of sexual assault and domestic violence. For example, data from the NCTSN Core Data Set shows that girls in the juvenile justice system are four times more likely than boys to have experienced sexual assault and twice as likely to report sexual abuse. Another study found that 76% of girls placed in foster homes reported being sexually abused, and 93% had records of physical or sexual abuse (Malvaso et al., 2022). While boys are more likely to have witnessed violence in the community, girls are significantly more likely to report experiencing sexual abuse and family violence. Girls involved in the justice system are also more likely to have been sexually abused and severely neglected in the past compared to boys. In one study comparing detained and community youth, girls in the justice system were nearly 10 times more likely than boys to report having been raped or sexually abused.

There is also a subset of young people known as polyvictims who have experienced multiple forms of victimization. In samples involving the court system, polyvictimization rates are high and are associated with the most serious emotional and behavioral health issues. Gender differences exist in the pathways to polyvictimization, with exposure to community violence being more common for boys and girls who experience polyvictimization being more likely to reside in homes with high levels of conflict, violence, and parental mental health issues (Malvaso et al., 2022). Living in families where traumatic adversity persists, often due to external structural factors like socioeconomic and racial/ethnic disparities, as well as intergenerational victimization patterns, can put girls at a higher risk of experiencing pervasive traumatic victimization and becoming involved in the juvenile justice system (Malvaso et al., 2022).

7.4. GENDER-RESPONSIVE PROGRAMMING FOR FEMALE JUVENILES

Gender-responsive programming for female juveniles is crucial in addressing the unique needs and experiences of girls involved in the juvenile justice system. Many girls who enter the system have experienced trauma, such as abuse, neglect, or assault, which often leads to their involvement in the system (Watson & Edelman, 2012). However, there is a lack of resources and successful therapies available to help girls identify and address their needs (Watson & Edelman, 2012).

Girls make up the largest and fastest-growing demographic within the juvenile justice system, yet there is a dearth of programming that takes their gender into account. Additionally, there is a lack of data collection efforts aimed at understanding how girls and LGBTQ/GNC youth, who are overrepresented in the system, are affected by the problems these reforms seek to address. As a result, few juvenile justice reforms are tailored to meet the specific needs and pathways of girls and LGBTQ/GNC youth, limiting their potential to benefit from these reforms (Watson & Edelman, 2012).

To develop effective gender-responsive programming for female juveniles, several essential components should be considered.

These components include:

1. **Relational:** Adolescence is a period of significant change and development, and it is crucial to foster healthy relationships and social environments for girls. This includes promoting both romantic and non-romantic connections and facilitating ongoing interactions with friends, family, and older women.
2. **Restorative:** Programs should assist girls in navigating the legal system while considering their histories of trauma and victimization. This approach acknowledges the impact of trauma on girls' lives and aims to support their healing and recovery.
3. **Intersectional and Sociocultural Relevant:** Gender-responsive programming should address the various marginalities that girls face due to their gender, sexual orientation, age, race, immigration status, and socioeconomic background. By recognizing and addressing these intersecting identities, programs can better meet the needs of diverse groups of young women.
4. **Tailored:** Programs should be specifically designed to address the unique requirements of a diverse cohort of young ladies. This includes considering their individual strengths, challenges, and developmental needs.
5. **Multi-Level:** Gender-responsive programming should address girls' involvement in multiple systems, such as child welfare, school, and juvenile justice. It should also consider their involvement on an individual, peer, family, and community level. This holistic approach recognizes the interconnectedness of various systems and the importance of addressing girls' needs at multiple levels.
6. **Community-based:** Programs should offer adaptable services to young people in their local communities, addressing their specific needs and circumstances.

7.5. THE CRIMINALIZATION OF GIRLS OF COLOR

According to Heipt (2015), girls and young women make up over 30% of all juveniles detained, and this percentage has been steadily rising over the past 20 years. Girls involved in the juvenile justice system often face numerous obstacles, including destitution, racism, misogyny, and past experiences with sexual assault, domestic abuse, and exploitation.

Black females, in particular, are the group in the juvenile justice system that is expanding the fastest and are disproportionately represented in various stages of the juvenile justice process, such as referral and imprisonment.

It is important to note that 40% of females involved in the juvenile justice system self-identify as transgender, gender nonconforming, lesbian, or bisexual. These statistics and inequalities persist even though girls in the court system often pose little to no threat to society. The criminalization of girls of color, especially Black girls, is a significant issue that needs to be addressed.

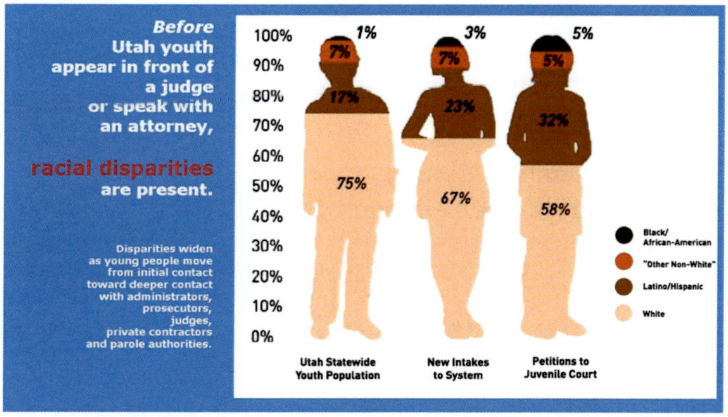

Figure 7.2. *Racial disparities in Utah's juvenile justice system.*

Source: Gunderson (2020).

Black girls may feel endangered and unsafe, leading them to resist or take actions they believe will help them defend themselves when they are hurt or subjected to emotionally abusive messaging. The human brain is wired to protect the body from perceived or actual threats (Sherman & Balck, 2015). This can manifest as low-level crimes like stealing to pay for necessities or status violations like fleeing from home to avoid abuse. It may also appear as arguments with family members or friends, as an attempt to regain control over their lives.

However, these actions are often labeled as "aggressive" by individuals who are meant to support Black girls. Claims of abuse by Black females are frequently not taken seriously, and they are often blamed for their own misbehavior instead of being asked about the underlying factors that influenced their actions (Figure 7.2).

To address the criminalization of girls of color, Sherman & Balck (2015) suggest several approaches for working with justice-involved Black girls who are suffering from persistent trauma:

- Apply trauma-informed techniques. Use trauma screening tools and recognize that "problem behaviors" are often trauma reactions that require support rather than punishment.
- Recognize the role of racism, sexism, ableism, heterocentrism, and poverty in girls' lived experiences.
- Meet girls where they are. Seek safety, wellbeing, and healing as defined by the girls themselves.
- Capitalize on girls' resiliency. Remind them of their strengths and empower them to overcome challenges.
- Utilize culturally diverse activities and curriculums that are relevant and relatable to the girls' experiences.
- Hire personnel who relate to the girls, such as members of the same communities, formerly incarcerated girls, or survivor leaders. Provide each girl with a supporting adult to help navigate the reentry process.
- Establish customized plans that take into account each girl's strengths, risks, and needs, including educational, mental health, employment, housing, and childcare support.
- Invest in girls' education and consider initiatives like the EMERGE program of the National Black Women's Justice Institute, which aims to help young girls who have previously dealt with the criminal or juvenile justice systems find a "confinement to college and career" track.
- Incorporate activities that promote social and emotional learning, such as art therapy, journaling, storytelling, and drama.

7.6. LGBTQ+ YOUTH IN THE JUVENILE JUSTICE SYSTEM

In the juvenile justice system, there are significant shortcomings that need to be addressed, particularly in relation to LGBTQ+ youth (Buist, 2019). These adolescents are disproportionately overrepresented in both the juvenile and adult justice systems, with queer women and trans, non-binary, and gender non-conforming individuals being the most affected. This overrepresentation highlights a systemic problem that needs to be addressed. In order to improve the situation, changes need to be made in various institutions such as the judicial branch, police departments, schools, and prisons (Figure 7.3).

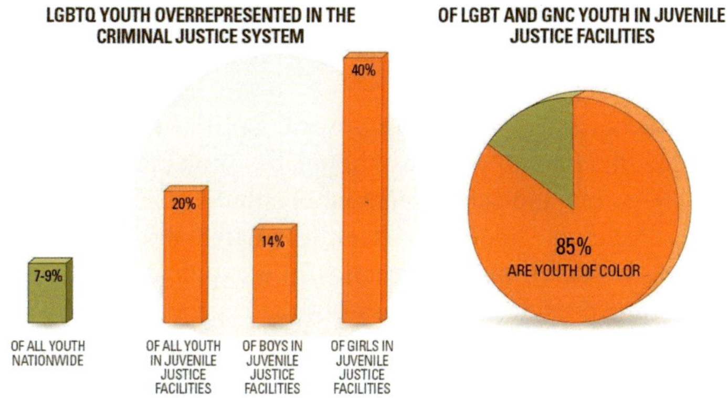

Figure 7.3. *LGBTQ+ youth overrepresented in juvenile justice system.*

Source: Shelton (2023).

The history of the Western notion of aberrant sexual activities can be traced back to the confusion felt by colonists upon discovering gender and sexual manifestations in North America. Even in the present day, LGBTQ+ individuals still have to overcome the belief that their sexual orientation and gender identity are inherently evil or incorrect. Early prison planners observed a high prevalence of homosexual behavior within correctional facilities and concluded that spending time in these facilities "encouraged" such behavior (Buist, 2019).

Research indicates that LGBTQ+ youth have different experiences with the police compared to their cisgender/heterosexual peers. For example, they may be stopped by the police for displaying emotive behavior in public. Many LGBTQ+ individuals also recall police officers calling them derogatory names. Furthermore, the legal system often fails to provide competent legal representation or advocacy for LGBTQ+ adolescents. In jail facilities, LGBTQ+ individuals are frequently segregated for safety reasons, but this practice reinforces gender norms and discrimination against the LGBTQ+ community (Buist, 2019). LGBTQ+ homeless youth are more likely to be involved in the juvenile justice system compared to their non-LGBTQ+ peers. These youth may be forced to commit "survival crimes," such as sex work, in order to pay for housing, food, and other essentials. Homelessness often leads to incarceration, and being released from a correctional facility can result in homelessness once again, creating a vicious cycle.

In schools, LGBTQ+ youth are three times more likely to be hurt or threatened with a weapon compared to their non-LGBTQ+ peers. Students who experience bullying due to their sexual orientation are also more likely to carry guns to school for self-defense, which often leads to encounters with the authorities. When a young person is suspended from school, the likelihood of further suspensions and greater involvement in the justice system increases. Arrest rates are higher for suspended students compared to non-suspended students (Buist, 2019).

To address these issues, there are several policy implications that need to be considered. In schools, policies should be implemented to support and protect LGBTQ+ youth, and school personnel should receive more training on LGBTQ+ issues. Schools should also seek less harsh and disruptive solutions instead of relying on discriminatory tactics like expulsions, suspensions, and "self-reflection" time outside of the classroom.

7.7. THE ROLE OF FAMILIES IN GIRLS' INVOLVEMENT IN CRIME

The role of families in girls' involvement in crime is significant and cannot be ignored. Families play a crucial role in the socialization of children, shaping their behavior, values, and beliefs. However, certain factors within the family environment can contribute to women's criminality.

One important factor is the type of family and the environment in which a child grows up. Research has shown that there is a strong association between women's crime and the type of home they come from. For example, studies have found that a significant number of female offenders come from broken homes or single-parent households (Nilsson, 2017). These families often struggle to meet the child's needs and may not be able to provide proper supervision, making the girls more vulnerable to being influenced by others into engaging in criminal activities.

Parental abuse, particularly physical violence, is another factor that contributes to women's criminality. Girls who experience physical abuse from their parents may become emotionally dependent on others outside of their household, making them more susceptible to engaging in antisocial behavior (Nilsson, 2017). Studies have also shown that women who have experienced parental abuse or witnessed their parents engaging in criminal behavior are more likely to exhibit behavioral problems from an early age.

Family history of criminality is another important factor to consider. Research has found that women who commit crimes often come from families where their husbands or in-laws have engaged in antisocial behavior and have been incarcerated for felonies (Nilsson, 2017). In Indian society, where women are often financially dependent on their husbands, they may be compelled to support their husbands in their illegal activities, further perpetuating the cycle of criminal behavior within the family.

The role of in-laws is also significant. Studies have shown that many women who are charged with property crimes are actually victims of their husbands' or in-laws' wrongdoings. In some cases, women may be unfairly implicated in crimes as a form of retaliation from their in-laws or husbands. For example, if a husband is detained for illegal activities, the wife may also be detained for supporting him, even if she was acting out of financial dependence rather than personal desire (Nilsson, 2017).

Overall, families have a significant influence on girls' involvement in crime. Factors such as family type, parental abuse, family history of criminality, and the role of in-laws all contribute to the likelihood of women engaging in criminal activities. Understanding these factors is crucial for developing effective strategies to prevent and address women's criminality.

7.8. RESTORATIVE JUSTICE APPROACHES FOR FEMALE JUVENILES

Restorative justice approaches for female juveniles are a flexible and interactive way to address criminal behavior and provide an alternative to the traditional legal system. These approaches aim to enhance access to justice, particularly for disadvantaged and marginalized groups, as well as crime victims, aligning with the goal of creating inclusive and effective institutions (Hodgson, 2022).

Restorative justice programs are based on the principle that those who have been harmed by crime should actively participate in the process of making amends, alleviating their suffering, and preventing further harm. This approach also promotes inclusivity, tolerance, truth-seeking, peaceful dispute resolution, diversity appreciation, and civic responsibility (Hodgson, 2022). While restorative justice is not a new concept, it has historical roots in traditional methods of resolving disputes and administering justice in many societies. The procedures can be adapted to meet the specific needs and cultural contexts of different communities.

Both new and established restorative justice models offer communities effective ways to address conflicts and mitigate the harm caused by criminal behavior. These models involve the participation of individuals directly involved in or impacted by the crime, including community members. The success of restorative justice processes relies on the willingness of all parties to participate and engage in a secure dialogue facilitated by a neutral third party to reach a consensus. Restorative justice provides an alternative path to justice for offenders, victims, and the community. It encourages victims to safely participate in the resolution process and gives offenders an opportunity to take responsibility for the harm they have caused (Hodgson, 2022). This approach recognizes that criminal behavior not only violates the law but also harms victims and the community.

Practitioners of restorative justice agree that what distinguishes a response to crime as "restorative" is not just the specific practices or procedures used but rather the adherence to a set of values that guide the involvement of all parties in responding to a criminal incident and its aftermath. These values include truth, justice, physical and mental safety of participants, inclusion, empowerment, protection of the rights of victims and offenders, reparations, solidarity, respect, dignity, voluntariness, and transparency in the process and outcomes (Hodgson, 2022).

Over the past two decades, there has been a growing recognition of the need for criminal justice systems to prioritize the needs and interests of victims. The Declaration of Basic Principles on Justice for Victims of Crime and Abuse of Power emphasizes the importance of utilizing informal mechanisms, such as mediation, arbitration, and customary justice, to facilitate conciliation and redress for victims. Restorative justice approaches can uniquely address many of the pressing demands of victims, including the need for information, empowerment through involvement, expression, empathy, reparation, and the restoration of control and security (Hodgson, 2022).

7.9. ADVOCACY AND SUPPORT FOR GIRLS IN THE JUVENILE JUSTICE SYSTEM

Advocacy and support for girls in the juvenile justice system is crucial, as girls and young women make up a significant portion of juvenile offenders. Over the past two decades, there has been a consistent rise in court proceedings, arrests, and detentions involving girls. Unfortunately, girls of color and those from impoverished backgrounds are disproportionately affected. These girls often experience violence, including sexual and physical assault, and are generally non-violent and pose little risk to public safety (Parrish, 2020).

However, the involvement of girls in the juvenile justice system often does more harm than good. They receive less support and access to resources compared to boys, particularly in terms of education and therapy. This disparity becomes even more pronounced when girls' numbers in the juvenile justice system increase, especially for violent crimes, status offenses, and technical probation violations (Parrish, 2020).

Black girls, in particular, may enter the juvenile justice system due to experiences of abuse, trauma, poverty, and discrimination based on their race, ethnicity, and gender. It is important to recognize the various pathways through which young women enter and exit the system in order to ensure that only those who pose a genuine threat to public safety are involved. This requires reducing reliance on secure placements and implementing gender- and culturally-responsive, trauma-informed, and developmentally appropriate approaches for the few girls and young women who do require intervention (Parrish, 2020).

Creating healthy social contexts for girls and young women involves a national commitment from various stakeholders, including families, friends, communities, social institutions, and society as a whole.

Practical gender-responsiveness is essential in addressing the unique needs of girls in the juvenile justice system. Despite historically fewer girls being involved in the system, recent trends show that more girls are being arrested and incarcerated compared to boys. Status offenses are often the reason for girls' involvement in the system. Therefore, practices, policies, and interventions need to be adapted to meet the specific needs of girls, as the services and supports that are most effective for them are often different (Parrish, 2020).

While research on effective programming for boys has been more extensive, gender-responsive programming for girls requires a theoretical framework that establishes research-based guidelines for successful interventions. Many of the benefits of this approach can also be applied to boys, including being relational, culturally sensitive, strength-based, developmentally appropriate, trauma-informed, and strength-informed. It is important to provide physical, psychological, and emotional safety to clients.

7.10. PREVENTING GIRLS' ENTRY INTO THE JUSTICE SYSTEM

To prevent girls from entering the justice system, it is important to recognize the specific risks and requirements that apply to them. Girls who are considered at-risk often face trauma, mental health issues, substance misuse, and unstable families. To break this cycle and establish a fairer system for girls, gender-informed approaches, early intervention, and cooperation between community and correctional providers are necessary. One crucial method is gender-responsive programming, which involves creating treatments that consider the particular needs, experiences, and risk factors that apply to girls. This can include gender-specific counseling, mental health assistance, and trauma-informed care. By tailoring interventions to address these specific needs, positive outcomes can be promoted and the involvement of girls in the juvenile justice system can be reduced. Early intervention and diversion are also important strategies to prevent girls from entering the formal legal system. By identifying at-risk females early on and providing them with alternative interventions, deeper engagement with the justice system can be avoided. School-based treatments, restorative justice, and community-based programs can all play a role in diverting girls away from the justice system.

Education and skill development are essential in equipping girls with the tools they need to succeed. By providing life skills development, career training, and education, girls can enhance their decision-making abilities, self-worth, and resilience. These skills can help prevent their involvement in the justice system and contribute to their overall well-being.

Community and family support are crucial in preventing girls from entering the justice system. Encouraging good parenting and reinforcing family ties can provide a supportive environment for girls. Involving mentors, positive role models, and community organizations can also have a positive impact on girls' lives and help steer them away from the justice system.

Addressing victimization and trauma is another important aspect of preventing girls' entry into the justice system. Many girls in the system have been victims of abuse or trauma, and it is essential to provide them with safe environments, psychotherapy, and trauma-focused therapy.

CHAPTER 8

WOMEN AND CRIMINALIZED HEALTH BEHAVIORS

Contents

There is a need for research on the intricate and significant correlation between women, the criminal justice system, and their health behaviors (Sered & Norton-Hawk, 2013). Women within the criminal justice system often encounter specific health concerns, including trauma, substance abuse, and mental health issues. Understanding the factors that lead women to engage in criminalized health-related offenses, such as drug addiction, prostitution, and property offenses, is essential for developing effective strategies and promoting overall well-being among this vulnerable group.

This chapter will provide a comprehensive examination of Substance Abuse and Women's Criminal Behavior, Mental Health Issues and the Criminalization of Women, Reproductive Health and the Legal System, HIV/AIDS and Women in the Criminal Justice System, and Homelessness and Criminal Justice Involvement. The effects of poverty on women's health and legal status, the availability of healthcare for incarcerated women, approaches that consider gender when addressing health needs, perspectives that consider the intersection of gender and health in relation to crime, and the role of public health in preventing health behaviors that lead to criminalization.

8.1. SUBSTANCE ABUSE AND WOMEN'S CRIMINAL BEHAVIOR

Drug use is a contributing factor to women's involvement in the criminal court system. The prevalence of drug use is high among female offenders, and research has shown a strong correlation between drug use and repeated engagement with the criminal justice system (Tuchman, 2014). Based on national statistics, 43% of women held in federal correctional facilities and 60% of women held in state prisons met the criteria for drug addiction or dependency. Research on drug misuse and criminal activity indicates that female prisoners exhibited a higher frequency of drug experimentation compared to male prisoners before becoming involved in the criminal justice system (Figure 8.1).

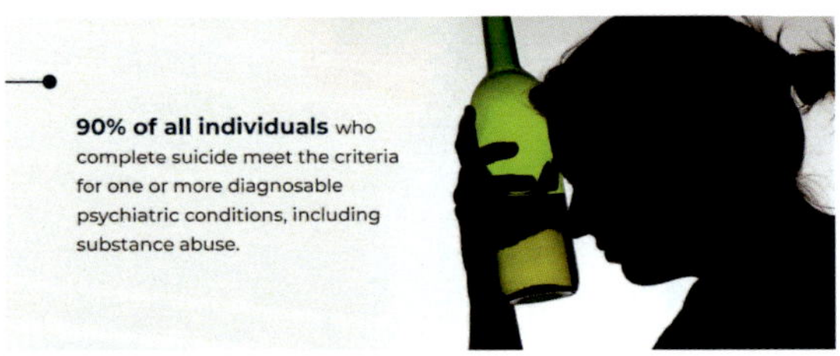

Figure 8.1. *Substance abuse and violence against oneself.*

Source: Gateway Foundation (2023).

According to Tuchman (2014), violent crimes are the primary and most direct pathway for males to become involved in the criminal justice system. However, drug-related offenses and drug use also play a significant role in men's interaction with the legal system. Tuchman (2014) proposes a hypothesis suggesting a potential direct correlation between women's drug usage and their experience of interpersonal violence. It is argued that while men may express their anger outwardly in response to a negative event, women are more likely to turn to drug use as a way to cope with internalized feelings of shame, which may be a result of past abuse.

Previous research has established that men are the main instigators of drug use in women. Female offenders attribute drug misuse to a previous incident of physical abuse, commonly referred to as a "battering incident," where drugs were utilized as a method of reestablishing a connection with men. Imprisoned women have also emphasized how their romantic partners manipulated the criminal justice system and how they became involved in drug trafficking. Studies on female drug dealers and traffickers contradict this claim, demonstrating that men do not always play a central role in women's involvement in drug use and the drug market economy. Women participating in the drug market have demonstrated a degree of independence and decision-making power in selecting their own involvement and have actively resisted the negative perception of being helpless victims.

Drug use is often not isolated, but instead serves as a mediator for criminal behavior that arises from interconnected issues in women's lives, such as victimization. Extensive evidence suggests that both males and females are more likely to engage in drug use and criminal behavior if they have been victimized beforehand. According to Tuchman (2014), the prevailing belief in the literature on child victimization is that individuals who have been subjected to maltreatment during their childhood are more prone to engaging in criminal behavior during their adolescence and adulthood. Research on the "cycle of violence" indicates that children who have experienced abuse and neglect are more prone to being arrested at a young age for delinquent behavior, engaging in criminal activities as adults, and participating in violent crimes.

Gender-specific analyses indicated that girls who experienced abuse and neglect during their early childhood were more prone to developing depression and potentially being hospitalized, while boys were more inclined to exhibit outward and violent behavior as a reaction. However, it is widely believed that child abuse or neglect does not directly cause criminality or delinquency. Instead, women's transgressions were associated with victimization, regardless of the type (e.g., physical, sexual, or neglect), due to their misuse of substances, feelings of sadness, and anxiety.

8.2. THE RELATIONSHIP BETWEEN MENTAL HEALTH ISSUES AND THE CRIMINALIZATION OF WOMEN

Given the recent increase in mass shootings, there has been extensive deliberation and analysis regarding the correlation between mental illness and criminal behavior. The association between mental illness and criminal behavior is often misunderstood, despite the positive impact of increased media coverage and renewed emphasis on the importance of mental health in the aftermath of such disasters (Bloom & Covington, 2008) (Figure 8.2).

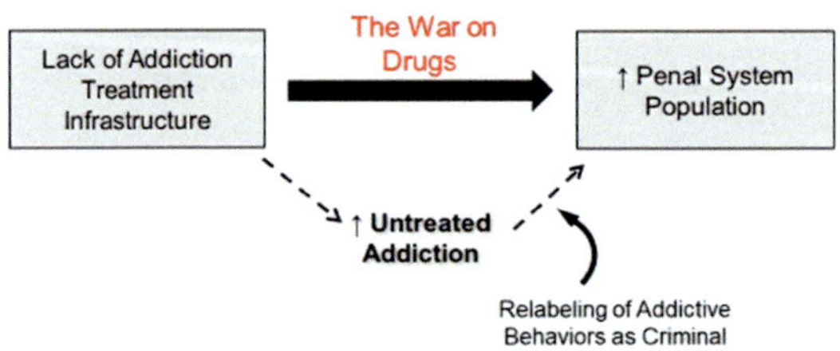

Figure 8.2. *Dotted arrows show how the lack of mental health resources leads to more mentally ill people in prisons.*

Source: Grecco & Chambers (2019).

There is a widespread misunderstanding that individuals with mental illness are more prone to displaying aggressive and violent behavior. The media's inclination to portray criminals as "mentally unstable" individuals significantly influences the public's perception of psychiatric patients as individuals who pose a threat. Multiple data points suggest otherwise. According to Bloom & Covington (2008), individuals who have mental illnesses are more prone to being victims of violent crimes compared to those who commit the crimes. Even the criminal justice system exhibits this bias, treating individuals with mental illnesses as if they were criminals, subjecting them to prosecution, arrest, and longer periods of incarceration compared to the general population.

The act of categorizing all criminals as having mental illnesses is a vital factor that leads to the misleading association between psychiatric disorders and criminal behavior. The misconception held by the general public that criminality and mental illness are interchangeable stems from society's perception that behavioral and conduct problems indicate a psychological disorder. The misclassification of criminals as having psychiatric illnesses is the main factor contributing to the elevated prevalence of mental illness observed in jail and prison populations. According to Bloom & Covington (2008), these numbers frequently result from social factors rather than a thorough medical and mental assessment and diagnosis.

Antisocial personality disorder (ASPD) is a diagnosis that is often given to individuals in the prison population without much thought or reason. As a result, there is a lack of consensus regarding the legitimacy of ASPD as a genuine mental health disorder or merely a social stigma. The term is increasingly employed to depict criminals as individuals with mental health conditions. To prevent criminals from using mental diagnoses as a means to evade punishment, it is imperative for psychiatrists to ensure that diagnoses are only assigned when specific criteria are met.

While it may require a significant upfront investment, implementing a comprehensive and sustained national mental health policy that enhances the accessibility and availability of treatment options could ultimately be a wise and cost-effective decision. Based on certain calculations, an individual suffering from mental illness has the potential to evade a decade-long imprisonment by undergoing a 90-day therapy program at a mental hospital. Enhanced availability of mental health services would result in significant cost savings for both society and individuals affected by crime. Moreover, it would significantly improve the quality of life for individuals afflicted with mental illness and facilitate their integration as productive members of society.

The complex correlation between mental health disorders and criminal behavior has substantial implications for society). There is a pressing need for thorough research and innovative strategies to enhance the availability and accessibility of mental health treatment. Currently, there is insufficient data to substantiate the autonomous forecasting of criminal conduct based on mental illness. On the other hand, extensive research shows that individuals with mental illness are much more prone to being victims rather than perpetrators of violent crimes (Bloom & Covington, 2008).

A multidisciplinary team consisting of psychiatrists, social workers, and patient advocates must identify, mitigate, or eliminate risk factors that contribute to individuals with mental illness engaging in criminal behavior, with the goal of breaking the association between mental illness and criminality. The team approach includes a multi-tiered system that aims to identify mentally ill patients who are at risk at an early stage and provide assistance to address issues such as medical non-compliance and food and housing insecurity. This approach aims to prevent mentally ill individuals from coming into contact with the criminal justice system. Individuals already engaged in the criminal justice system necessitate a targeted approach that encompasses empowerment, education, and rehabilitation. Finally, to eliminate misunderstandings and prevent the incorrect categorization of criminals as individuals with mental illness and vice versa, a focused endeavor is required to educate the general public and professionals in the criminal justice system (Bloom & Covington, 2008).

8.3. REPRODUCTIVE HEALTH AND THE LEGAL SYSTEM

The field of reproductive health intersects with the legal system in various ways, and understanding the laws and regulations surrounding reproductive health is crucial for ensuring access to essential services and protecting individuals' rights and well-being. This article explores the legal frameworks, challenges, and complexities related to reproductive health, including abortion rights, access to contraception, racial disparities in maternal health, teens' rights, assisted reproductive technologies, and global perspectives on reproductive health.

One of the key aspects of reproductive health and the legal system is the guarantee of legal safeguards that enable individuals to access crucial reproductive health services, such as safe abortion, prenatal care, and contraception. The Affordable Care Act (ACA) in the United States, for example, requires cost-sharing-free coverage of family planning and other preventive care, ensuring that individuals have access to these services without financial barriers (Glasier et al., 2006).

Abortion rights continue to be a divisive topic, with state laws in the United States varying significantly despite the constitutional right to abortion established by the landmark Roe v. Wade case. Targeted Regulation of Abortion Providers (TRAP) laws impose unnecessary regulations on clinics, making it more difficult for individuals to access abortion services (Glasier et al., 2006).

Access to contraception is essential for reproductive autonomy, but the issue becomes complicated when medical professionals are granted the right to refuse patients based on their moral or religious beliefs. Conscience clauses allow healthcare providers to decline providing contraception or other reproductive health services, raising questions about striking a balance between patient needs and individual rights.

Racial disparities in maternal health outcomes are still prevalent, with higher maternal mortality rates among Black women and inadequate prenatal care. Legal action aims to improve access to maternal health care and address systemic racism in order to reduce these disparities.

The reproductive rights of minors also present a nuanced legal issue. Some states allow minors to access abortion and contraceptive services without parental permission, recognizing the importance of minor autonomy. However, finding a balance between parental involvement and minor autonomy remains a legal challenge.

Assisted Reproductive Technologies (ART), such as surrogacy and in vitro fertilization (IVF), raise legal issues related to parentage, custody, and contractual rights. As these technologies continue to advance, laws must adapt to reflect the changing dynamics of modern families.

Reproductive health is a global concern, and international human rights frameworks recognize the fundamental right to reproductive autonomy. Advocacy efforts aim to eliminate gender-based violence, promote sexual education, and ensure universal access to reproductive health care. Legal safeguards, lobbying, and informed policies play a critical role in navigating this complex terrain and protecting reproductive health rights (Glasier et al., 2006).

8.4. HIV/AIDS AND WOMEN IN THE CRIMINAL JUSTICE SYSTEM

HIV/AIDS is a significant issue for women in the criminal justice system, as they face unique challenges and vulnerabilities that increase their risk of infection. According to Meyer et al. (2011), women in prison are more likely to use drugs and have HIV compared to men. They are also more likely to engage in dangerous behaviors such as injecting drug usage, unsafe tattooing, and self-harm. Additionally, women in prison are more vulnerable to gender-based sexual abuse.

One of the reasons why women are at risk of HIV in prisons is due to vulnerability, stigma, and prejudice. Socially marginalized women, who make up the majority of incarcerated women, are more likely to have used drugs or engaged in sex work. Many of them have also experienced high-risk sexual behavior or have been victims of gender-based violence. These factors make women more susceptible to HIV infection (Meyer et al., 2011).

Furthermore, women in prison have limited access to facilities and services, as prisons are often overcrowded and understaffed. The current programs and services designed for women in prison are often ineffective or menial, preventing them from taking advantage of available opportunities. Basic necessities such as clean sanitary towels and sanitary napkins are often lacking, which is essential for maintaining menstrual hygiene.

Another factor that increases the risk of HIV for women in prison is the disproportionate imprisonment of women far from their homes. This distance increases their sense of isolation and can lead to additional stressors such as anxiety and financial hardship for both the women and their families. After release, the stigma of incarceration carries a greater weight on women than on men, and they may face discrimination and difficulties reintegrating into their communities. Drug consumption and injection are also significant factors contributing to the risk of HIV for women in prison. Many women are incarcerated for drug-related offenses, and while some may start using drugs while in prison, others continue to use and inject narcotics. Due to the lack of access to safe injecting equipment and health services, women who inject drugs are more likely to contract HIV compared to men. They often use homemade syringes or discarded needles, which increases the risk of infection.

Sexual assault and high-risk sexual activity are additional factors that increase the risk of HIV for women in prison. Women are more vulnerable to sexual assault, including rape, in the restricted atmosphere of prisons, both from male staff members and other male inmates. In some cases, female inmates are housed in close proximity to or inside male jails, and they may not have their own cells or be under the supervision of male inmates. This vulnerability to sexual exploitation puts women at risk of HIV transmission (Meyer et al., 2011).

Tattooing is another risky behavior for HIV transmission in prison. Women in prison often get tattoos using unsafe methods and equipment, such as using shared needles that haven't been sanitized. The lack of safety measures and protective gear increases the risk of HIV transmission through tattooing.

Nutrition and well-being are also important factors to consider in relation to HIV risk for women in prison. Compared to men, women have limited access to medical treatments and reproductive health care in prison. Resources for health promotion, information, and treatment, including HIV and drug addiction treatment, are often more restricted in women's prisons. Women are also more physically susceptible to HIV than men, and the presence of sexually transmitted infections (STIs) further increases their risk of HIV infection. The prevalence of HIV among women in prison is higher due to these factors.

Incarcerated women who are mothers face additional challenges. Many of them are young women, and some are pregnant or become pregnant while in prison. Access to reproductive, prenatal, and postnatal care is often limited for women in prison. Antiretroviral therapy, which prevents mother-to-child transmission of HIV, is frequently unavailable to incarcerated women, including pregnant women living with HIV. Special care and attention are needed for children born in prison, particularly to mothers living with HIV.

8.5. HOMELESSNESS AND CRIMINAL JUSTICE INVOLVEMENT

Homelessness and criminal justice involvement are interconnected issues that have serious implications for individuals, communities, and the criminal justice system as a whole (Greenberg & Rosenheck, 2008). Homelessness is a complex problem that requires attention from federal, state, and local governments, and it is particularly prevalent among individuals who have contact with the criminal justice system.

According to the Department of Housing and Urban Development (HUD), individuals who are staying in shelters, escaping institutions (including jails), or residing in unfit places fall under the definition of homelessness. Additionally, those who will be leaving their temporary accommodation in two weeks or are escaping domestic abuse and unable to find shelter or support are also considered homeless. However, homeless advocacy groups argue that the definition of homelessness should include individuals who are "doubling up" or staying with family or friends, even if they are not required to leave within two weeks (Greenberg & Rosenheck, 2008) (Figure 8.3).

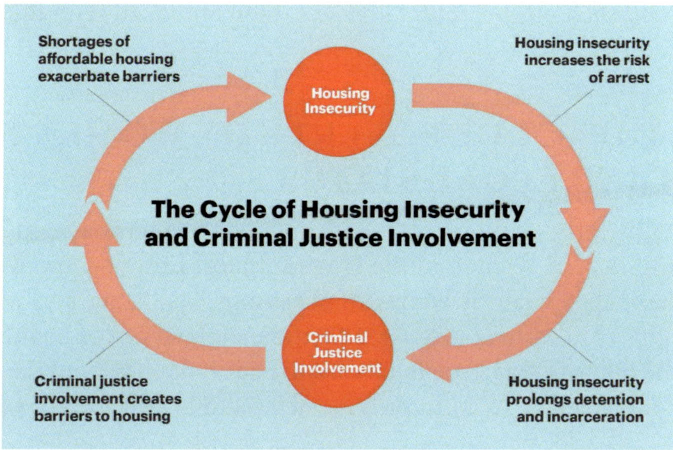

Figure 8.3. *The cycle of housing insecurity and criminal justice involvement.*

Source: Local Housing Solutions (2024).

There are several risk factors that contribute to homelessness, and these factors vary for families and individuals. Structural factors such as unemployment, poverty, and a lack of suitable housing are more common among families experiencing homelessness. On the other hand, factors such as substance abuse, eviction, and mental illness are more prevalent among single individuals who end up homeless.

Substance abuse and mental health conditions are significant issues among the homeless population. According to the Substance Abuse and Mental Health Services Administration, 35% of the homeless population has a substance use disorder. Substance abuse can both contribute to and be a coping mechanism for the difficulties and trauma associated with homelessness. However, homelessness poses significant barriers to accessing treatment and can hinder the prognosis of therapy. Factors such as social isolation, lack of transportation, and an uncoordinated system of treatment delivery make it challenging for homeless individuals to receive the necessary support.

Domestic abuse is another significant factor contributing to homelessness. Survivors of domestic abuse may become homeless after leaving an abusive relationship, often due to shame, discriminatory legislation, and limited access to financial resources.

Finally, trauma is a significant factor that can lead to homelessness, particularly among women who have experienced emotional, physical, or sexual abuse. These traumatic events can have a profound impact on an individual's mental and emotional well-being, often resulting in a loss of stability and a need for homeless services or shelters. When individuals leave an abusive relationship and seek out homeless services, they are faced with the additional trauma.

8.6. THE IMPACT OF POVERTY ON WOMEN'S HEALTH AND LEGAL STATUS

The impact of poverty on women's health and legal status is a significant issue that affects millions of women in the United States. Low-income women face numerous challenges when it comes to accessing healthcare and maintaining their legal rights. This article discusses the financial burden of healthcare costs on women, the barriers they face in obtaining necessary care, and the role of the Affordable Care Act (ACA) in improving access to healthcare for low-income women.

Women, particularly those living in poverty, are more likely to require healthcare throughout their lives. They are more prone to long-term illnesses that require ongoing care and are more likely to take prescription medications. Additionally, women experience mental health issues such as depression at higher rates than men. Women also require more interaction with medical professionals during their reproductive years, even if they are childless. These factors contribute to higher healthcare expenses for women (Hankivsky, 2012).

However, women's ability to afford healthcare is often hindered by their lower incomes. Women, on average, earn less than men and are more likely to live in poverty or have extremely low incomes. This disparity in income means that women's out-of-pocket medical expenses account for a larger portion of their income.

The financial strain of healthcare costs often leads women to postpone or forgo necessary care. Women with low incomes also face additional barriers to accessing care, such as difficulties finding childcare, taking time off work, or transportation issues. These barriers can delay the identification of dangerous illnesses or prevent women from receiving necessary treatment (Asad & Clair, 2018). The financial instability caused by the high cost of medical care further exacerbates the challenges faced by low-income women. Many women working low-paying jobs with inflexible schedules do not have paid sick leave or the ability to take time off for medical care.

This means that if they miss work due to illness or medical appointments, they risk losing their jobs or incurring financial damages. Additionally, women are more likely than men to struggle with medical debt or expenses. In 2016, one in four women reported having difficulty paying medical costs and had to use most of their savings or borrow money (Asad & Clair, 2018).

The Affordable Care Act (ACA) has played a crucial role in improving access to healthcare for low-income women. The ACA has expanded health insurance coverage, making it more affordable and accessible for millions of women. However, despite these improvements, women with low incomes are still more likely to be uninsured. In 2016, half of the uninsured women reported forgoing medical care due to financial constraints. Lack of insurance often leads to poorer health outcomes, as uninsured individuals receive diagnoses at later stages and have higher mortality rates (Asad & Clair, 2018).

The ACA has made significant progress in addressing the discrimination that women face in the individual market. It has prohibited insurance companies from denying coverage to women with pre-existing conditions specific to them, such as having undergone a Cesarean section or having been pregnant in the past. The ACA also addresses discriminatory practices against women, such as charging them more for the same coverage as men. Additionally, the ACA ensures that women's major medical needs, including maternity care, prescription medication, treatment for substance misuse and mental health issues, and preventive care, are covered by insurance.

8.7. ACCESS TO HEALTHCARE FOR INCARCERATED WOMEN

The lack of access to healthcare for incarcerated women is a significant issue that compounds and worsens negative health outcomes for this population. There are several factors that contribute to this problem, including inadequate trauma care, inadequate infrastructure, unsatisfactory living conditions in prison, the possibility of physical or sexual abuse, solitary confinement, intimidation, and harassment by correctional officers, and restricted access to counseling services and social support (Davis et al., 2018) (Figure 8.4).

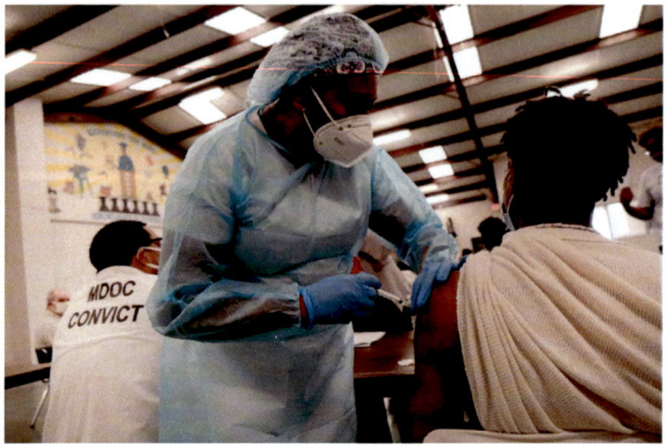

Figure 8.4. *Prisoner at bolivar county correctional facility in Mississippi receives COVID-19 vaccination from medical workers.*

Source: Avila (2022).

One of the consequences of this lack of access to healthcare is the high mortality rate and deteriorating health among female inmates. Many prisoners continue to pass away or experience worsening health conditions due to the inadequate healthcare provided in prisons. For example, federal prisons often lack obstetricians and gynecologists with the necessary training, leading to lower screening rates and incorrect interpretation of test results. This puts women at risk for diseases that can be prevented, such as ovarian and breast cancers.

Reproductive health care and family planning services are also major issues in the federal prison system. A significant number of female inmates are pregnant, but they often do not have access to prenatal care, screenings, and social support necessary for a safe and healthy pregnancy and delivery. The separation of mothers from their babies shortly after birth increases the likelihood of postpartum depression and emotional distress, which can have long-term negative effects on both the mother and the child.

In addition to the lack of healthcare, incarcerated women also face the challenge of supporting and taking care of their families while in prison. Many women are the primary caretakers for their children, and their incarceration often leads to the disruption of their families and the uprooting of their children (Davis et al., 2018). This adds to the stress and emotional harm experienced by incarcerated women, both during their time in prison and upon their release and return to their communities.

The current situation in prisons not only fails to meet the basic medical needs of female inmates but also violates their human rights. The inhumane conditions in prisons, combined with the lack of access to healthcare, increase the likelihood of negative health outcomes for a population that is already at risk. It is crucial to provide a caring and restorative environment for female prisoners to ensure their long-term health and well-being. Prison reform that prioritizes trauma care, social support, counseling services, educational opportunities, increased time for family bonding, greater allowance for early release, and meaningful post-release services is necessary to improve the health outcomes of incarcerated women (Davis et al., 2018). Such reforms would not only benefit the health of female inmates but also contribute to a smaller prison population and lower rates of recidivism.

Overall, poverty has a profound impact on women's health and legal status. Low-income women face higher healthcare costs, struggle to afford necessary care, and often have limited access to healthcare services. The ACA has made significant strides in improving access to healthcare for low-income women, but there is still work to be done to ensure that all women have equal access to affordable and comprehensive healthcare.

8.8. GENDER-RESPONSIVE APPROACHES TO ADDRESSING HEALTH NEEDS

Gender-responsive approaches to addressing health needs are an essential component of person-centered health services. These approaches aim to provide comprehensive care that takes into account the distinct requirements, backgrounds, and vulnerabilities of different genders (Messina et al., 2019). By implementing gender-sensitive service delivery, addressing health needs specific to gender, promoting gender-transformative leadership and policies, considering equity and social determinants of health, and upholding human rights and global perspectives, health systems can ensure that they are truly serving all individuals.

1. **Gender-Sensitive Service Delivery:** Gender-sensitive service delivery involves using communication techniques that are sensitive to gender differences. Healthcare professionals should practice active listening, empathy, and respect for patients' choices. Building a relationship of trust between patients and providers is crucial, as patients who receive respectful treatment are more empowered to actively participate in their healthcare decisions. Additionally, health education should be gender-responsive, providing information about specific gender-related health risks, prevention strategies, and treatment options (Messina et al., 2019).
2. **Taking Care of Health Needs Specific to Gender:** Addressing health needs specific to gender is another important aspect of gender-responsive care. Maternal health requires gender-specific care during

pregnancy, labor, and the postpartum period. Access to prenatal care, safe deliveries, and postnatal support are essential for ensuring the well-being of pregnant individuals. Sexual and reproductive health services, including family planning, contraception, and sexual health, should be easily accessible and inclusive. Mental health care should also be gender-responsive, recognizing that men and women may have different experiences with mental health issues and incorporating trauma-informed approaches (Messina et al., 2019).

3. **Gender-Transformative Leadership and Policies:** Gender-transformative leadership and policies play a crucial role in promoting gender-responsive health systems. Increasing the representation of women in leadership roles within the health sector is essential for advancing equity, fairness in decision-making, and creating respectful working conditions. Workforce development is also important, as educating medical personnel in gender-responsive care ensures that they recognize and address the unique health needs of women.
4. **Equity and Social Determinants of Health:** Equity and social determinants of health are key considerations in gender-responsive approaches. Gender-responsive health systems take into account social determinants such as social support networks, education, and income. Addressing economic inequities, discrimination, and gender-based violence is crucial for improving health outcomes. By addressing these social determinants, health systems can work towards achieving health equity for all individuals (Messina et al., 2019).
5. **Human Rights and Global Perspectives:** In recent years, there has been a growing recognition of the importance of gender-responsive health as a worldwide concern. Gender equality, sexual rights, and reproductive autonomy are now acknowledged as fundamental human rights in international frameworks (Messina et al., 2019). As a result, advocacy work has focused on abolishing gender-based violence, advancing sexual education, and ensuring that everyone has access to high-quality healthcare globally.

8.9. INTERSECTIONAL PERSPECTIVES ON WOMEN'S HEALTH AND CRIME

Intersectionality is a concept that recognizes the ways in which different social identities intersect and interact to create unique experiences and disadvantages for individuals. When applied to the intersection of women's health and crime, an intersectional perspective allows for a deeper understanding of the various factors that contribute to health disparities among women involved in the legal system (Borras, 2021). This perspective considers how age, sexual orientation, class, and race, among other factors, influence women's experiences and access to healthcare.

One of the benefits of using an intersectional lens is that it helps to uncover the structural and representational barriers that women face in terms of their health before they become involved in the criminal justice system. These barriers can include limited access to healthcare services due to socioeconomic factors, discrimination based on race or sexual orientation, and age-related health issues (Borras, 2021). By understanding these barriers, policymakers and healthcare providers can work towards addressing them and improving the overall health outcomes for women.

Additionally, an intersectional perspective sheds light on the health and well-being of women while they are detained. This perspective highlights the institutional impediments to providing adequate healthcare within carceral settings, as well as the role that stigma plays in perpetuating harmful behaviors and preventing access to necessary treatments. By recognizing these challenges, efforts can be made to improve healthcare services within prisons and address the stigma associated with women's health issues.

However, there are also potential drawbacks and challenges associated with using an intersectional lens in the study of women's health and crime. One concern is the risk of unintentional scholarly use, where researchers may inadvertently promote preexisting biases or damaging narratives (Borras, 2021). It is important for researchers to approach their work with caution and be mindful of the potential impact of their findings on marginalized communities.

Another challenge is the need for gender-sensitive services and reentry programs that take into account the intersecting identities of women involved in the legal system. While gender-sensitive programs are important, an intersectional perspective highlights the need to also consider other marginalization axes, such as race, class, and sexual orientation, in order to provide comprehensive and effective care. This requires a more nuanced understanding of the intersecting identities and experiences of women, and the development of programs that address their specific needs.

In order to fully incorporate intersectionality into the study of women's health and crime, there are several obstacles that need to be addressed. One is the inadequate knowledge and training of criminal justice professionals in understanding and applying intersectional perspectives. Without proper training, the implementation of intersectionality may be hindered. It is important to provide education and training to criminal justice professionals to ensure that they have the necessary tools to address the unique needs of women.

Another obstacle is the siloed approach of criminal justice systems, where different components such as the police, courts, and prisons often operate in isolation. This lack of collaboration hinders the integration of intersectionality, as it requires interdisciplinary collaboration and the removal of these obstacles (Borras, 2021). The second is the inadequacy of current data gathering techniques in capturing intersectional identities. It is crucial to create reliable data systems that consider variables such as disability, gender, sexual orientation, and race. Without accurate and comprehensive data, it becomes difficult to understand the experiences and needs of individuals with intersecting identities.

The third is the need to reform policies and practices within the criminal justice system. Intersectionality calls into question established policies and procedures, as biases, discriminatory behaviors, and uneven treatment among different identities must be addressed. Reforms are necessary to ensure fairness and equal. The fourth is opposition to change. Some stakeholders may resist adopting intersectional approaches due to inertia or a fear of disrupting the status quo. This resistance can hinder progress and prevent the adoption of more inclusive and equitable practices. To overcome this challenge, advocacy and leadership are essential. Advocates for intersectionality need to effectively communicate the benefits and importance of adopting intersectional approaches, while leaders need to champion and drive the change (Borras, 2021).

The fifth is resource allocation. It can be difficult to allocate resources to meet the demands of intersectionality. It is essential to prioritize equity and make sure that initiatives serving underrepresented communities receive sufficient financing. The sixth is legal and ethical considerations. It can be difficult from a legal and moral standpoint to fairly balance the rights of various groups inside the criminal justice system. It takes careful navigation to ensure fairness when taking intersecting identities into account. Criminal justice systems can advance toward more inclusive, egalitarian, and productive practices by overcoming these obstacles (Borras, 2021).

8.10. THE ROLE OF PUBLIC HEALTH IN PREVENTING CRIMINALIZED HEALTH BEHAVIORS

Public health plays a crucial role in addressing criminalized health practices due to the strong connection between justice and health (Massoglia & Remster, 2019). The subsequent strategies are crucial:

1. **Holistic Approaches:** Interventions in public health should go beyond punitive ideologies. Promoting alternatives to imprisonment, addressing structural inequalities, and emphasizing public health measures are all integral to prioritizing health.
2. **Decreasing Incarceration:** It is crucial to significantly reduce the population of individuals in prison. Allocating resources towards social determinants of health, such as housing and employment, rather than focusing on carceral systems, improves overall well-being.
3. **Noncarceral Accountability Measures:** To enhance safety, well-being, and accountability, public health can explore noncarceral approaches.

Other options encompass tactics for minimizing harm, community-driven endeavors, and approaches rooted in restorative justice.

4. **Restoring Voting Rights:** Granting incarcerated individuals the chance to vote once more promotes active participation in civic affairs. Public health advocates for inclusive legislation that recognizes the detrimental impact of voting disenfranchisement on an individual's well-being.
5. **Research and Evaluation:** It is imperative to allocate funds for studies that examine the policy variables that impact individuals' exposure to the criminal justice system and propose alternative solutions. Methods that are effective are based on approaches that are supported by evidence.

Through enhancing public health interventions, we can dismantle detrimental systems and establish equitable structures that prioritize justice and health.

CHAPTER 9

GENDER EQUALITY AND REFORM IN THE CRIMINAL JUSTICE SYSTEM

Contents

The intersection of women's rights and criminal justice reform is a critical point where gender equity and systemic change converge. Considering the unique challenges that women encounter in the criminal justice system, any attempts to enhance it should consider the gender-specific barriers they face (Schneider, 2013). In order to address issues such as unfair sentencing practices and ensure trauma-informed care, it is essential to approach the pursuit of justice with a gender-responsive lens. Individuals strive for a more equitable and inclusive criminal justice system through the advocacy of just policies and the eradication of gender-based biases. This chapter will discuss the progression of women's rights within the legal system. The Influence of Feminist Movements on the Criminal Justice System Advocacy by women for policy change and gender equity in legal representation. The significance of international law in safeguarding women's rights, promoting restorative justice, and enhancing women's empowerment. The Convergence of Gender, Race, and LGBTQ+ Rights Grassroots mobilization for gender equality, the impact of media on women's rights and criminal justice, as well as strategies for advancing gender equality in the legal system.

9.1. THE PROGRESSION OF WOMEN'S RIGHTS WITHIN THE LEGAL SYSTEM

The 1979 UN Convention on the Elimination of All Forms of Discrimination Against Women provided a comprehensive framework for the worldwide advancement of women's rights. In 1981, the UN General Assembly promptly established the International Bill of Rights for Women, which has subsequently received approval from 189 member nations. Nevertheless, the objective of achieving gender equality for women remains incomplete. In the year 2000, women in 25 countries faced more difficulty in obtaining passports compared to men. In over 30% of countries, women were prohibited from working the night shift on equal terms as men. Women in the majority of countries lacked adequate protection against sexual harassment and domestic violence, while a small number of countries did offer such protection (Sheets, 2007).

The presence or absence of women's rights has a significant impact. Women's motivation to invest and generate economic opportunities is affected by property rights. Additionally, labor laws that limit access to abortion and contraception have a negative impact on female employment. Furthermore, these factors also influence women's decisions regarding marriage. Hence, it is imperative to understand the underlying reasons for the significant disparities in women's legal standing across different regions. Certain nations have effectively implemented reforms over time, while others have failed to do so.

Academic inquiries analyze these different experiences by using political-economic theories to understand why individual voters and politicians support women's rights.

Throughout the past five decades, significant advancements have occurred in all regions, despite notable variations in the pace of change. Sub-Saharan Africa experienced the most significant improvement, with the average score increasing from 38.5 to 69.9 between 1970 and the present, representing an 81% shift (Sheets, 2007). Despite variations in the pace of change across different economies, numerous regional trends have remained consistent. Although high-income OECD economies achieved the highest regional average score in 2019, it is worth noting that economies in the Europe and Central Asia region held the highest score in 1970. During the specified time period, affluent OECD economies achieved significant advancements in implementing legal reforms related to gender equality. Indeed, the high-income OECD economies experienced the second-largest percentage increase in their average WBL score compared to all other regions, reaching 70.2%. During the 1970s, high-income OECD economies implemented significant changes in their gender legislation. By the end of the decade, these economies surpassed Central Asia and Eastern Europe to become the top-ranked region, a position they still maintain today. From 1970 to 2019, these two regions accounted for 50% of the documented reforms (Sheets, 2007). The development of the Middle East and North Africa region is progressing at a slow pace, which is worth mentioning. During the year 1970, women in this particular region had fewer rights compared to men in the areas evaluated by the WBL index, with an average score of 31.0 in The World Baseball League. Although the rate of improvement has been modest, the average score of 49.6 in 2019 indicates that there has been progress. The bulk of advancements in the field of women's rights has taken place in recent times. Specifically, during the 1970s, 1980s, and to a lesser extent, the 1990s, the average Women's Business and Law (WBL) score in the region remained relatively stable. From 2000 to the present, there has been an improvement in women's economic opportunity equality in the region over the last 20 years. Nevertheless, women in the region continue to face a higher number of legal obstacles in comparison to men in the same area, and even in comparison to women in other regions globally (Sheets, 2007).

9.2. THE IMPACT OF FEMINIST MOVEMENTS ON CRIMINAL JUSTICE

Feminism is founded on the fundamental principle that women should have full and equal rights in society, the economy, and politics. Feminist theory originated as a response to Western traditions that imposed restrictions on women's rights, although it has since evolved into a global phenomenon with various expressions and adaptations (Schneider, 2013). The feminist movement is a strong advocate for achieving social, economic, and political equality between genders. Feminism is endorsed by a diverse range of organizations committed to enhancing women's rights and interests globally, with its origins primarily in Western societies.

Throughout the majority of Western history, women were confined to domestic roles, while men were granted access to engage in public affairs. In medieval Europe, women were prohibited from owning property, receiving education, or participating in public activities. As of the early 1900s, women in many regions were still deprived of the right to vote and hold public positions (Schneider, 2013). Due to the absence of male representation, they were often marginalized from participating in commercial transactions, accessing education, and pursuing professional careers. These restrictions persisted in specific regions, even in contemporary times. The fundamental objective of feminism is to achieve absolute parity for women. By challenging entrenched traditions and prejudiced actions, it aims to eliminate barriers that hinder the progress of women. Originating from Western cultures, feminism has exerted a significant influence on various subjects, such as intersectionality, reproductive rights, and gender-based violence.

Feminism ultimately benefits society as a whole by prioritizing the most marginalized individuals and fostering a more equitable and righteous social order.

9.2.1. The Convergence of Feminism and Criminal Justice

1. **Carceral Feminism:** The term "law and order feminism" refers to the commitment of feminists to an agenda that emphasizes strict enforcement of laws, often advocating for punitive measures as a means to address gender inequality and violence against women. While feminist movements have expanded women's opportunities, certain strategies employed by feminist elites have been shaped by their privileges, potentially overlooking the experiences of underprivileged women. The "Other" women often marginalized due to factors such as poverty, homosexuality, immigration status, race, lower levels of education, or disability, have individual reasons for refraining from engaging with the legal system of the state. Black feminists have not only focused on punitive measures, but also on systemic factors that contribute to women being vulnerable to assault.

2. **The Feminist Campaign against Crime:** Professor Aya Gruber, in her book The Feminist War on Crime, offers a critique of feminists who advocate for punishment as a means of resolving issues related to crime. Gruber argues that jails are not an effective solution for addressing sexual offenses or domestic abuse. She advocates for a fresh feminist storyline that incorporates abolitionism, denounces imprisonment, and strives to improve the circumstances of all women (Burgess-Proctor, 2006). The emphasis in shaping societal ideals should be placed on the expressive function of criminal law, rather than on punishment.
3. **Advances in Feminist Criminology:** The discipline of feminist studies has transformed our understanding of criminal behavior and unlawful activities. Feminists have surpassed basic explanations by recognizing gender disparities in victimization and criminal behavior.

They perceive gender dynamics as complex, shaped by interconnected factors that contribute to social injustices. Feminist efforts have led to significant changes in the criminal justice system, particularly in the treatment of victims (Burgess-Proctor, 2006).

4. **Criminal Law Reform and Feminism:** Throughout history, the women's movement has advocated for modifications to the legal system, specifically in regard to the crime of rape. Conversely, feminist legal criticism has had an influence on criminal law, resulting in changes to institutions, processes, and doctrines.

Feminists continue to scrutinize and enhance the criminal justice system, advocating for equitable treatment of victims and leveraging innovative research. Ultimately, feminist perspectives have transformed the field of criminal justice by advocating for a more compassionate and pragmatic approach that prioritizes justice, equality, and the well-being of all individuals. Feminism is a positive and influential movement that advocates for the recognition and respect of women's rights. It strives to create a society where gender equality is not limited or constrained.

9.3. WOMEN'S ADVOCACY FOR POLICY CHANGE

Women's advocacy for policy change is crucial for enhancing sustainability, resource allocation, and governance. Including women in policy formation processes not only benefits the government but also empowers women to exercise agency and voice (Junk et al., 2021). Women become more competent and self-assured as they have more opportunities to participate in these procedures.

One area where women's advocacy for policy change is particularly important is women's economic empowerment (WEE). WEE is a global priority due to its effects on sustainable livelihoods, poverty eradication, and peace promotion. When women are economically empowered, up to 90% of their income is allocated to their families, resulting in homes with better nutrition, improved health, and higher levels of education. Additionally, agreements that arise from empowered women's participation in peace processes have a 35% higher chance of lasting at least 15 years (Junk et al., 2021). Women also play a significant role in entrepreneurship, with nearly 10 million small and medium-sized businesses owned by women, which greatly contributes to job creation. Therefore, policy change that takes into account the distinct lifestyles of men and women is essential, going beyond gender-neutral approaches.

There are five key lessons for evidence-based policy reform that can enhance women's advocacy for policy change:

1. **Apply a Gender Lens:** Policies should acknowledge that men and women have distinct perspectives on life. Gender-neutral policies might not fully empower women.
2. **Address Unofficial Policy Gaps:** In addition to overcoming official legal obstacles, it is important to address unofficial policy gaps and silences that impede women entrepreneurs.
3. **Expand on Women's Policy Assets:** Well-executed reform should make better use of already-existing policy assets and enhance their execution.
4. **Encourage Collective Action:** Empowering women often serves as a precursor to larger reform movements.
5. **Promote Women's Leadership and Advocacy Experiences:** Women should be provided with opportunities to apply their leadership and advocacy experiences gained through involvement in associations, voluntary work, and political parties.

Policy advocacy plays a crucial role in promoting gender-responsive norms and policies. It involves influencing decision-makers, institutions, and civil society to adopt, develop, and uphold policies that benefit women's and girls' lives and rights. Advocacy efforts aim to bring about changes in policies that support gender justice, promoting equality and gender rights. Legislative action is one effective way to bring about social change.

Organizations like Women for Women International play a significant role in advocating for policy change at local, national, regional, and international levels (Junk et al., 2021). They work with influential individuals and groups to prioritize the needs of women impacted by conflict. Women's lobbying for legislative changes is essential for achieving gender equality, leveling the playing field, and building a more inclusive and just society.

There are various strategies and initiatives that support women's advocacy for policy change. These include:

1. **Find Ways for Women to Apply Their Leadership and Advocacy Experiences:** Women can acquire and utilize leadership abilities through their involvement in associations, voluntary work, and political parties. Projects should be flexible enough to seize advocacy opportunities when the environment shifts.
2. **Knowledge Fairs:** These are organized events aimed at spreading knowledge to a wide audience. They can be used as awareness-raising initiatives or platforms for sharing research and information on specific subjects.
3. **Development and Presentation of Women's Initiatives:** Local governments and donors can support women's initiatives that focus on various sectors, such as agriculture, small businesses, and community development. These initiatives contribute to women's economic empowerment and overall development.

9.4. GENDER EQUITY IN LEGAL REPRESENTATION

Gender equity in legal representation plays a crucial role in the broader pursuit of gender equality. Promoting equitable involvement in decision-making, creating inclusive and just communities, ensuring access to basic public services, and fostering prosperity for all in the economy and environment are all crucial aspects to consider (Riccucci & Van Ryzin, 2017). Despite significant advancements, discriminatory laws continue to persist across the globe, impeding the progress towards achieving gender equality and restricting the opportunities available to women and girls. The laws in question have distinct requirements for individuals based on their gender in a range of areas, including acquiring a passport, selecting employment, changing nationality, participating in legal proceedings, inheriting assets, and determining marital partners (Riccucci & Van Ryzin, 2017). When it comes to tackling gender inequality in the legal sector, there are a number of strategies that individuals can consider implementing. First and foremost, it is crucial to emphasize the significance of advocating for laws that uphold gender equality and firmly reject any form of gender-based discrimination. Advocating for more stringent legislation against gender-based violence, advocating for the elimination of discriminatory laws and practices, and advocating for the use of gender-neutral language in legal documents are all important actions to take.

One impactful way to contribute is by providing pro bono legal services to individuals and groups dedicated to promoting gender equality. One possible way to contribute is by offering legal advice and assistance to organizations that work towards gender equality. Another way is to stand up for individuals who have experienced gender-based discrimination or violence and support the initiatives they are involved in. Several organizations, including the Gender Equality Law Center, the National Women's Law Center, and ENOUGH, provide lawyers with opportunities to offer pro bono assistance in the field of gender equality.

Another effective approach to tackling gender inequality is by assuming the role of a subject matter expert. When lawyers testify as expert witnesses, they have the opportunity to delve into the ways in which certain legislation or policies can have a direct impact on important aspects of women's lives, such as their health, access to education, and economic stability. Furthermore, they can provide valuable insights into the presence of gender discrimination within specific fields or work environments. Providing testimony as an expert witness holds immense weight in court proceedings, as it guarantees that legal judgments are made with a thorough grasp of the pertinent matters at hand (Riccucci & Van Ryzin, 2017).

Another crucial strategy is to disseminate knowledge about gender equality. Lawyers have various avenues to disseminate knowledge on gender equality issues and the corresponding legal framework. They can conduct seminars or workshops, contribute articles or opinion pieces, or deliver speeches to legislators or community associations, effectively educating others on these important matters (Riccucci & Van Ryzin, 2017). Participating in organizations like the Above the Law Commission on Domestic and Sexual Violence or Above the Law's Civil Rights and Social Justice Group can offer valuable chances to make a meaningful impact on gender equity initiatives.

Finally, it is essential to challenge and debunk gender preconceptions and stereotypes in order to advance the cause of gender equality. By actively challenging gender stereotypes and discrimination in their personal lives and professional endeavors, individuals have the power to make a meaningful impact on promoting gender equality every single day. Active participation in challenging gender stereotypes and biases is crucial for both men and women.

To effectively combat gender stereotypes in the workplace, it is crucial for individuals to address their own unconscious biases and potential microaggressions. Unconscious bias is the natural inclination to make implicit connections without conscious deliberation. Individuals of all genders must acknowledge and comprehend the impact of biases on their careers and actively work towards addressing them (Riccucci & Van Ryzin, 2017).

It is imperative to emphasize the significance of attaining gender equity in legal representation in order to promote gender equality as a whole. There are various strategies that individuals can employ to tackle gender inequality in the legal sector. These strategies include advocating for laws that take gender into account, providing pro bono legal services, serving as experts in the field, sharing knowledge about gender equality, and challenging gender stereotypes. Through active engagement with these strategies, individuals have the power to create a meaningful impact in advancing gender equality not only in the legal sector but also in other areas (Riccucci & Van Ryzin, 2017).

9.5. THE ROLE OF INTERNATIONAL LAW IN PROTECTING WOMEN'S RIGHTS

According to Smith (2022), one of the fundamental aspects of human rights is the attainment of gender equality and the eradication of any kind of discrimination against women. However, it is important to acknowledge that women often face numerous violations of their human rights throughout their lives, and unfortunately, the issue of women's rights has not always been given the attention it deserves. To effectively address discrimination against women, it is crucial to have a comprehensive understanding of the various forms of discrimination they experience and the barriers they face in achieving gender equality (Smith, 2022).

Throughout history, there has been a profound focus on the issue of women's human rights. Over the past few decades, remarkable strides have been taken to advance women's rights on a global scale. However, it is important to acknowledge that there are still notable disparities, and the lives of women are constantly evolving, with the emergence of fresh types of discrimination against them on a regular basis. Furthermore, various factors such as age, social situation, education, marital status, ethnicity, nationality, religion, health, and disability can contribute to the prejudice faced by certain groups of women (Smith, 2022). It is crucial to consider all intersecting types of discrimination when developing policies and strategies to address discrimination against women.

The International Covenant on Civil and Political Rights and the International Covenant on Economic, Social, and Cultural Rights are two significant human rights treaties that were developed by the Commission on Human Rights in response to the Universal Declaration's adoption. These are part of the International Bill of Human Rights, along with the Universal Declaration. According to Smith (2022), when states ratify or accede to the provisions of the two Covenants, along with other human rights agreements, they become legally obligated to abide by them. When states ratify these agreements, they have a responsibility to regularly submit reports to expert groups. These groups then provide recommendations on the necessary actions to fulfill the obligations outlined in the treaties. Furthermore, these treaty-monitoring agencies consider individual complaints of alleged infringement, as long as the States have given their consent to do so (Smith, 2022).

International law provides significant protection for women's rights, although the challenge lies in effectively implementing these laws. Here are a few strategies that can be implemented to enhance enforcement:

- Promoting the ratification of significant agreements such as the Convention on the Elimination of All Forms of Discrimination Against Women (CEDAW) in order to effectively facilitate its implementation across nations.
- Ensuring the protection of women's rights necessitates the alignment of national legislation and international standards (Smith, 2022).
- Providing judges and attorneys with the necessary knowledge to effectively interpret and implement the law with consideration for gender-related issues.
- Equipping human rights advocates and women's organizations with the necessary resources to effectively monitor policy implementation and advocate for necessary changes.
- Providing women with easily accessible and reasonably priced legal assistance services. One possible approach to address cases involving gender-based violence is the establishment of specialized courts or tribunals.
- Collecting and presenting gender-disaggregated data. This is an essential tool for understanding and addressing gender disparities. It provides valuable insights into the different experiences and outcomes of men and women in various areas of life. By analyzing and interpreting this data, we can identify patterns, trends, and gaps that exist between genders. This knowledge is Gather data on female violence to inform policy decisions and track progress.
- Enhancing the reporting procedures for cases of rights abuses against women.
- Using international organizations and procedures to hold states accountable for their transgressions.
- Engaging men and boys in awareness-raising and educational initiatives in order to promote and advance gender equality.

Ultimately, the effective enforcement of international law requires a comprehensive approach that encompasses legal procedures, knowledge, access to justice, data, accountability, and societal reform.

9.6. RESTORATIVE JUSTICE AND WOMEN'S EMPOWERMENT

Restorative techniques have been approached with caution by women, particularly in cases involving gender-based injustices (Goodmark, 2018). There are several important issues that require attention, such as the undervaluation of gender-based damages, the condemnation of violence against women, and the need for rehabilitation professionals to improve victim safety. In this section, we will argue that restorative justice can be seen as a feminist practice. It stems from a shared skepticism towards government-run institutions and a desire for community engagement, which were key drivers of the early feminist movement. Restorative justice plays a crucial role in advancing feminist objectives. It focuses on elevating the voices of women, supporting their independence and empowerment, involving the community, rejecting gender essentialism, adopting an intersectional perspective, challenging patriarchal structures, and working towards ending violence against women (Goodmark, 2018).

Restorative justice and carceral feminism are clearly in conflict with each other. According to Goodmark (2018), this aligns perfectly with the core principles and ideologies of feminism. The feminist agenda involves a range of important objectives that can be accomplished through the implementation of restorative justice. These include providing a platform for women's voices to be heard, promoting their autonomy and empowerment, engaging with the community, adopting an intersectional analysis that rejects gender essentialism, challenging patriarchal structures, and eradicating violence against women (Goodmark, 2018).

1. **Voice:** The foundation of feminism is rooted in the real-world experiences of women. The phrase "the personal is political" was initially coined by feminists. In the early days of their movement, one of their main strategies was to raise awareness and situate women's distinct experiences within a broader political context (Goodmark, 2018). It is crucial, as feminism emphasizes, that the narratives of marginalized individuals have a profound influence on law and policy, particularly in amplifying the voices of women. Restorative justice places a strong emphasis on valuing the personal experiences of those who have been harmed. Understanding the potential harm that can arise from each of the primary restorative justice questions

is crucial. What was the impact of the injury? In order for the procedure to move forward, it is imperative that the individual who has been affected provides a response. What steps can be taken to address and rectify the damage? Through a comprehensive analysis of the negative consequences and the corresponding requirements, the individual who has been affected takes charge of facilitating the restorative conversation (Goodmark, 2018).

2. **Empowerment:** In the context of restorative justice, the concept of empowerment is closely linked to the idea of amplifying one's voice. In his work on Restorative justice and responsive regulation, Goodmark emphasizes the importance of actively listening to the stories of individuals and giving them the recognition they deserve. He argues that this aspect of restorative justice has the potential to empower those who have been marginalized and disenfranchised. Restorative justice has the potential to empower victims of gender-based abuses by addressing the disempowerment they may have experienced as a result of their assault (Goodmark, 2018).

9.7. THE INTERSECTION OF GENDER, RACE, AND LGBTQ+ RIGHTS

Activists focused on sexual orientation and gender identity and expression (SOGIE) often overlook the different settings in which oppression is expressed, including race, ethnicity, gender, disability, age, and class. These contexts serve as the backdrop for various forms of discrimination, violence, and other violations of human rights. It is worth noting that due to the intersectionality of various forms of oppression, LGBTQ individuals may not always be able to pinpoint the exact type of oppression that impacts them the most (Swank & Fahs, 2013).

Considering the rights of LGBTQ individuals, just like any other group or individual, or those associated with any particular issue, requires acknowledging the diverse range of identities and circumstances that shape people's lives. An integrated strategy is crucial in addressing inequality and violations, which can be perpetuated by both State and non-State actors.

While it is true that we are all equal, it is important to acknowledge that we possess unique qualities and differences. Do human rights violations based on sexual orientation, gender identity, and expression have an equal impact on individuals within the LGBT community? Does the infringement of any right, such as the freedom to choose a job, participate in governance, or have a reasonable standard of life, have the same impact on LGBTI individuals as it does on the general public (Swank & Fahs, 2013)? Do the reasons behind acts of violence targeting lesbians and gay men exhibit any similarities or commonalities? Is the discrimination faced by a homosexual man who identifies as masculine comparable to that faced by a man who identifies as more feminine according to cultural norms?

When we examine the experiences of indigenous homosexual men in Latin American metropolises, we find distinct differences compared to their white counterparts in the same urban setting. Just like any other group, individuals with different identities, such as lesbian, elderly, crippled, impoverished, transgender, or any other, have their own unique experiences.

In various settings, such as LGBT communities, workplaces, public spaces, and online platforms, individuals who identify as LGBTI may unfortunately encounter instances of racism. Moreover, they may also face discrimination and prejudice from their own family members, who may exhibit homophobia, biphobia, or transphobia.

An intersectional perspective allows us to uncover and confront the various identities that individuals possess, shedding light on the different ways in which prejudice and disadvantages can intersect and impact their lives. This strategy aims to tackle the inequalities that arise from systems of discrimination, such as patriarchy, class oppression, and ethnicity. The analysis takes into account various social, political, and historical factors, while also recognizing the unique personal experiences that arise from the blending of multiple identities.

In addition, addressing inquiries such as the ones mentioned above highlights the interconnectedness of the rights of LGBTI individuals with the rights of various other groups, including women, children, youth, individuals with disabilities, and members of ethnic minorities (Swank & Fahs, 2013). It is important to note that LGBTQ individuals are encompassed within the scope of any interconnected mechanism or instrument that acknowledges and upholds their rights, and vice versa. As Swank & Fahs (2013) argue, it is important to view the mixing of identities through an intersectional analysis. This perspective emphasizes that such mixing results in unique and distinct experiences, rather than simply adding to an individual's existing burdens. In other words, the objective is to emphasize notable distinctions and similarities rather than to establish that one group has more advantages or is more oppressed than another.

Furthermore, it is crucial for leaders and activists advocating for the rights of LGBTI individuals to understand that social injustice cannot be eliminated in isolation. By adopting an intersectional approach, they can recognize the interconnectedness of various forms of oppression and discrimination. It is crucial to note that intersectionality should foster collaboration among advocates and human rights defenders across different movements and initiatives for human rights. These include but are not limited to women's rights, workers' rights, environmental rights, rights of people with disabilities, indigenous rights, and migrant rights). An intersectional approach has the potential to bring about positive outcomes for all groups that face marginalization, exclusion, and rights violations. This is particularly important in a world where certain mechanisms are used to maintain privileges based on sexual orientation, gender identity, and social class.

9.8. GRASSROOTS ORGANIZING FOR GENDER JUSTICE

Grassroots organizing for gender justice is a powerful movement that focuses on the interests and experiences of women, queer, trans, and non-binary individuals who have been impacted by the intersecting forces of capitalism, white supremacy, and patriarchy. This movement aims to mobilize and empower the voices of those most affected by gender inequity, challenging oppressive practices, dismantling institutional barriers, and working towards a more equitable world where everyone's rights are valued and celebrated through community-led initiatives (Ellsworth, 2024).

There are several organizations that are actively fighting for gender equality and working towards achieving gender justice. One such organization is UN Women, the United Nations Entity for Gender Equality, and the Empowerment of Women. UN Women was founded with the goal of advancing global efforts to address the concerns of women and works closely with governments, civil society organizations, and policymakers to develop and implement laws, policies, and services that empower women. UN Women focuses on four main areas: eliminating violence against women and girls, promoting women's leadership and participation in governance systems, ensuring women's economic security and autonomy, and enabling women's contribution to building sustainable peace and resilience (Ellsworth, 2024).

Another organization that is actively working towards gender justice is the Association for Women's Rights in Development (AWID). AWID is an international organization that aims to advance women's human rights and gender equality worldwide. AWID collaborates closely with activists and decision-makers across the globe to impact gender policies and practices. It promotes discourse and strategies on important issues, supports coordinated efforts with feminist causes, and works towards a fair distribution of wealth by promoting corporate responsibility and tax fairness (Ellsworth, 2024).

Womankind Worldwide is another organization dedicated to women's rights and gender justice. Womankind Worldwide collaborates and stands in solidarity with other women's rights movements and organizations to improve the lives of women. The organization advocates for international organizations and governments to promote and protect women's rights, works with women's rights organizations and movements in various countries, and provides safe havens for women and girls fleeing abuse (Ellsworth, 2024). Womankind Worldwide also offers funding opportunities, advocacy platforms, and technical assistance to women's rights movements, and uses its knowledge to push for legislative changes and ensure that women's rights are prioritized globally (Ellsworth, 2024).

These organizations, along with many others, play a crucial role in grassroots organizing for gender justice. They work tirelessly to address the systemic barriers and inequalities that women, queer, trans, and non-binary individuals face, and strive to create a world where everyone's rights are respected and upheld. Through their efforts, they are making significant strides towards achieving gender equality and justice for all (Ellsworth, 2024).

9.9. THE INFLUENCE OF MEDIA ON WOMEN'S RIGHTS AND CRIMINAL JUSTICE

The influence of media on women's rights and criminal justice is a significant and complex issue. Media coverage plays a crucial role in shaping public attitudes and perceptions on these topics. The way the media portrays violence against women and the criminal justice system can have a profound impact on viewers' emotional reactions and sense of accountability. However, there are several concerning trends and biases in media coverage that need to be addressed in order to promote gender justice (Roberts, 2018).

One study found that media coverage of violence against women tends to focus on individual cases rather than providing a broader social context. This incident-based reporting often fails to delve deeper into the problem and understand the underlying causes and systemic issues. The study also revealed that the majority of sources in these articles came from the police and the criminal justice system, while only a small percentage came from advocates for domestic abuse and survivors themselves. This imbalance in sources can contribute to a skewed understanding of the issue and perpetuate existing power dynamics (Roberts, 2018).

Another concerning trend in media coverage is the "murder centric" framework, where the focus is primarily on homicides. While these cases are undoubtedly newsworthy, they do not accurately represent the various ways that women experience violence. Physical abuse against intimate partners and sexual assault were the most commonly reported forms of violence, while other forms such as emotional abuse, threats, and sexual harassment were essentially ignored. This narrow focus can limit public understanding of the full extent of violence against women and hinder efforts to address these issues comprehensively.

Falsehoods and victim-blaming also persist in media reporting on violence against women. The study found that a significant percentage of incident-based reporting involved victim-blaming, such as suggesting that the victim was at fault for being drunk, flirting with the offender, or going home with him. Justifications for the offender were also present in a significant portion of the reporting, such as attributing their actions to being under the influence of drugs or seeking retribution. These biases can perpetuate harmful stereotypes and contribute to a culture of victim-blaming and impunity (Roberts, 2018).

Interestingly, the study also identified a tendency to make the offender invisible in media reporting, with a large percentage of incident-based reporting containing no information about the offender. This omission can further contribute to a lack of accountability and understanding of the perpetrators of violence against women.

Language choice in media reporting is another important aspect to consider. The study found that a significant percentage of newspaper and web headlines were sensationalistic, and some incident-based news articles employed sensationalistic language, including graphic or sexually explicit details. This sensationalism can contribute to the objectification and dehumanization of victims, as well as desensitize the public to the seriousness of the issue.

9.10. STRATEGIES FOR PROMOTING GENDER EQUALITY IN THE LEGAL SYSTEM

Promoting gender equality in the legal system is crucial for creating a fair and just society. In order to achieve this goal, there are several strategies that can be implemented.

Firstly, it is important to promote equal partnership in household chores and childcare. In many parts of the world, women still bear the majority of the responsibility for childcare and household duties. This unequal distribution of tasks not only affects women's productivity at work but also increases the risk of mental health issues. Research has shown that women in developing nations perform nearly three hours more per day than men in unpaid labor, while women in affluent nations perform, on average, two hours more (Sever, 2022). Therefore, it is essential to encourage men to take an equal share of household chores and childcare responsibilities.

Secondly, it is crucial to seek out indications of domestic violence and provide support to those who are experiencing abuse. Domestic violence is not limited to physical aggression but also includes psychological abuse and verbal attacks. Unfortunately, many women who experience abuse do not seek assistance. According to UN research, less than 40% of women who experience abuse in most countries seek any form of help, and of those who do, most turn to friends and family rather than official organizations and systems (Sever, 2022). Therefore, it is important to raise awareness about domestic violence and provide resources and support for those who are affected.

Thirdly, supporting parents and mothers is essential for promoting gender equality. Pregnant women should be offered assistance, such as a bus seat, and facilities for changing children should be available in all public spaces. Additionally, businesses should be encouraged to provide maternity and paternity leave. Unfortunately, many countries still do not offer adequate maternity and paternity leave. According to UN statistics, only 53% of nations provide maternity leave that lasts at least 14 weeks, and paternity leave is only provided in 48% of the world's nations (Sever, 2022). Therefore, it is important to advocate for policies that support parents and ensure equal opportunities for both mothers and fathers.

Another important strategy for promoting gender equality is to challenge and reject racist and chauvinist attitudes. Derogatory language and discriminatory remarks towards women, racial minorities, LGBTQI individuals, and other marginalized groups should not be tolerated. It is important to speak up and educate others about the harmful effects of such language and attitudes.

CHAPTER 10

WOMEN, GENDER, AND GLOBAL CRIME TRENDS

Contents

When examining women's experiences with crime in the interconnected world, it becomes apparent that these experiences are viewed from multiple perspectives, which are intricately tied to their gender identity. This chapter aims to explore the complex connections between criminal behavior, women, and the broader sociocultural context. Our goal is to analyze the intricate patterns of criminal activity in different cultural and geographical contexts. We will be examining the prevailing gender norms, power dynamics, and systemic inequalities that contribute to these patterns (Heiskanen & Lietonen, 2016). This journey offers us the opportunity to engage in a thorough examination, illuminating the profound impact of gender on crime and justice on a global scale. We will explore topics ranging from the devastating consequences of intimate partner abuse to the hidden webs of multinational criminal operations. We will delve into specific topics related to global crime and its impact on women.

10.1. TRANSNATIONAL CRIME AND WOMEN

It is imperative for institutions involved in criminal justice and crime prevention to ensure that women are provided with authentic and efficient protection against abuse, exploitation, and discrimination. Whether these crimes have an international nature is relevant because it may require specific preventive or control measures. It is important to address the matter of women's access to protection from organized crime. Additionally, we must examine how the criminal justice system can play a role in preventing exploitative behavior and other forms of violence against women. Transnational organized crime is increasingly emerging as a significant threat. It is evident that the current level of protection provided by the criminal justice system for women against various forms of abuse and exploitation inflicted by multinational criminal organizations is insufficient. Furthermore, it is crucial to conduct a comprehensive and timely analysis of the impact that criminal law, the criminal justice system, and crime prevention strategies have on the lives of women.

There is ongoing debate regarding the presence of gender-based violence and exploitation in modern international crimes. However, it is undeniable that certain cases unequivocally involve such elements. There is clear evidence pointing to the involvement of various organized criminal enterprises in the trafficking of women and children for the purpose of exploitation. There is substantial evidence indicating that certain forms of international organized crime specifically focus on women and children. Furthermore, it has been suggested that there has been a rise in the number of women being recruited into criminal organizations (Arsovska & Allum, 2014).

The surge in global travel and extensive media coverage has significantly heightened awareness of international opportunities, resulting in a notable increase in both legal and illegal migration. According to Arsovska & Allum (2014), human trafficking and smuggling have become significant factors in migration patterns in recent decades. Despite the implementation of stricter regulations and more stringent admission criteria, there continues to be a persistent demand for migration.

This demand has inadvertently created new opportunities for criminal entrepreneurs to exploit and profit from. It is possible to achieve high earnings. Currently, organized crime, which includes the trafficking of migrants, is found in various parts of the world and is recognized internationally as a major challenge for law enforcement, human security, and human rights. Illegal migrants often find themselves vulnerable to exploitation by traffickers who offer a variety of services.

These services can include job brokering, transportation, lodging, smuggling, and even training on evading border guards or seeking asylum. Criminal organizations often exploit vulnerable illegal migrants, using deceptive tactics and intimidation to further their own agendas. The bonded status of individuals who are trafficked serves as a powerful example of the oppressive conditions that are widely acknowledged in contemporary global discussions.

According to Arsovska & Allum (2014), there is a significant increase in the trafficking of women from the South to both the North and the South. The individuals are being transported from countries where the state economy has been devastated by structural adjustment, villages have been destroyed due to deforestation, and families have been compelled to move to urban areas. Additionally, the phenomenon of feminization of poverty is particularly evident in these nations. They are being taken to countries with higher GDP and a better standard of living for the average citizen. Sexism, racism, and poverty are all factors that contribute to the issue of women being trafficked (Arsovska & Allum, 2014).

Although trafficking has been a pressing global issue for many years, there has been a lack of effective measures taken to put an end to the highly profitable trade in women.

Undoubtedly, the complex and widespread issue of women trafficking presents significant challenges when it comes to enforcement. In many cases, countries involved in the process of trafficking tend to avoid the responsibility of protecting women who have been trafficked. Many States prioritize the victim's unlawful status as they are inclined to promptly pursue deportation if the victim is discovered.

10.2. HUMAN TRAFFICKING AND EXPLOITATION OF WOMEN

According to Hume & Sidun (2017), human trafficking is a global issue that disproportionately affects women and girls. In fact, 71% of victims of human trafficking are women and girls, while nearly 75% of identified victims of child trafficking are young females. However, it is important to note that the percentage of identified male victims has been increasing, from 16% in 2004 to 29% in 2014 (Figure 10.1).

Figure 10.1. *Women more likely to be impacted by human trafficking.*

Source: Dressember (2021).

The harms of trafficking are known to be more severe for women and girls compared to men and boys. This is due to the specific forms of exploitation that women and girls are exposed to, such as sexual exploitation and violence, domestic servitude, and forced marriage. The Secretary General Report on trafficking in women and girls acknowledges this disparity.

The most common type of trafficking worldwide is for the purpose of sexual exploitation, accounting for 54% of all cases. In fact, 96% of victims of sexual exploitation are women. Traffickers who use women for other illicit activities, such as forced labor, begging, and domestic slavery, often use sexual abuse as a form of coercion and control. In recent years, there has been an increase in the percentage of victims trafficked for forced labor, with 4 out of 10 victims between 2012 and 2014 being trafficked for this purpose. Of these victims, 63% were men. In cases of organ trafficking, 82% of victims are men.

There are several root causes and risk factors that contribute to the disproportionate impact of trafficking on women and girls. Gender inequality plays a significant role, as women and girls who experience gendered poverty, limited access to education, insufficient work possibilities, and a lack of control over their financial resources are more vulnerable to trafficking. Gender-based violence also contributes to this vulnerability, as it perpetuates a cycle of violence against women and normalizes such abuse.

Discriminatory immigration or labor laws, as well as gender-neutral policies, also contribute to the vulnerability of women to trafficking. Human rights and gender-sensitive labor and migration regulations may limit women's freedom of movement and job switching, making it more likely for them to seek work in unregulated and informal sectors where they are more susceptible to exploitation.

Humanitarian crises, post-conflict environments, and conflict also increase the vulnerability of women and girls to trafficking. During these times, when the rule of law is absent, armed groups may target women and girls for forced and child marriages, domestic servitude, and sexual slavery.

Migration is closely linked to trafficking, and the gender aspect of this connection is often overlooked. Between 2000 and 2015, there was a significant increase in international migration. Women make up more than half of all migrant workers worldwide, leading to the feminization of the global labor market. However, women face specific hazards and vulnerabilities related to their gender during their migratory journey, making them more susceptible to trafficking. They are often concentrated in low-skilled, low-paying industries, such as domestic work, which fall under unregulated and informal sectors with little to no legal protection. This is a result of gender discrimination and the undervaluation of low-skilled occupations. As a result, women are more vulnerable to assault, forced labor, extortion, debt bondage, and gender-specific exploitation.

10.3. GENDERED IMPACTS OF WAR AND CONFLICT

According to Reynolds (2021), approximately 80% of internally displaced individuals and refugees globally are women and girls. This statistic highlights the disproportionate impact of armed conflict on women and girls, who often face discrimination, violence, and a lack of access to essential services during and after conflicts. The effects of war on women and girls are wide-ranging and include physical and psychological trauma, reproductive health issues, increased vulnerability to sexually transmitted infections (STIs), and limited educational and economic opportunities.

One of the major consequences of armed conflict on women and girls is the disruption of healthcare services. During times of conflict, basic healthcare, including reproductive health services, is often interrupted, or rendered unavailable. This puts women and girls at risk of complications during pregnancy and childbirth, as well as other reproductive health issues. Additionally, the use of rape and sexual assault as weapons of war specifically targets women and girls, leading to long-term physical and psychological consequences. Efforts to address these issues must focus on providing support and protection for women and girls, as well as promoting human rights and gender education.

The prevalence of STIs, including HIV/AIDS, is also significantly higher among women and girls in conflict-affected areas. Reynolds (2021) cites a study conducted in Africa that found teenage girls had an HIV infection rate four times higher than that of teenage boys in post-conflict settings. This disparity can be attributed to factors such as sexual exploitation, high-risk behaviors, and the inability to negotiate safe sex.

Addressing the systemic use of gender-based violence and promoting safe sexual practices are crucial in reducing the spread of STIs among women and girls in conflict-affected areas.

Adolescents, both boys and girls, are particularly vulnerable during times of armed conflict. The trauma and lack of social services and support can have long-term impacts on their mental and physical well-being. However, the risks are even greater for girls, as they face additional challenges related to gender-based violence and discrimination. The collapse of social systems in conflict-affected areas often leads to high-risk behaviors, such as drug use and early sexual activity, among young people. Providing comprehensive support and services for adolescents, including mental health care and education, is essential in mitigating the negative effects of war on their well-being.

In post-conflict environments, the presence of peacekeeping forces can have unintended consequences for public health, particularly for women and girls. Reynolds (2021) notes that the majority of military personnel and peacekeeping mission staff are adult men with different cultural backgrounds and expectations regarding behavior. This can lead to an increase in the demand for the commercial sex trade, which in turn contributes to economic, physical, and sexual exploitation. Efforts to address these issues should include measures to prevent and respond to gender-based violence, as well as promote gender equality and women's empowerment.

Despite the challenges faced by women and girls in conflict situations, there are examples of successful outcomes and resilience. Reynolds (2021) highlights the importance of women's mobilization at the local level to address conflict and promote women's and girls' empowerment. Women's leadership can be harnessed to drive change and contribute to post-conflict reconstruction initiatives.

10.4. WOMEN'S INVOLVEMENT IN TERRORISM AND EXTREMISM

Women's involvement in violent extremism is a complex and multifaceted issue that requires a comprehensive understanding in order to effectively address and prevent it. Historically, women have actively participated in armed rebel groups, often taking on crucial roles such as recruits, fighters, and fundraisers (Carter, 2013). Despite being overlooked in stereotypes of violent political figures, women have been involved in 60% of armed rebel groups in recent decades. For example, female fighters for the National Liberation Front in Algeria in the 1950s were able to bypass checkpoints and plant bombs in key targets. In Sri Lanka, all-female battalions gained notoriety for their brutal warfare and strict discipline. Women also made up a significant portion of the Revolutionary Armed Forces of Colombia (FARC), serving in all operational capacities and contributing to the group's military strength (Carter, 2013) (Figure 10.2).

Figure 10.2. *ISIS' feared all female Al-Khansaa Brigade.*

Source: Ulas (2019).

In recent years, there has been an increase in women leading attacks and participating in all-female extremist networks. Examples include a mother and her two children in London plotting an attack on the British Museum, and 11 women in Morocco acquiring chemicals for bomb-making. Female members of Boko Haram have become the majority of the group's suicide attackers, responsible for killing over 1,200 people between 2014 and 2018. Female suicide attacks are often more deadly than those carried out by men, with higher casualty rates and lower failure rates (Carter, 2013).

The motivations for women joining extremist groups are similar to those of male recruits, including social ties and ideological commitment. However, some women are also forced into violent acts through kidnapping and coercion.

In Nigeria, for example, some women join Boko Haram in order to receive an education in an area where educational opportunities for females are limited. Others join in the hopes of gaining freedom and access to resources (Carter, 2013).

Women also play a significant role in recruitment, fundraising, and the dissemination of propaganda for extremist groups. In 2014, 15 American women were accused of sending funds to al-Shabab insurgents in Somalia using coded language and small transactions to avoid detection. In Palestine, 11 women were arrested for operating fraudulent charity organizations that provided funding to the Islamic Jihad (True & Eddyono, 2017).

Furthermore, women perform various supporting roles that are crucial to the functioning of extremist organizations. Women-led armed insurgencies have been found to be more successful against government forces and to control larger territories.

10.5. THE GLOBALIZATION OF GENDER-BASED VIOLENCE

Globalization has had a significant impact on women's lives, particularly in terms of their economic opportunities and their fight for gender equality. In the past, women were expected to stay at home and take care of the household, while men were the primary breadwinners. However, as globalization progressed, women gained greater awareness of their rights and their desire to seek employment and financial independence (Baker & Leicht, 2017).

One of the ways in which globalization has affected women is through the advancement of technology and the opening up of job opportunities. With the establishment of multinational companies and the growth of the global market, women now have more options for employment. They are no longer limited to traditional roles and can pursue careers in various fields. This has not only provided them with financial stability but has also given them a sense of empowerment and independence.

Furthermore, globalization has played a crucial role in promoting gender equality. Women have become more aware of their rights and have started demanding equal opportunities in all aspects of life. They no longer wish to be discriminated against based on their gender and are fighting for equal pay, equal representation in leadership positions, and equal access to education and healthcare.

Globalization has also exposed women to different cultures and ideas, allowing them to challenge traditional norms and expectations. They have become more aware of the injustices and inequalities that exist in society and are actively working towards creating a more inclusive and equal world.

However, it is important to note that globalization has not been entirely positive for women. While it has provided them with new opportunities, it has also exposed them to new forms of violence and exploitation. In some countries, globalization has resulted in increased opportunities for violence against women, particularly those who are impoverished and marginalized. They are more susceptible to exploitation, abuse, enslavement, and entrapment.

For example, in the UK and Japan, globalization has led to an increase in domestic violence against women. Economic pressures and changing gender roles have created tension within households, leading to an increase in violence. Studies have shown that a significant number of women in these countries have experienced physical abuse from their male partners.

Furthermore, globalization has also contributed to the objectification and sexualization of women. The media, influenced by global trends, often portrays women in a sexualized manner, perpetuating harmful stereotypes and contributing to a culture of violence against women (Baker & Leicht, 2017).

10.6. THE ROLE OF TECHNOLOGY IN GLOBAL CRIME

One of the key advancements in technology that has revolutionized crime prevention is the use of artificial intelligence (AI) and machine learning. AI technology allows computer systems to perform tasks that require human intelligence, such as interpreting patterns and trends in crime. By analyzing large amounts of data, including emails, files, and conversations, AI can help law enforcement predict and prevent criminal activity more effectively (Wall, 2024).

Predictive policing and data analysis are also important tools in crime prevention. By using analytical tools and data analysis techniques, law enforcement can identify individuals and areas with a higher risk of crime. This allows them to allocate resources and personnel more efficiently, ensuring that they are present where they are most needed. For example, sex offender management software can monitor offenders' mobile devices and alert probation and parole officials if illegal items are discovered, potentially preventing future crimes (Wall, 2024).

Another benefit of technology in crime prevention is the ability to deploy personnel and resources effectively. By using precise and efficient crime analytics, law enforcement can determine the most effective way to allocate manpower and resources. This is achieved through the generation of geospatial data using heuristic methods and advanced mathematical models, which are run through AI systems (Wall, 2024).

The combination of hard and soft technology has also enhanced law enforcement's ability to recognize and address new dangers. Social media forensics, facial recognition, and digital forensic tools like the Digital Evidence Investigator PRO (DEI PRO) have provided law enforcement agencies with powerful tools to combat crime in the digital age. DEI PRO, for example, is a portable tool loaded with automated digital forensics software that allows investigators to quickly and efficiently analyze digital evidence.

Overall, the use of technology in crime prevention has transformed safety and the ability to detect crimes. AI and machine learning have enabled law enforcement to predict and prevent criminal activity more effectively, while predictive policing and data analysis have allowed for more efficient allocation of resources. The combination of hard and soft technology has given law enforcement agencies greater capacity to recognize and address new dangers. With the continued advancements in technology, the fight against crime is likely to become even more effective in the future (Wall, 2024).

10.7. THE INTERSECTION OF GENDER AND ENVIRONMENTAL CRIME

Gender-based violence (GBV) is a violation of human rights that has far-reaching consequences for individuals, communities, and nations. It perpetuates gender inequality and hinders development objectives. GBV is prevalent in all environments and is rooted in discriminatory laws, norms, and gender roles. It affects access to and control over natural resources, exacerbating gender inequality and increasing vulnerabilities to violence.

One of the ways GBV is used to reinforce gender norms and maintain power disparities is through control over natural resources such as land, forests, agriculture, water, and fisheries. Women often face gender-specific roles and expectations when it comes to accessing and managing these resources, making them more susceptible to experiencing GBV during daily tasks. GBV can be used to prevent women from pursuing economic opportunities or leaving abusive relationships by enforcing land and property grabs and extorting them when they try to secure their rights (Nightingale, 2006).

Property grabbing, also known as disinheritance, is a form of economic violence that undermines women's agency and ability to generate income from land. It is often accompanied by other forms of GBV, such as evictions and physical and mental abuse. The insecurity of land rights and the intersectionality of violence and discrimination put women, particularly indigenous women, at greater risk of being targeted by large-scale land grabs and other forms of GBV. Women may also be subjected to sexual extortion by corrupt authorities in exchange for land titles and agricultural land.

Advancing women's land rights has numerous benefits, including increased food security, economic opportunities, decision-making power, and participation in sustainable land practices. It can also reduce other forms of GBV and intimate partner violence. However, the relationship between expanded land rights for women and higher rates of GBV is context-specific and varies in different settings.

GBV is also prevalent in the agriculture industry, where it is used to uphold unequal power dynamics. Women who question the unequal decision-making authority over agricultural yields and production may become victims of marital violence. Male managers in agricultural workforces have been found to sexually harass and abuse women, forcing them into hazardous jobs or limiting their hours if their advances are rejected.

The linkages between GBV and the environment are complex and multifaceted. GBV not only perpetuates gender inequality but also leads to the loss of traditional knowledge, biodiversity, and ecosystem services. The threats and pressures on the environment and its resources further exacerbate gender inequality and power imbalances in communities and households dealing with resource scarcity and societal stress. Despite these challenges, there is hope for protecting human rights and thriving ecosystems. Taking immediate action to stop GBV, advance gender equality, and safeguard the environment is crucial. Preventing and responding to GBV in environmental contexts can open doors for improved conservation, sustainable development, human rights, and gender equality (Nightingale, 2006).

10.8. WOMEN'S PARTICIPATION IN ORGANIZED CRIME NETWORKS

Gender studies of organized crime go beyond discussing the roles and crimes that males play and the crimes that women commit. It also involves understanding how gender is structured and expressed in human behavior. People's interactions with each other and the law are influenced by long-standing forms of discrimination such as racism, sexism, and classism. An intersectional, gender-based perspective allows for a more nuanced understanding of why both men and women engage in criminal activities and how their roles are often connected to systemic conditions that have existed for a long time (Paoli, 2017) (Figure 10.3).

Figure 10.3. *Female gangs in the world.*

Source: Discoverize (2023).

Incorporating intersectionality into the study of crime helps to clarify the causes of criminality and how control and enforcement affect men and women differently. Gender, birth location, and social class are not the sole factors that lead someone to commit a crime. By considering the gendered dynamics of organized crime and how gender is operationalized in the structure and organization of criminal groups, researchers can gain valuable insights into the experiences of men and women in the world of organized crime.

While there has been a significant focus on the relationship between masculinity and crime, the gendered aspects of women's involvement in organized crime and criminal activity are not as well-documented. For many years, women were often portrayed as the mothers, sisters, spouses, or lovers of organized crime members or leaders, and their close relationships with these men drove them into a life of crime. However, recent research has shed light on the various roles that women can have in organized crime groups, including organizers, leaders, traffickers, recruiters, and other members of the criminal community such as lawyers, couriers, and accountants.

The limited research on the subject reveals the distinct dynamics faced by women in organized crime groups. According to the Global Initiative against Transnational Organized Crime, women and girls are typically excluded from positions of leadership within these groups. They are also more likely to experience sexual assault and engage in sexual activities as part of their interactions with other gang members and the criminal justice system. Additionally, women and girls often bear the brunt of the consequences of gang activities, such as incarceration, family dissolution, and loss of parental rights.

The Global Initiative against Transnational Organized Crime has identified several drivers of recruitment for women into organized crime. One of these drivers is a sense of kinship and belonging. Many women who get involved in the gang scene do so because it provides them with a sense of community that they may not have experienced in their own families. Gang membership offers resources, such as money, clothing, and jewelry, as well as protection from violence and abuse.

Another driver of recruitment is the defense that gangs provide. Women may join gangs to seek protection in a dangerous environment where they are vulnerable to domestic and sexual abuse. However, it is important to note that some women continue to experience violence from gang members, including their boyfriends (Paoli, 2017).

Access to resources is also a significant factor in women's involvement in organized crime. Gangs often provide women with access to material goods, such as jewelry, cars, and clothes, which they may not be able to afford otherwise. Boyfriends and gang leaders are often the means through which women gain access to these commodities.

For some women, joining a gang is seen as the path of least resistance. They may receive immediate rewards and find more exciting opportunities with better compensation compared to the limited options available to them in the legal economy. Many women express dissatisfaction with their regular jobs, which are often low-paying and unfulfilling (Paoli, 2017).

Substance misuse is another driver of recruitment for women into organized crime. Some women may turn to gangs as a result of their struggles with addiction, as it provides them with access to drugs and a certain level of protection. Substance misuse can make women more vulnerable to violence and hinder their ability to find stable, legal employment.

10.9. INTERNATIONAL RESPONSES TO GENDERED CRIME TRENDS

In the world today, gender-based violence disproportionately affects women and girls. Shockingly, one in three women have experienced sexual assault or other forms of abuse. Women are also more likely to be murdered by family members or intimate partners.

Unfortunately, crimes against women are often underreported and have low conviction rates. This is due to flaws in the criminal justice system, victim blaming, gender stereotypes, and inadequate responses from professionals and institutions, leading to secondary victimization of survivors (Frank et al., 2010).

To address this issue, comprehensive and multi-sectoral solutions are needed to achieve Sustainable Development Goal 5.2, which aims to eliminate all forms of gender-based violence against women and girls by 2030. Criminal justice remedies and crime prevention play a crucial role in this strategy. The United Nations Office on Drugs and Crime (UNODC) has been assisting countries since 2010 in implementing victim-centered approaches to combat gender-based violence, in line with international standards and norms.

The UNODC supports various initiatives, such as the UN-EU Spotlight Initiative, the Joint UN Global Program on Essential Services for Women and Girls Subject to Violence, and the Global Program on Strengthening Crime Prevention and Criminal Justice Responses to Violence against Women (GLOW65) (Frank et al., 2010). Through these programs, the UNODC provides technical assistance to enhance public advocacy, operational guidance, and access to criminal justice remedies for violence against women.

Efforts to combat gendered crime on an international level include improving data collection and analysis on gender-based violence, evaluating the implementation of national laws and policies, closing legal gaps, and eliminating discriminatory practices, and promoting victim-centered responses. This involves creating and implementing initiatives to enhance the capacity of criminal justice professionals, including judges, prosecutors, police, and others, and establishing standard operating procedures or coordination mechanisms within the criminal justice system (Frank et al., 2010).

In 2019, the UNODC launched the Global Program on Strengthening Crime Prevention and Criminal Justice Responses to Violence against Women to complement existing UN programs and national projects. The program aims to provide women who are victims of violence with accessible and high-quality criminal justice and crime prevention services that adhere to global standards and guidelines. It focuses on three main interventions: enhancing knowledge on how the criminal justice system responds to violence against women through data gathering and analysis, aligning national laws and policies with international norms, and improving the responsiveness and support provided by criminal justice institutions to victims and survivors (Frank et al., 2010).

10.10. PROMOTING GENDER EQUITY IN GLOBAL JUSTICE INITIATIVES

Gender continues to play a significant role in health and wellbeing worldwide, with women and girls facing greater risks and susceptibility to infection. They also often experience lack of decision-making authority and resource control, as well as barriers to accessing health information and treatments. Rigid gender norms and roles contribute to poorer health outcomes for women, girls, men, and gender diverse communities. Disadvantaged groups, who are already vulnerable, face additional discrimination exacerbated by negative gender norms and inequality (Cornwall & Rivas, 2015).

Gender inequality has been identified as a major contributing factor to the HIV epidemic, particularly impacting young women and teenage girls. In sub-Saharan Africa, six out of seven adolescents aged 15–19 who are HIV positive are female. Gender disparities and inequities also influence the consequences of tuberculosis (TB), with men being more likely to have active TB despite women facing obstacles to receiving treatment. Negative gender norms around masculinity can increase men's exposure to risk factors and decrease their likelihood of seeking medical attention. Gender dynamics, roles, and relationships also affect the malaria epidemic, as limited economic and decision-making power for women hinders their access to preventive measures and treatment (Cornwall & Rivas, 2015).

Gender equality in health means ensuring that all individuals have the same rights and access to the best possible care. Health equity recognizes that marginalized groups may require additional resources and support to achieve the same health outcomes as other groups. The Global Fund is committed to promoting this equitable approach and actively works with and invests in marginalized populations.

The Global Fund prioritizes the needs of adolescent girls and young women in its efforts to combat HIV. Between 2018 and 2020, the 13 priority countries with the highest HIV burden saw a 107% increase in Global Fund investments in HIV prevention and testing for this population. As a result, the HIV incidence rate among adolescent girls and young women has decreased by 56% since 2010 (Cornwall & Rivas, 2015).

BIBLIOGRAPHY

1. Amaechi, E. C. (2018). The future of women in leadership: Breaking the glass ceiling: A global perspective. In *The Future of Leadership: Addressing Complex Global Issues* (pp. 145–167).
2. Arsovska, J., & Allum, F. (2014). Introduction: Women and transnational organized crime. *Trends in Organized Crime, 17*, 1–15.
3. Asad, A. L., & Clair, M. (2018). Racialized legal status as a social determinant of health. *Social Science & Medicine, 199*, 19–28.
4. Avalos, L. (2020). Reversing the decriminalization of sexual violence. *Nevada Law Journal, 21*, 1.
5. Avila, C. J. (2022). Prison health care is only available if you can afford it. *Prism*. Retrieved from: https://prismreports.org/2022/10/31/prison-health-care-hidden-costs/ (accessed on 2 August 2024).
6. Baker, P. L., & Leicht, K. T. (2017). Globalization, gender, and development: Toward a theoretical understanding of public gender-based violence against women and girls. *Sociology of Development, 3*(4), 323–345.
7. Baldry, E., & Cunneen, C. (2014). Imprisoned Indigenous women and the shadow of colonial patriarchy. *Australian & New Zealand Journal of Criminology, 47*(2), 276–298.
8. Balfour, G., & Comack, E. (2021). *Criminalizing Women: Gender and (in)Justice in Neoliberal Times*. Fernwood Publishing.
9. Barak, G., Leighton, P., & Flavin, J. (2010). *Class, Race, Gender, and Crime: The Social Realities of Justice in America*. Rowman & Littlefield Publishers.

10. BBC. (2020). Women offenders: Prison alternative to open in Wales first. Retrieved from: https://www.bbc.com/news/uk-wales-52533929 (accessed on 2 August 2024).
11. Bloom, B. E., & Covington, S. (2008). Addressing the mental health needs of women offenders. In *Women's Mental Health Issues Across the Criminal Justice System* (pp. 160–176).
12. Bontrager, S., Barrick, K., & Stupi, E. (2013). Gender and sentencing: A meta-analysis of contemporary research. *Journal of Gender, Race & Justice, 16*, 349–367.
13. Borras, A. M. (2021). Toward an intersectional approach to health justice. *International Journal of Health Services, 51*(2), 206–225.
14. Brezina, T. (2017). General strain theory. In *Oxford Research Encyclopedia of Criminology and Criminal Justice.*
15. Brown, G. A. (2004). Gender as a factor in the response of the law-enforcement system to violence against partners. *Sexuality and Culture, 8*(3), 3–139.
16. Brown, M., & Ross, S. (2010). Assisting and supporting women released from prison: Is mentoring the answer? *Current Issues in Criminal Justice, 22*(2), 217–232.
17. Bruinius, H. (2016). Number of women in jail rising faster than men: What's driving the trend? *The Christian Science Monitor*. Retrieved from: https://www.csmonitor.com/USA/Justice/2016/0819/Number-of-women-in-jail-rising-faster-than-men-What-s-driving-the-trend (accessed on 2 August 2024).
18. Buist, C. L. (2019). LGBTQ rights in the fields of criminal law and law enforcement. *University of Richmond Law Review, 54*, 877–895.
19. Bukuluki, P., Kisaakye, P., Wandiembe, S. P., Bulenzi-Gulere, G., Letiyo, E., Namirembe, H. N. L., Schmidt, I., Kakande, P. N., & Nissling, S. (2023). Access to information on gender-based violence prevention during COVID-19 lockdown in Uganda: A cross-sectional study. *The Lancet*. Retrieved from: https://www.thelancet.com/journals/eclinm/article/PIIS2589-5370%2823%2900023-8/fulltext (accessed on 2 August 2024).
20. Burfeind, J., & Bartusch, D. (2015). *Juvenile Delinquency: An Integrated Approach*. Routledge.
21. Burgess-Proctor, A. (2006). Intersections of race, class, gender, and crime: Future directions for feminist criminology. *Feminist Criminology, 1*(1), 27–47.
22. Burman, M., & McIvor, G. (2004). Breaking the mould. In *Women Who Offend* (p. 38).

23. Campbell, R., & Feeney, H. (2022). "On the shelves, covered in dust": The history of untested sexual assault kits in the United States. In *Sexual Assault Kits and Reforming the Response to Rape* (pp. 9–23). Routledge.

24. Carrabine, E., et al. (2020). *Criminology: A Sociological Introduction*. Routledge.

25. Carrington, K., & Death, J. (2014). Feminist criminologies' contribution to understandings of sex, gender, and crime. In *The Oxford Handbook of Gender, Sex, and Crime* (p. 99).

26. Carter, B., (2013). *Women and violent extremism* (GSDRC Helpdesk Research Report 898). Birmingham, UK: GSDRC, University of Birmingham. 1–13.

27. Catalano, S. (2012). Stalking victims in the United States—Revised. *Age, 18*(19), 8–047.

28. Chamberlain, L., & Levenson, R. (2010). Reproductive health and partner violence guidelines: An integrated response to intimate partner violence and reproductive coercion. San Francisco, CA: Family Violence Prevention Fund.

29. Children's Action Corps. (2014). *The Trajectory of a Traumatized Youth: A Three System Perspective - Desktop Guide to Good Juvenile Probation Practice*. Retrieved from: https://www.goodjuvenileprobationpractice.org/resources/the-trajectory-of-a-traumatized-youth-a-three-system-perspective (accessed on 2 August 2024).

30. Chinkin, Christine M. and Lisa Gormley. "Violence against Women." In *The UN Convention on the*

31. Elimination of All Forms of Discrimination against Women and Its Optional Protocol: A Commentary, edited by Patricia Schulz, Ruth Halperin-Kaddari, Beate Rudolf, and Marsha A. Freeman, 627-684. 2nd ed. Oxford: Oxford University Press, 2022..

32. Chowdhury, N., & Gibson, K. (2019). This is (still) a man's world: Young professional women's identity struggles in gendered workplaces. *Feminism & Psychology, 29*(4), 475–493.

33. Collica-Cox, K., & Schulz, D. M. (2019). Women wardens and correction executives: Paths to leadership. *Corrections, 4*(2), 89–111.

34. Cook, S. (2024). How working from home is impacting women. *Business Because*. Retrieved from: https://www.businessbecause.com/news/insights/7539/working-from-home-impact-women (accessed on 2 August 2024).

35. Cornwall, A., & Rivas, A. M. (2015). From 'gender equality' and 'women's empowerment' to global justice: Reclaiming a transformative agenda for gender and development. *Third World Quarterly, 36*(2), 396–415.

36. Creaney, S. (2012). Risk, prevention, and early intervention: Youth justice responses to girls. *Safer Communities, 11*(2), 111–120.

37. Creek, S., & Dunn, J. L. (2014). Intersectionality and the study of sex, gender, and crime. In *The Oxford Handbook of Gender, Sex, and Crime* (pp. 40–65). Oxford University Press.

38. Cretsinger, Mollie, et al. (2023), "Improving policy implementation to end gender-based violence", in OECD, *Joining Forces for Gender Equality: What is Holding us Back?*, OECD Publishing, Paris. DOI: https://doi.org/10.1787/c940e13f-en.

39. Criminology. (2024). *Wikipedia*. Retrieved from: https://en.wikipedia.org/wiki/Criminology (accessed on 2 August 2024).

40. CSG Justice Center. (2022). Adopting a gender-responsive approach for women in the justice system: A resource guide. Retrieved from: https://csgjusticecenter.org/publications/adopting-a-gender-responsive-approach-for-women-in-the-justice-system-a-resource-guide/ (accessed on 2 August 2024).

41. Dalacoura, K. (2019). Women and gender in the Middle East and North Africa: Mapping the field and addressing policy dilemmas at the post-2011 juncture. Retrieved from: http://www.menaraproject.eu/ (accessed on 2 August 2024).

42. Dancig-Rosenberg, H., & Yosef, N. (2019). Crime victimhood and intersectionality. *Fordham Urban Law Journal, 47*, 85–104.

43. Davis, D. M., Bello, J. K., & Rottnek, F. (2018). Care of incarcerated patients. *American Family Physician, 98*(10), 577–583.

44. Deshpande, N. A., & Nour, N. M. (2013). Sex trafficking of women and girls. *Reviews in Obstetrics and Gynecology, 6*(1), e22.

45. Dhatt, R., Theobald, S., Buzuzi, S., Ros, B., Vong, S., Muraya, K., & Jackson, C. (2017). The role of women's leadership and gender equity in leadership and health system strengthening. *Global Health, Epidemiology and Genomics, 2*, e8.

46. Dima. (2023). Women's movements. *The MENA Chronicle | Fanack*. Retrieved from: https://fanack.com/society/gender-equality-in-the-middle-east-and-north-africa/womens-movements-in-the-middle-east-and-north-africa/ (accessed on 2 August 2024).

47. Discoverize. (2023). 10 most dangerous female gangs in the world [Video]. *YouTube*. Retrieved from: https://www.youtube.com/watch?v=ePw7NXHrcA4 (accessed on 2 August 2024).

48. Djamba, Y. K., & Kimuna, S. R. (2015). Gender-based violence. *Springer International Publishing Switzerland*. DOI 10.1007/978-3-319-05561-7_6.

49. Dressember. (2021). Why are women more likely to be impacted by human trafficking? *Dressember*. Retrieved from: https://www.dressember.org/blog/dressemberreading3 (accessed on 2 August 2024).

50. Dudouet, V. (2014). *Civil Resistance and Conflict Transformation*. Taylor & Francis.

51. Einwohner, R. L., Kelly-Thompson, K., Sinclair-Chapman, V., Tormos-Aponte, F., Weldon, S. L., Wright, J. M., & Wu, C. (2021). Active solidarity: Intersectional solidarity in action. *Social Politics: International Studies in Gender, State & Society, 28*(3), 704–729.

52. Ellsworth, Madison Ruth, "The utilization of grassroots organizing by Black women pioneers to achieve reproductive justice." (2024). *Electronic Theses and Dissertations*. Paper 4317. https://doi.org/10.18297/etd/4317.

53. Elsesser, K. (2018). Female lawyers face widespread gender bias, according to new study. *Forbes*. Retrieved from: https://www.forbes.com/sites/kimelsesser/2018/10/01/female-lawyers-face-widespread-gender-bias-according-to-new-study/ (accessed on 2 August 2024).

54. Essentials, L. (2021). Violence against women. *Law Essentials*. Retrieved from: https://lawessential.com/criminal-law/f/violence-against-women?blogcategory=Criminal+Law (accessed on 2 August 2024).

55. European Institute for Gender Equality. (2024). What is gender-based violence? Retrieved from: https://eige.europa.eu/gender-based-violence/what-is-gender-based-violence (accessed on 2 August 2024).

56. Evaluation of the Family Violence Prevention Program. (2019). Retrieved from: https://www.rcaanc-cirnac.gc.ca/eng/1555071142332/1555071210727 (accessed on 2 August 2024).

57. Evans, K., & Jamieson, J. (2008). *Gender and Crime: A Reader*. McGraw-Hill Education.

58. Ferguson, K. E. (2017). Feminist theory today. *Annual Review of Political Science, 20*, 269–286.

59. Frank, D. J., Camp, B. J., & Boutcher, S. A. (2010). Worldwide trends in the criminal regulation of sex, 1945 to 2005. *American Sociological Review, 75*(6), 867–893.

60. Gateway Foundation. (2023). Violence, substance abuse, and mental illness. Retrieved from: https://www.gatewayfoundation.org/addiction-blog/relationship-between-alcohol-and-violence/ (accessed on 2 August 2024).

61. Glasier, A., Gülmezoglu, A. M., Schmid, G. P., Moreno, C. G., & Van Look, P. F. (2006). Sexual and reproductive health: A matter of life and death. *The Lancet, 368*(9547), 1595–1607.

62. Goodkind, S. (2005). Gender-specific services in the juvenile justice system: A critical examination. *Affilia, 20*(1), 52–70.

63. Goodmark, L. (2018). Restorative justice as feminist practice. *International Journal of Restorative Justice, 1*, 372–388.

64. GOV.UK. (2020). *Women and the Criminal Justice System, 2019*. Retrieved from: https://www.gov.uk/government/statistics/women-and-the-criminal-justice-system-2019/women-and-the-criminal-justice-system-2019 (accessed on 2 August 2024).

65. Grecco, G. G., & Chambers, R. A. (2019). The Penrose Effect and its acceleration by the war on drugs: A crisis of untranslated neuroscience and untreated addiction and mental illness. *Translational Psychiatry, 9*(1). https://doi.org/10.1038/s41398-019-0661-9.

66. Greenberg, G. A., & Rosenheck, R. A. (2008). Homelessness in the state and federal prison population. *Criminal Behaviour and Mental Health, 18*(2), 88–103.

67. Greene, H. T. (2000). Black females in law enforcement: A foundation for future research. *Journal of Contemporary Criminal Justice, 16*(2), 230–239.

68. Gunderson, S. (2020). Voices for Utah children–Let's end racial disparities in Utah's juvenile justice system. *Voices for Utah Children*. Retrieved from: https://utahchildren.org/newsroom/speaking-of-kids-blog/item/806-let-s-end-racial-disparities-in-utah-s-juvenile-justice-system (accessed on 2 August 2024).

69. Halder, D., & Jaishankar, K. (2011). *Cyber Crime and the Victimization of Women: Laws, Rights and Regulations*. IGI Global.

70. Hankivsky, O. (2012). Women's health, men's health, and gender and health: Implications of intersectionality. *Social Science & Medicine, 74*(11), 1712–1720.

71. Heidensohn, F. (2012). The future of feminist criminology. *Crime, Media, Culture, 8*(2), 123–134.

72. Heipt, W. S. (2015). Girls' court: A gender responsive juvenile court alternative. *Seattle Journal for Social Justice, 13*(3), 10–28.

73. Heiskanen, M., & Lietonen, A. (2016). *Crime and Gender: A Study on How Men and Women are Represented in International Crime Statistics*. Universität Tübingen.

74. Helfgott, J. B., Gunnison, E., Murtagh, A., & Navejar, B. (2018). Badasses: The rise of women in criminal justice. *Women & Criminal Justice, 28*(4), 235–261.

75. Hodgson, J. (2022). Offending girls and restorative justice: A critical analysis. *Youth Justice, 22*(2), 166–188.

76. Hume, D. L., & Sidun, N. M. (2017). *Human Trafficking of Women and Girls: Characteristics, Commonalities, and Complexities*. Taylor & Francis.

77. Initiative, J. L. (2013). Local faith communities and the promotion of resilience in humanitarian situations: A scoping study. *Communities*.

78. Interpol. (2021). Colombian police take down criminal group behind human trafficking. Retrieved from: https://www.interpol.int/News-and-Events/News/2021/Colombian-police-take-down-criminal-group-behind-human-trafficking (accessed on 2 August 2024).

79. Junk, W. M., Romeijn, J., & Rasmussen, A. (2021). Is this a men's world? On the need to study descriptive representation of women in lobbying and policy advocacy. *Journal of European Public Policy, 28*(6), 943–957.

80. Kajstura, A. (2017). *Women's Mass Incarceration: The Whole Pie 2017*. ACLU Smart Justice New York.

81. Kerig, P. K. (2018). Polyvictimization and girls' involvement in the juvenile justice system: Investigating gender-differentiated patterns of risk, recidivism, and resilience. *Journal of Interpersonal Violence, 33*(5), 789–809.

82. Kiamba, J. M. (2009). Women and leadership positions: Social and cultural barriers to success. *Wagadu: A Journal of International Women's Studies, 6*(1), 89–104.

83. Koski, S. V., & Costanza, S. (2015). An examination of narratives from women offenders: Are gender-specific reentry efforts needed? *Qualitative Sociology Review, 11*(1), 70–89.

84. Kruttschnitt, C., Kalsbeek, W. D., & House, C. C. (2014). *Estimating the Incidence of Rape and Sexual Assault*. Washington, DC: National Academies Press.

85. Law Journal for Social Justice. (2023). The challenges of comparing intimate partner violence statistics on a global scale. Retrieved from: https://lawjournalforsocialjustice.com/2023/11/30/the-challenges-of-comparing-intimate-partner-violence-statistics-on-a-global-scale/ (accessed on 2 August 2024).

86. Lawson, M. A., Martin, A. E., Huda, I., & Matz, S. C. (2022). Hiring women into senior leadership positions is associated with a reduction in gender stereotypes in organizational language. *Proceedings of the National Academy of Sciences, 119*(9), e2026443119.

87. Leaper, C., & Friedman, C. K. (2007). The socialization of gender. In J. E. Grusec & P. D. Hastings (Eds.), *Handbook of Socialization: Theory and Research* (pp. 561–587). Guilford Press.

88. Local Housing Solutions. (2024). Housing and criminal justice agencies can work together. Retrieved from: https://localhousingsolutions.org/bridge/housing-criminal-justice-agencies-can-work-together/ (accessed on 2 August 2024).

89. Lopez, V., & Pasko, L. (2017). Bringing Latinas to the forefront: Latina girls, women, and the justice system. *Feminist Criminology, 12*(3), 195–198.

90. Malvaso, C. G., et al. (2022). Associations between adverse childhood experiences and trauma among young people who offend: A systematic literature review. *Trauma, Violence, & Abuse, 23*(5), 1677–1694.

91. Massoglia, M., & Remster, B. (2019). Linkages between incarceration and health. *Public Health Reports, 134*(1_suppl), 8S–14S.

92. Maule, A. (2016). The power of teaching race and wrongful conviction to women in prison. *Innocence Project*. Retrieved from: https://innocenceproject.org/power-teaching-race-wrongful-conviction-women-prison/ (accessed on 2 August 2024).

93. Messina, N. P., et al. (2019). Gender-responsive approaches for women in the United States. In T. C. L. Van Cleve & M. M. B. M. T. T. P. (Eds.), *The Routledge Companion to Rehabilitative Work in Criminal Justice* (pp. 633–650). Routledge.

94. Meyer, J. P., Chen, N. E., & Springer, S. A. (2011). HIV treatment in the criminal justice system: Critical knowledge and intervention gaps. *AIDS Research and Treatment, 2011*, 680617.

95. Miller, H. V. (2021). Female re-entry and gender-responsive programming. *Corrections Today, 13*(2), 20–25.

96. Modrowski, C. A., et al. (2021). Victimization profiles in girls involved in

the juvenile justice system: A latent class analysis. *Child Abuse & Neglect, 111*, 104774.

97. Moffitt, T. E., & Caspi, A. (2001). Childhood predictors differentiate life-course persistent and adolescence-limited antisocial pathways among males and females. *Development and Psychopathology, 13*(2), 355–375.
98. Momsen, J. (2019). *Gender and Development*. Routledge.
99. Morrison, A., Ellsberg, M., & Bott, S. (2007). Addressing gender-based violence: A critical review of interventions. *The World Bank Research Observer, 22*(1), 25–51.
100. Myers Jr, S. L., & Radhakrishna, V. (2018). Hate crimes, crimes of atrocity, and affirmative action in India and the US. Paper prepared for the Government of Karnataka International Conference: Reclaiming Social Justice, Revisiting Ambedkar.
101. Niau, A. (2021). Female offender, victim of the patriarchal system: A critical discourse analysis of the case of Lisa Montgomery.
102. Nightingale, A. (2006). The nature of gender: Work, gender, and environment. *Environment and Planning D: Society and Space, 24*(2), 165–185.
103. Nilsson, E. L. (2017). Analyzing gender differences in the relationship between family influences and adolescent offending among boys and girls. *Child Indicators Research, 10*(4), 1079–1094.
104. Oberwittler, D. (2019). Lethal violence: A global view on homicide. In *Oxford Research Encyclopedia of Criminology and Criminal Justice.* Oxford University Press.
105. Obudho, N., & Ntonjira, L. (2024). Silent no more: Leaders must be held accountable to end femicide. *The East African*. Retrieved from: https://www.theeastafrican.co.ke/tea/oped/comment/leaders-must-be-held-accountable-to-end-femicide-4509466 (accessed on 2 August 2024).
106. Paoli, L. (2017). The paradoxes of organized crime. In *Transnational Organized Crime* (pp. 295–342). Routledge.
107. Parrish, D. E. (2020). Achieving justice for girls in the juvenile justice system. *Social Work, 65*(2), 149–158.
108. Passel, J. S., & D'Vera Cohn, S. W. (2009). A portrait of unauthorized immigrants in the United States. *Pew Hispanic Center*, 311–328.
109. Passel, J. S., & D'Vera Cohn, S. W. (2011). Unauthorized immigrant population: National and state trends, 2010 (p. 31). Washington, DC: Pew Hispanic Center.
110. PCARE. (2017). PCARE@10: Reflecting on a decade of prison

communication, activism, research, and education, while looking ahead to new challenges and opportunities. *Communication and Critical/Cultural Studies, 14*(3), 288–310.

111. Peresie, J. L. (2004). Female judges matter: Gender and collegial decision-making in the federal appellate courts. *Yale Law Journal, 114*, 1759–1809.
112. Pertek, S., Block, K., Goodson, L., Hassan, P., Hourani, J., & Phillimore, J. (2023). Gender-based violence, religion and forced displacement: Protective and risk factors. *Frontiers in Human Dynamics, 5*, 1058822.
113. Puhrmann, A. M. (2015). Gender and general strain theory: An examination of the role of gendered strains and negative emotions on crime (Doctoral dissertation, University of Miami).
114. RAINN. (2024). Victims of sexual violence: Statistics. Retrieved from: https://www.rainn.org/statistics/victims-sexual-violence (accessed on 2 August 2024).
115. Ramsey, C. B. (2002). The discretionary power of public prosecutors in historical perspective. *American Criminal Law Review, 39*, 1309–1328.
116. Reisig, M. D., et al. (2006). Assessing recidivism risk across female pathways to crime. *Justice Quarterly, 23*(3), 384–405.
117. Reynolds, A. N. (2021). Women at work and war: Integrating gender and conflict into impact assessment. *Impact Assessment and Project Appraisal, 39*(3), 196–205.
118. Riccucci, N. M., & Van Ryzin, G. G. (2017). Representative bureaucracy: A lever to enhance social equity, coproduction, and democracy. *Public Administration Review, 77*(1), 21–30.
119. Rivas, C., Ramsay, J., Sadowski, L., Davidson, L. L., Dunnes, D., Eldridge, S., & Feder, G. (2016). Advocacy interventions to reduce or eliminate violence and promote the physical and psychosocial well-being of women who experience intimate partner abuse: A systematic review. *Campbell Systematic Reviews, 12*(1), 1–202.
120. Roberts, J. (2018). *Public Opinion, Crime, and Criminal Justice*. Routledge.
121. Salisbury, E. J., & Van Voorhis, P. (2009). Gendered pathways: A quantitative investigation of women probationers' paths to incarceration. *Criminal Justice and Behavior, 36*(6), 541–566.
122. Sanjel, S. (2013). Gender-based violence: A crucial challenge for public health. *Kathmandu University Medical Journal, 11*(2), 179–184.
123. SBS News. (2018). Australian woman charged with drug trafficking in Cambodia. Retrieved from: https://www.sbs.com.au/news/article/

australian-woman-charged-with-drug-trafficking-in-cambodia/h3kr2dh9r (accessed on 2 August 2024).

124. Schneider, E. M. (2013). The dialectics of rights and politics: Perspectives from the women's movement. In *At the Boundaries of Law (RLE Feminist Theory)* (pp. 301–319). Routledge.

125. Schwartz, J., et al. (2015). 30 years of sex stratification in violent crime partnerships and groups. *Feminist Criminology, 10*(1), 60–91.

126. Sears, E. W. (2023). Black women looking back: Reflections on the impact of Black women's support. Northern Kentucky University, 1–15.

127. Sered, S., & Norton-Hawk, M. (2013). Criminalized women and the health care system: The case for continuity of services. *Journal of Correctional Health Care, 19*(3), 164–177.

128. Servon, L., Esquier, A., & Tiley, G. (2021). Gender and financialization of the criminal justice system. *Social Sciences, 10*(11), 446. https://doi.org/10.3390/socsci10110446.

129. Sever, C. (2022). Legal gender equality as a catalyst for convergence. International Monetary Fund.

130. Sheets, B. (2007). Women in the criminal justice system. *Research and Advocacy for Reform.*

131. Shelton, J. S. (2023). Report highlights need to create justice for LGBT youth. *True Colors United.* Retrieved from: https://truecolorsunited.org/report-highlights-need-to-create-justice-for-lgbt-youth/ (accessed on 2 August 2024).

132. Sherman, F., & Black, A. (2015). Gender injustice: System-level juvenile justice reforms for girls.

133. Smith, R. K. (2022). *International Human Rights Law.* Oxford University Press.

134. Steffensmeier, D., et al. (2006). Gender gap trends for violent crimes, 1980 to 2003: A UCR-NCVS comparison. *Feminist Criminology, 1*(1), 72–98.

135. Swank, E., & Fahs, B. (2013). An intersectional analysis of gender and race for sexual minorities who engage in gay and lesbian rights activism. *Sex Roles, 68*, 660–674.

136. Tomsen, S. (2008). Masculinities, crime, and criminalization. In *The Critical Criminology Companion* (pp. 94–104).

137. Treskon, L., & Bright, C. L. (2017). Bringing gender-responsive principles into practice. Center for Criminal Justice Research. Retrieved from: www.mdrc.org/sites/default/files/PACE_brief_March2017_web.pdf (accessed on 2 August 2024).

138. True, J., & Eddyono, S. W. (2017). Preventing violent extremism: *Gender perspectives and women's roles*. 20-55. http://docs.wixstatic.com/ugd/b4aef1_5fb20e84855b45aabb5437fe96fc3616.pdf

139. Tuchman, E. (2014). Women and addiction: The importance of gender issues in substance abuse research. In *Women, Children, and Addiction* (pp. 15–26). Routledge.

140. Ulas, G. (2019). Female radicalization: Why do women join ISIS? *Middle East Centre*. Retrieved from: https://blogs.lse.ac.uk/mec/2019/08/15/female-radicalisation-why-do-women-join-isis/ (accessed on 2 August 2024).

141. United Nations Office on Drugs and Crime. (2024). To achieve justice, we need more women in justice: The first International Day of Women Judges inaugurates a gender-responsive justice initiative. Retrieved from: https://www.unodc.org/unodc/frontpage/2022/March/to-achieve-justice--we-need-more-women-in-justice_-the-first-international-day-of-women-judges-inaugurates-a-gender-responsive-justice-initiative.html (accessed on 2 August 2024).

142. UNODC. (2024). Organized crime module 15 key issues: Gender and different types of organized crime. Retrieved from: https://sherloc.unodc.org/cld/en/education/tertiary/organized-crime/module-15/key-issues/gender-and-different-types-of-organized-crime.html (accessed on 2 August 2024).

143. Wall, D. S. (2024). *Cybercrime: The Transformation of Crime in The Information Age*. John Wiley & Sons.

144. Watson, L., & Edelman, P. (2012). Improving the juvenile justice system for girls: Lessons from the states. *Georgetown Journal on Poverty Law & Policy, 20*, 215–230.

145. Welch, K. (2007). Black criminal stereotypes and racial profiling. *Journal of Contemporary Criminal Justice, 23*(3), 276–288.

146. Williams, A. A. (2000). Criminality of women in the 18th century in the Southwest of England (Doctoral dissertation, University of Plymouth).

147. Winterdyk, J. A. (2020). Exploring a 'new' perspective for criminological inquiry: Global criminology. *Macedonian Review for Criminal Law & Criminology, 27*, 1–16.

148. World Health Organization. (2023). HRP at 50: Harnessing the power of science, research, data and digital technologies to improve sexual and reproductive health and rights. World Health Organization.

INDEX

G

H

I

FSC
www.fsc.org
MIX
Papier | Fördert gute Waldnutzung
FSC® C083411

Kolibri 360 GmbH
Ferdinand-Jühlke-Straße 7
99095 Erfurt, Deutschland
produktsicherheit@kolibri360.de